Jens Damm, Andreas Steen (Eds.)

Postmodern China

Berliner China-Hefte
Chinese History and Society

Edited by
Mechthild Leutner

Assistant Editors
Jens Damm, Nathalie van Looy
and Hauke Neddermann

Ostasiatisches Seminar
der Freien Universität Berlin

Volume 34

LIT

Postmodern China

edited by

Jens Damm and Andreas Steen

LIT

Bibliographic information published by the Deutsche Nationalbibliothek
The Deutsche Nationalbibliothek lists this publication in the Deutsche Nationalbibliografie; detailed bibliographic data are available in the Internet at http://dnb.d-nb.de.

ISBN 978-3-8258-1705-3

A catalogue record for this book is available from the British Library

Verlagskontakt:
Fresnostr. 2 D-48159 Münster
Tel. +49 (0) 2 51/620 32 - 22 Fax +49 (0) 2 51/922 60 99
e-Mail: lit@lit-verlag.de http://www.lit-verlag.de

Auslieferung:

Deutschland/Schweiz: LIT Verlag Fresnostr. 2, D-48159 Münster
Tel. +49 (0) 2 51/620 32 - 22, Fax +49 (0) 2 51/922 60 99, e-Mail: vertrieb@lit-verlag.de

Österreich: Medienlogistik Pichler-ÖBZ GmbH & Co KG
IZ-NÖ, Süd, Straße 1, Objekt 34, A-2355 Wiener Neudorf
Tel. +43 (0) 2236/63 535-290, +43 (0) 2236/63 535 - 243, mlo@medien-logistik.at

Distributed in the UK by: Global Book Marketing, 99B Wallis Rd, London, E9 5LN
Phone: +44 (0) 20 8533 5800 – Fax: +44 (0) 1600 775 663
http://www.centralbooks.co.uk/html

Distributed in North America by:

Transaction Publishers
New Brunswick (U.S.A.) and London (U.K.)

Transaction Publishers
Rutgers University
35 Berrue Circle
Piscataway, NJ 08854

Phone: +1 (732) 445 - 2280
Fax: + 1 (732) 445 - 3138
for orders (U. S. only):
toll free (888) 999 - 6778
e-mail:
orders@transactionspub.com

Contents

Postmodern China

Conference Reports

Reviews

Calligraphy: Chen Ning
Orders: Lit-Verlag Münster-Hamburg-London, Grevener Str. 179, D-48159 Münster, Germany, lit@lit-verlag.de.
Submission of Manuscripts (Articles, Reports, and Reviews):
Chinese History and Society/Berliner China-Hefte, Freie Universität Berlin, Ostasiatisches Seminar, Ehrenbergstr. 26-28, 14195 Berlin, eChina@zedat.fu-berlin.de.
Manuscripts should conform to the style of Chinese History and Society/Berliner China-Hefte: <http://www.chinesehistoryandsociety.de>

Jens Damm and Andreas Steen

Introduction: Postmodern China

The articles collected in this volume look at various cultural activities in "Postmodern China," concentrating on music, advertising, literature, film, and the Internet. Our purpose is to provide insights into different spaces of "postmodernism in action," describing and analyzing both reflected and non-reflected practices in the culture and everyday life of the People's Republic of China (PRC), Hong Kong and Taiwan. *Postmodern China* takes for granted that "postmodernism in China and Asia today is no longer a residue of some ancient mentality, but a real socioeconomic presence" (Lu 2001a: 65). It looks, in particular, at the PRC's cultural development since the 1990s, following the notion that postmodernism as a new cultural, literary and artistic formation is connected to globalization, political and economic liberalization and an increasing variety of transnational transfers.

In the PRC, the postmodern moment can be divided into two – if not three – phases. The reform policy of the "New Era" (*xin shiqi*), 1977-1989, paved the way for the arrival of new foreign literature and theories in China, and inspired a small group of authors to discuss topics, such as the concept of postmodernism. Interest increased after Frederic Jameson's guest lectures at Peking University in 1985, which one year later were published in Chinese as "Postmodernism and Cultural Theory."[1] This book continued to inspire Chinese discussions far into the next decade. Meanwhile, other western works on postmodern theory were translated and became influential, for example, those of Jean-Francoise Lyotard, Linda Hutcheon, Douwe Fokkema, and Jürgen Habermas. Debates intensified after the early 1990s, when "postmodernism arrived in China as a full-fledged reality" (Lu 2001a: 66). Thus, the second period began after the suppression of the democracy movement in 1989, coinciding with what is termed the post-New Era (*hou xin shiqi*), also understood as "post-Tiananmen," "post-revolutionary" and "post-socialist." Yang Xiaobin, in addition, characterizes Chinese postmodernism as "postcatastrophic, posttraumatic, post-Cultural Revolution and post-Mao-Deng" (Yang 2002: 231).

The particular circumstances that boosted the popularity of "post-studies" (*houxue*) and the production of postmodern culture during these two periods in China are well-researched and can be summarized as follows: when the Chinese Communist Party (CCP) launched its "socialist market economy" policy in 1992, China's economic boom and her transformation into a consumer society began. In addition, nationalism was propagated as the new unifying ideology, inspiring, for example, the populist-popular anti-American bestseller "China can say no!" (*Zhongguo keyi shuo bu!*, 1996). Meanwhile, the intellectuals' role was restricted to the academic world, also due to the new climate of economic liberalism, mass-culture, and consumerism, in which they had lost their former influence and power in the public discourse. Postmodern theory was perceived as offering an opportunity to position oneself as a critical observer both in China and vis-à-vis the West. Different aspects of the debate are reflected in a number of articles that appeared between 1995-97, some of which were republished in the volume "Postmodernism and China," edited by Arif Dirlik and Xudong

1 Chinese title: „*Houxiandai zhuyi yu wenhua lilun.*" On the early history, see Dirlik/Zhang 1997, Münchau 2002 and Xiaobin Yang 2002.

Zhang (2000).[2] In their introduction, first published in 1997, the editors formulated the following argument:

While Chinese postmodernism may be most striking as an antirevolutionary repudiation of a socialist modernity, what may make Chinese postmodernity unique is that, within a postsocialist situation, postmodernity itself may serve as a site of struggle between the legacy of the past and the forces of the present (Dirlik/Zhang 2000: 7).

In other words, Chinese postmodernity is be grasped "also in the relationship to a socialist and revolutionary modernity" (ibid.) and serves as a periodizing concept that goes beyond the two dominant categories of the previous century, namely modernity and enlightenment. With this volume, however, we also want to highlight postmodernity as a condition of China's reality and everyday life after her entry into the global capitalist system. This moment is captured in a statement of Sheldon H. Lu, another well-known and prolific writer on Chinese postmodernity:

Chinese postmodernity *is a marker of profound social anomalies and ideological contradictions in contemporary China, and Chinese* postmodernism *is the most forceful expression of these anomalies and contradictions in the realm of art and culture* (Lu 2001: 66).

One of these "contradictions" can be found in Lu's observation that "contemporary China consists of the superimposition of multiple temporalities; the premodern, the modern, and the postmodern coexist in the same space and at the same moment" (Lu 1997: 66). There are, of course, other arguments to emphasize the existence of a postmodernity with Chinese characteristics, and yet other critics who also express different views.[3] Today, however, the debate on Chinese postmodernity has cooled down. It could be argued that "Postmodern China" has reached a third phase, one in which the many possibilities and "anomalies" appear to be accepted and less reflected upon because they can be effectively exploited for either individual or collective purposes, such as, commerce and entertainment, politics and propaganda.

Notwithstanding theoretical disagreements, the post-New Era prepared the ground for new forms of cultural production and consumption, based on increasing patterns of globalization and China's economic integration into the world market. The transfer of goods was accompanied by new technologies, such as, mobile phones, CDs/DVDs, and the Internet, all of which led to a rapid increase in the mobility of information, images and sounds, and also of money and subversion. As China became imbedded in new transnational structures of communication and exchange, it experienced what Lyotard (1984: 76) once called the realism of "anything goes," which is, in fact, that of money. If commercialization is one aspect, the democratizing effects of postmodern forces is another which cannot be disregarded, for example, the impact of Western (popular) culture and the new creative syntheses of various elements of history, tradition, and politics in the realms of culture and art. Other aspects to be included are the revival of several expressions of nostalgia, negotiations of new gender-roles, and discourses on Chineseness and the Chinese diaspora. In this volume, we address these questions in the context of three fields of research: first, the broad area of popular music, including performance, advertising and performance venues.

---

2 First published in a special issue of the journal *boundary 2* 24/3, 1974.

3 For more details on the debate, see, for example, Wang Ning 1997; Guo Jian 1999; Liu Kang 1997; Ben Xu 2001; Sheldon H. Lu 1997, 2001, 2007 and Münchau 2001.

Second, postmodernity and literature, ranging from novels to poetry, from "traditional" novels to anonymous Internet postings, and, third, postmodern aspects related to film and the Internet, focusing on transnational issues between Taiwan, Hong Kong and the PRC.

In the first part, popular music, the authors share some common understanding of the postmodern situation in China with regard to history and nostalgia – the inclusion of "classic" pop venues in Hong Kong adds a further element – but differ in other aspects. *Andrew Field* and *Jeroen Groenewegen*, although dealing with Beijing punk rock as a marginalized form of the music scene, show how group dynamics in the concerts are essential for the specific performances. For them, punk rock bands keep the "flame of revolutionary discourse alive," while, at the same time, commoditization takes place. Thus, as the case of the marginalized punk rock shows, postmodernity in China is more than a "depoliticized culture of urban consumption" which – although carefully monitored by officials – has gained enormous influence since 1992. Postmodernity as expressed in the performances of punk rock tends to satirize China's mainstream involvement in a "mad dash to gain money, sex and power," while, at the same time, the discussions on a new Chinese nationalism are hollowed out. Building on an analysis of CD covers since 1989, *Andreas Steen* emphasizes that in the PRC, postmodernity should be equated with postsocialism – a defragmented discourse which is shaped by globalization, consumer revolution, and the commercialization of Chinese cultural and historical memory, with reference to both to the traditional historiography of China and to the experience of the more recent turbulent past of Communist China. Steen is critical of the idea that a revolutionary discourse is really being kept alive. Images of the revolutionary past, as displayed on CD covers, carry new meanings and say more about the creative employment of sales and commoditization strategies than about musical content. However, although they are used for political propaganda and for rock music alike, both in China and abroad, they still reflect the ideological struggle in the realm of popular culture. *Jeroen de Kloet* and *Yiu Fai Chow* deal with the changing landscape of Hong Kong and the memory of pop venues associated with Cantopop (or the proclaimed death of these mass phenomena of the 1980s and early 1990s). Their concern is the relation between public space, with reference to the pop venues, and the production of identification through the lens of collective memory. They argue persuasively that Hong Kong itself is imagined in terms of "money and tradition."

In the second part, focusing on literature, *Anne Wedell-Wedellsborg* and *Heather Inwood* conclude that the period of more theoretically inspired discussions on the relationship between realism, modernism and post-modernism has been abandoned since the 1990s and in the new millennium. The Chinese literary scene since the 1990s has been shaped by the break-up of any centralized discourse, marketization and commoditization of culture, or to employ the term used by Sheldon Lu, a "postmodern turn" has occurred (Lu 1997: 130). Wedell-Wedellsborg, to a far greater extent than the authors in the first section, follows the idea put forward by Lu that the simultaneous existence of multiple temporalities forms the essence of postmodernism in the PRC, where multiple temporalities are available to the individual as different paths or choices. In the novel, which she discusses in great detail, Yu Hua's "Brother" (*Xiongdi*), can be regarded as a "small story" which at the same time is intertwined with the grand narrative of the history of the PRC including the Cultural Revolution and the reform and opening period. Wedell-Wedellsborg concludes that Yu Hua's novel may truly be called a postmodern Chinese novel – an opinion which is also shared by a large group of Chinese critics who praise the novel as postmodern because it "turn(s) upside down established values and social classes:" Inwood's contribution on identity politics in online Chinese poetry groups and her special focus on the "School of Rubbish" deals with marginalized groups and the relation between postmodernity and multiple identities. Her example, the poetry of the "School of Rubbish;" starts with the quoted line "The East is Black" which demonstrates how master narratives such as "The East is Red"-ideology are re-configured and played with in contemporary China. New forms of poetry develop alongside new forms of distribution, production and consumption practices. Despite the multiple identities of the online-poet, the desire to belong to various well-known literary circles could hinder him/her from fully appreciating and grasping all the opportunities available. *Carsten Storm*, in his theoretically and empirically founded article on new historical novels and films, asks whether postmodernism should be understood as a globalized phenomenon or whether a form of postmodernism with Chinese characteristics exists. He concludes that there are various hybrid forms which transcend the exclusiveness and dichotomy of both concepts. His detailed analysis of films and novels show quite clearly that the deconstruction of master narratives, in this case both the CCP's version of history and older forms of historiographies, is an intrinsic sign of postmodern literary and filmic expression. Storm remarks that Western postmodern theory has been adapted to particular circumstances in China, and some Chinese critics even equate postmodernism with the disposition of folk culture, the history of familiarization and individualization.

In the third part, the authors focus on transitional aspects of postmodern China. With his focus on humor, *Martin Gieselmann* provides a new and refreshing perspective on a selection of contemporary "Chinese" films from the PRC, Hong Kong and Taiwan. Gieselmann's definition of postmodernity derives from the use of parody and irony. He embeds his argument within the specific historical development of China, but enlarges the analyzed space to "transnational China," so that his comparative approach allows him not only to highlight differences between China and the West, but also within the "Chinese world." The volume closes with an article by Jens Damm and his analysis of the role of the Internet for the Chinese diaspora. While Damm does not deny that the Internet may help to encourage the circulation of nationalist ideas within the Chinese community, he concludes that a global, postmodern and hybrid diasporic Chinese cyberspace is emerging, where especially the Web 2.0 applications offer space for the creation of postmodern hybrid identities which transcend the territorial boundedness of the traditional nation state and thus also transcend nationalist sentiments.

These articles cover a variety of different topics and demonstrate that there are recurring elements in any analysis of "postmodernity in action:" the importance of the ideological instabilities which created a moral vacuum where postmodernism could flourish, the interaction of the global with the local, and the creative – but also commercialized – handling of images derived from history. The authors describe a specific Chinese postmodern situation where the residual Chinese past is renegotiated within the emergent new capitalism and where the local and the global construct hybrid and unstable representations in various areas of cultural production. It was further shown that despite the decrease in intellectual debates on postmodernism, postmodern expressions are still strong. Although it is possible, it yet remains to be seen whether the Internet, in particular, will lead to the merging of the various postmodern forms of expression within the transnational Chinese world.

References

Dirlik, Arif and Zhang Xudong (1997) "Introduction: Postmodernism and China," in *boundary 2*, 24/3, pp. 1-18.

Dirlik, Arif and Zhang Xudong (2000) *Postmodernism and China*, Durham: Duke University Press.

Gu, Jian (1999) "Resisting Modernity in Contemporary China: The Cultural Revolution and Postmodernism," in *Modern China* 25/23, pp. 343-376.

Liu, Kang (1997) "Popular Culture and the Culture of the Masses in Contemporary China," in *boundary 2*, 24/3, pp. 99-122.

Lu, Sheldon H. (1996) "Postmodernity, Popular Culture, and the Intellectual: A Report on Post-Tiananmen China," in: *boundary 2* 23/2, pp. 139-169.

Lu, Sheldon H. (2001a) *China, Transnational Visuality, Global Postmodernity*, California: Stanford University Press.

Lu, Sheldon H. (2001b) "Global Post Modernization: The Intellectual, The Artist, and China's Condition," in *boundary 2* 24/3, pp. 65-97.

Lyotard, Jean-Francois (1984) *The Postmodern Condition: A Report on Knowledge*, transl. by Geoff Bennington and Brian Massumi, Manchester: Manchester University Press.

Münchau, Anne (2002) „Postmoderne Theorien in China und die Debatte über ihre Relevanz," in *Berliner China-Hefte. Beiträge zur Gesellschaft und Geschichte Chinas* 23, pp. 54-70.

Lu, Sheldon H. (2007) *Chinese Modernity and Global Biopolitics. Studies in Literature and Visual Culture*, Honolulu: University of Hawai'i Press.

Xu, Ben (2001) "Postmodern-Postcolonial Criticism and Pro-Democracy Enlightenment," in *Modern China* 27/1, pp. 117-147.

Wang, Ning (1997) "The Mapping of Chinese Postmodernity," in *boundary 2* 24/3, pp. 19-40.

Yang, Xiaobin (2002) „Postscript. Answering the Question. What is Postmodern/Post-Mao-Deng?" in Xiaobin Yang (ed.) *The Chinese Postmodern, Trauma and Irony in Chinese Avant-Garde Fiction*, Ann Arbor: University of Michigan Press, pp. 230-246.

Zhang, Xudong (1999) "Postmodernism and Post-Socialist Society: Cultural Politics in China after the 'New Era,'" in *New Left Review*, 237, pp. 77-105.

Andrew Field and Jeroen Groenewegen

Explosive Acts: Beijing's Punk Rock Scene in the Postmodern World of 2007

In this paper, we examine the musical and performance styles of several Chinese bands that fall loosely into the category of "Beijing punk rock." Analyses of punk rock music are often undertaken in the context of subcultural theory, to which punk rock served as a principle case (Hebdige 1978). A more fruitful line of inquiry, exemplified by Davies (1996) uses postmodern theory to study how punk rock challenges structures of power and authority while preventing co-optation by the market forces that drive the music and fashion industry in the Western world. In the West, the postmodern condition came to be associated with the malaise surrounding the global politics of the Cold War and the disenchantment with utopian visions of modernity that had arisen over the previous century embodied in the "isms" that professed a cure for the world's ills. In his study of punk rock in the UK, focusing on bands such as the Clash and the Sex Pistols, Davies demonstrates how these bands voiced strong critiques of post-war UK politics and US imperialism, while struggling against the commodification and ultimate dilution of the power and energy of their music, performance styles and ideas. Noting a similar trend in China, we connect the emergence of a punk rock scene in Beijing to the conditions of global postmodernity that are specific to the Chinese scene.

In the People's Republic of China, postmodernity emerges in the period after the Mao era (1949-1976), where disenchantment with socialist revolutionary practices is coupled with insecurities and opportunities created by the "opening and reforms" project initiated in the 1980s (Dirlik 2000). As Geremie Barmé argues, the shock that followed the Tiananmen Crisis of 1989 led to the sublimation of revolutionary and critical discourses into art and musical forms. Yet when marketized, the art and music scene came to constitute a "velvet prison" within which artists and musicians could continue to express criticism as long as they did not pose a serious threat to the basic structures of power and authority (Barmé 2000, Baranovitch 2003).

Born in the post-Tiananmen 1990s, but relying heavily on its Western counterpart from the late 1970s and early 1980s, Chinese punk rock has emerged as a powerful yet marginal musical genre. It is marginal in comparison to the Mandopop ballads that make up the mainstream and whose professed disinterest in politics render them more eligible for government approval and support. Nevertheless, punk performances are powerful and important. They offer sites for the more diverse and divergent opinions and life styles that emerge in the postmodern urban landscape, fanning flames of dissatisfaction and improper satisfaction through its violent dissonance. Punk rock in Beijing keeps the flame of revolutionary discourse alive through the act of performance, while continually struggling against the commodification and dilution of its energy, its signs, and its symbols.

The bands discussed in this article display their postmodernity through their performances: a *bricolage* of symbols, signs, and musical references. In China, the creation of group identity through style and fashion has a relatively short history and is still secondary to social cohesion on the basis of region, family, class, gender and generation. Based in Beijing and appealing to young people, Chinese punk rock reiterates certain of these older categories, but simultaneously its divergence from mainstream culture and its affinity with punk scenes in other places and times signify a trend in Chinese identity politics that legitimates a subcultural approach. However, in contrast to Hebdige's *Subculture: The Meaning of Style* our primary concerns are not signification, authenticity, and identity, but the creation and transmission of movements and effects (Gilbert 2004). Our main interest thus lies in the ways that punk rock bands in Beijing fan what we call the "intense fire of primal energy" during live shows, both through their performance and musical styles and through their cultural codes (i.e. clothing, hairstyle, body piercings).

Yet what constitutes this energy? And who is affected to what result? We do not offer any simple answers to these complex sociological questions, only avenues for further research. In the Beijing punk rock scene, the relation between the energetic event and subcultural signification is intricate. In the live arena or *xianchang*, experiences are forged that underlie notions of authenticity, identity, and belonging, but also of individuality and non-belonging – a paradoxical situation noted by other observers of the punk scene in the West (Tsitsos 1999: 399). Signs of a subcultural identity, such as dress code and group dance, enhance the intensity of the experience, and can indeed be part of the reason for the crowd to gather. To be sure, punk crowds are by no means unified in their reactions and motivations, let alone their styles of dress and behavior. Receptions and reactions to the bands and their music may differ according to the individual. Yet there are definite and discernable patterns in the way people engage in the music as a collective or crowd.

Rather than examine individual reactions to or interpretations of punk performances, our focus is thus on crowd dynamics. Here we draw inspiration from Elias Canetti's classic, *Crowds and Power*. Canetti studied the economy of energy in crowds. While written in the specific context of pre- and postwar Germany, his analysis is far more broadly applicable. All crowds are indebted with a propensity for growth, internal equality, density and direction (Canetti 1962: 32), traits that are easily recognized in Chinese punk audiences. In Canetti's taxonomy, punk audiences are a combination of rhythmic crowds and panicking flight crowds (Canetti 1962: 29, 35), where violent "panic" is contained within the broader harmony of a large crowd. This is apparent in the spontaneous outbursts of pogoing and moshing – a phenomenon we describe in this paper as "whirlpools of energy" – that sometimes burst forth within the audience during live performances of punk rock, usually towards the front of the stage (Tsitsos 1999). The image of a crowd within a crowd is reminiscent of subcultural theory, which posits subculture within mainstream culture. In this sense, punk shows offer a site for discharging the antagonism with daily, mainstream culture.[1] In the density of a punk crowd, there is hardly any other direction for venting violent energy than one's neighbor, even if the violence is, in this case, more playful and performative than destructive, though in some cases where authority figures are present, the energy can be directed at them.

Crowds react to the power of the performance. The physical performance of a punk rocker might include violent screaming, drumming, strumming, smashing instruments, jumping or leaping onstage or off into the crowd, or even kneeling or lying down on the stage as if wracked with convulsions. All of these are behaviors that we have witnessed during rock performances in Beijing, and some rock musicians discussed in this paper, such as Xie Tianxiao, integrate such behaviors into their act so frequently that they become expected and sometimes (in the case of Xie) even contracted. Rock concerts in Beijing are therefore no exception to the general rule of global rock culture that the performance is as much a

[1] See Canneti's sections on The Discharge and Destructiveness.

physical act as a musical act. The resulting transfer of energy between performers and audience (this is a two-way street after all), which takes place on both the physical plane of bodily motion and on the mental plane of emotion is vital to understanding the rock scene in China and its claims to a global authenticity, and yet few if any studies of rock music in China (let alone in other parts of the world) have explored this relationship in any detail.[2]

Each of the authors of this article has had his unique and long-term engagement with global music and dance cultures and their localizations in China.[3] Our approaches to recording and interpreting the punk music scene in Beijing complement each other. Field takes an audiovisual approach, collecting images and films of performances for analysis, while Groenewegen relies on field notes taken during and after the events. Both of us converge upon the notion that the most important space in the music scene is the nexus of interaction between performers and audience that takes place during live music events, especially at or near the front of the stage, and thus we spend most of our time in this nexus.

In undertaking this study, we collectively attended over 100 rock concerts, performances, and festivals held in Beijing between June and October 2007, when both authors were living in the city. Rather than attending these events as objective outside observers, we actively participated in the whirlpool of energy that a given *xianchang* might generate, and occasionally joined in the moshing and pogoing that often took place in the audience (though neither of us has crowd-surfed). We cultivated friendships with rock musicians, club managers, record producers, and audience members alike. We made copious notes on our experiences with the scene, and filmed many concerts, capturing both performers and audiences. We attended concerts in all the important live venues and festivals held during that time period.[4] While we cannot, for obvious reasons, relate all of the experiences, venues, and bands that we encountered, we have chosen to discuss several particular events, concerts, and bands that we feel are exemplary of the Beijing scene and the performative energy that is transferred between bands and fans on a nightly basis in clubs, concerts, and festivals.

---

[2] Important English-language studies of China's rock scene include Jones 1992, de Kloet 2001, Baranovich 2003, Steen 2000. Ian Condry's study of Japanese hip-hop culture in Tokyo also uses the *genba* (*xianchang*) as an important component for the study of localization of global musical forms.

[3] Andrew Field's fieldwork in China has focused on nightlife venues in Shanghai as a case study in the transmission of globalizing musical and dance cultures into China (Field 2008). His interest in rock music is more recent. Over the summer and fall of 2007, Field attended approximately thirty performance events in Beijing, Shanghai, Hunan, and Wuhan that featured punk or independent Chinese rock bands, including three major music festivals, and filmed and photographed over 100 bands and their audiences during these events. He also spoke with and interviewed several punk rock band members, punk/indie rock fans, record producers, and club owners in Beijing and Shanghai. Jeroen Groenewegen has been researching the live music scene since 2001. From August to October 2006 and from May to October 2007, Groenewegen conducted fieldwork for his dissertation research titled "The Performance of Identity in Chinese Popular Music."

[4] Nevertheless, it should be noted that this study necessarily incorporates our own particular musical biases and our own subject positions as Western male academics (though both of us are fluent in Mandarin). There are many other bands making up the punk rock music scene in Beijing that we simply do not have space for in this article.

Rock Music Clubs and Festivals in Beijing

Before launching into a discussion of specific performances, we will give the reader a general overview of the rock scene circa 2007. Rock music clubs function as the fulcrums around which the rock scene revolves in Beijing. As of 2007, these clubs are fairly evenly dispersed around the city. The rock music clubs with the most cachet include 1) Dos Kolegas on Liangmaqiao Road in the eastern Chaoyang District; 2) the Mao Livehouse on Big East Street of the Drum Tower; 3) D22 and 4) 13 Club located next to each other near Beida University's east entrance in the western Haidian District; 5) Yugong Yishan, originally located across from the Workers Stadium close to the nightlife district of Sanlitun, but closed down from late July to November and re-opened a few kilometers towards Lake Houhai; and 6) Star Live, just north of the Lama Temple (*Yonghe gong*) and the Second Ring Road. Between July and October 2007, we witnessed many concerts, festivals, and performances held nightly at each of these clubs. Each club caters to a mixed crowd of local Chinese and foreigners, often a fifty-fifty ratio but differing depending on the venue, night and the bands. Entrance fees range from 30 RMB at most clubs, to 80 or more RMB at the more commercial Star Live. Liquor is served in all these establishments, mostly in the form of beer. Drugs are rare, but occasional whiffs of marijuana can be sensed in the air. After shows, Chinese audiences usually leave the venue almost instantly. The audience members are usually but not exclusively people in their 20s or 30s, including both university students and young professionals. Men predominate, but there are significant numbers of females in the usual crowd. Some crowd members obviously belong to certain subcultures of rock – punk rockers, metal rockers, and so forth – while many others do not seem to profess any particular sartorial allegiance to a certain musical style. On a regular night, a club might attract a few dozen people, but on weekend nights and big "festival" events featuring a larger line-up of bands, hundreds of people might attend.

The size of the crowd also depends on that of the club itself. Star Live, by far the largest live music venue, can hold more than 1000 people, and tends to feature more big-name, popular artists who can draw a bigger audience. By way of contrast, D22, the smallest club, can hold only 150 people or so. Run by an American named Michael Pettis, D22 supports a small and loyal set of punk and post-punk bands and has the reputation of being an "incubator" for bands that Pettis and his club feel are worth supporting (Field, interview with Michael Pettis, October 2007). Its neighbor, 13 Club, tends to feature metal bands and cater to their fans. Dos Kolegas, run by two Chinese rock musicians, Liu Miao and Gao Feng, is a favored hangout for punk and post-punk rockers as well, but also features weekly sessions of experimental music held every Tuesday Night, a program known as "Waterland Sight and Sound" (*shuilu guanyin*) that invites avant-garde experimental musicians from all over the world to perform. Given its Japanese sponsors, Mao Livehouse boasts the best sound system among rock clubs in Beijing and can hold a few hundred people. It features a music hall physically separated from the bar and social area by concrete walls, and caters to a greater variety of bands than the other clubs.

Rock band, Hedgehog, consisting of bassist, Bo Xuan, drummer, Atom, and lead singer/guitarist, Zi Jian, perform at a special concert at the new *Yugong Yishan* organized by the Maybe Mars (Bing Masi) record label on November 10, 2007. Note the height of the stage – as tall as most of the audience – which creates a barrier between performers and audience not felt in other clubs where the stage is lower. Photo by Andrew Field.

Brain Failure's lead singer, Xiao Rong, with his trademark leopard-skin hairdo performs on the stage of the Mao Livehouse, August 11, 2007. Note the relatively low stage and close proximity to the audience, the strong audience reaction, and the ubiquitous presence of photographers and filmmakers, even onstage. Photo by Andrew Field.

Mao Livehouse often hosts festivals usually organized by a particular musical theme – for example, the summer and fall line – up for 2007 included festivals honoring Guns and Roses (where everyone performed tribute songs to this band), the Ramones (ditto), Brit Pop, Nu Metal, and many other themes. All of these clubs feature an elevated stage and standing room for the audience, creating an egalitarian atmosphere – though in the case of Star Live and the new Yugong Yishan, VIPs are catered for through special minimum-consumption tables in a lounge, on a balcony or even in the arena near the stage. Especially this last practice limits the amount of dancing and free roaming space – much to the chagrin of many fans who are there to rock en masse and as close to the stagefront as possible. Another factor in the transmission of energy that we discuss in this article is the size and height of the stage. Clubs with higher stages, such as Star Live and the new Yugong Yishan, tend to create more physical and psychological distance between rockers and their audience than the lower-stage clubs. At smaller clubs the only apparent barrier between bands and their audience lies in the use of photo cameras, camcorders and mobile phones. Given the lack of restrictions in this area, recording is a very popular strategy of engaging in rock shows. Notably, it represents an economy of desire that contrasts with that of dance. Another venue for performing rock music in Beijing is the outdoor music festival. During our period of observation between June and October, three major festivals took place in the city. The first was the CH+INDIE festival held at Dos Kolegas on July 7 and 8, featuring many of the city's top indie rock bands.[5]

The second was the Beijing Pop Festival held at Chaoyang Park on September 8 and 9, which was headlined by international acts such as the New York Dolls, Public Enemy, and the Nine Inch Nails, but also a large number of local bands. The third was the Modern Sky Festival, held at Haidian Park from October 2 to 4 2007, which also featured numerous

5 We designate this event the status of a festival because it took place over two days and was originally meant to be held outdoors, thus making it qualitatively different to the festivals held by rival clubs such as D22 and Mao Livehouse.

rock bands from all over the country as well as Hong Kong pop musicians and international acts, notably the New York-based indie band, The Yeah Yeah Yeahs.

These outdoor festivals offer a different dynamic to live venues, including multiple stages that are much larger and more separated from the crowd, squads of Chinese *bao'an* security guards placed conspicuously between the bands and the audience, and a much larger and more diverse crowd than the small, indoor clubs. One can still see similar performer-audience interactions to those of the more intimate clubs, though on a much grander, more epic scale as performers and audiences struggle to surmount the greater physical and psychological distance that separates them (for examples of this see our observations on the Beijing Pop Festival below). These large festivals, which gather crowds of thousands, also complicate the question of who constitutes the audience for rock performances in China. Yet it is safe to say that the great majority of people who attend these festivals do not regularly attend concerts in the city's rock music clubs. For the majority, going to a festival is simply a once-in-a-lifetime chance to see a Chinese rocker of the status of Cui Jian, or an international group with the cachet of the Nine Inch Nails. While most of the rockers featured in the regular line-ups of the city's rock music clubs do not have star status in China, there are a few exceptions. Among them is the artist, Xie Tianxiao.

Rock Star Energy: Xie Tianxiao at Star Live, June 8, 2007

When I arrived on June 8, 2007 at the Star Live, I could hardly get in.[6] Beijing's largest live venue was packed for what would be one of the most successful live shows of a Chinese rock band that I have ever witnessed.[7] With over 1000 people and tickets of 60 rmb (with a 10 rmb discount for students) the event must also have been a financial success for the organizers. Indeed, two months later, the organizing *danwei* (work unit), Thirteenth Month Independent Music Label, signed up Xie Tianxiao, thus moving from a folk and singer-songwriter label into louder music genres. As of the time of writing, Xie Tianxiao is recording his third studio album.

In the two-hour show, Xie plays almost all songs from his previous two albums. The back-up band puts everything into it. Drummer, Zhao Wei, hits the drums with all his might, nearly smashing the toms in the drum fill of "I Could Have Died Yesterday (*wo zuotian keneng sile*)," a fill reminiscent of the Nirvana song "Paper Cuts." Bass player, Guo Jian, with his dreads sways his hips and rhythm guitar player, Li Zhao, sporting cool sunglasses, shakes his shoulders. They walk across the stage, making sure they do not get in the way of Xie's energetic stage performance as his alter ego X.T.X., which is the focus of the concert. His white shirt with a slightly altered picture of Chairman Mao contrasts with the dark shirts of the band members, but in general the simple outfit of jeans and shirt suits the straightforwardness of the music. A large portion of the audience sings along with the uncomplicated, catchy melodies, suggesting a strong familiarity with his recorded music. It helps that the songs are in Mandarin Chinese and not English, unlike those of many punk bands in the city. Xie waves his long hair, runs across stage, screams, gesticulates, and pushes things over. During "Asima," Li Zhao throws his sunglasses away, as Xie gives the audience the finger. 'Fuck you' read his lips. I have never seen anything like that in a music

6 Jeroen Groenwegen is the author of this section.

7 Clips made by fans can be found on websites, such as www.ku6.com (中国摇滚新教父谢天笑的丑恶嘴脸 and 768 星光现场谢天笑阿诗玛等) and www.youku.com (谢天笑星光现场砸吉他 and 冷血乐队谢天笑).

concert in China before. The crowd in the fenced-off arena in front of the stage moshes even more vehemently. Some people make a circle and invite everyone to join. As it circles faster and faster it creates a large space and emits individuals who cannot cope with its speed. A girl gets hurt as one of the few remaining bar stools tips over. Her boyfriend picks it up and rushes furiously forwards, gesticulating and threatening to use it on the person he believed pushed his girlfriend over, but he is calmed down by bystanders. Soon the moshing and pogoing is as intensive as before. When the song is over, X.T.X. changes back to the typically humble Chinese stage persona and expresses happiness at seeing so many fans. His "I have really missed you" makes him suddenly sound like a pop singer, save for the out-of-town accent in his Chinese and shortage of breath. Male audience members shout "*niu bi*"[8] and "I love you, Xie Tianxiao" in Chinese.

Xie's rock star behavior is also evidenced by his relationship with the stage personnel. They help him with his frequent changes of guitar (a rare phenomenon in China), straighten up microphone and cymbal stands, and generally clean up Xie's mess. When agitated fans climb onto the one-and-a-half meter high stage to dance and stage dive, the stage personnel guides them backstage and releases them back into the arena through a side entrance. Although the stage personnel belong to the organizing party, and are most likely friendly with Xie he antagonizes them. They serve as a useful prop on which to vent his anger, which is encouraged by the audience. Had the stage personnel been dressed in uniform, the audience might have been more ready to develop its disobedience into hostility. The show accumulates more violence when Xie starts smashing his guitar. The audience reacts hysterically. Guo Jian waves his bass around and eventually breaks it. Zhao Wei pushes his drum kit over. Strings and pieces of wood scatter around, but Xie is far from satisfied. He circles around the stage, screaming, ranting, pushing at the amps and at fans that have climbed onto the stage, until finally the stage personnel force the tormented rock hero backstage.

The first time Xie smashed his guitar was in 1998. He comments in an article in the South China Weekly of November 2, 2006: "That time smashing my guitar wasn't a performance (*biaoyan*), I really felt there was too much sadness, I could only use this way to vent (*faxie*). [...] Back then no-one allowed me to, so when I did it, it was very satisfying. Nowadays, since they demand me to do it, it's become pointless (Cheng 2006)." Organizers of Xie Tianxiao's shows in Japan put the demand down in the performance contract, and Xie Tianxiao simply gives the organizer and the audience what it wants, resulting in guitar smashing in about half of his shows since 2004, most of them sponsored by a well-known American guitar label. The frequent guitar changes in Star Live and during other shows serve both as teasers and as a distraction so that the final change does not seem too staged.

Xie Tianxiao's music is rooted in the grunge and punk genres. His performance in Star Live in 2007 mimics Xie Tianxiao's development from the Nirvana-revering "punk" (liumang) he was when he still played in Cold Blooded Animal in the late 1990s to the propagator of a distinct and modern Chinese identity that he became after he stayed in America for a year in 2001. The show starts with the rawness of the first album, to move into a more Chinese sound, which Xie Tianxiao added as a 'taste enhancer' to the otherwise typical rock compositions of the second album (Anonymous 2005).[9] Two-thirds of the way into the

8 *Niubi* is Beijing slang, roughly meaning "awesome!" or "redhot."

9 The show also contained one new song, "Man of the House (Yeye)," starting with a Peking opera a-a-a, then escalating in a tormented scream.

show, Xie Tianxiao invites *guzheng*[10] player, Zhang Wei, onto the stage for the intro of "Who Brought Me Here (*shi shei ba wo dai dao zheli*)." They play the extended version of the song, which contains a dialogue between the two of them on the *guzheng*.

Who is it that brought me here?
At dawn I left the human crowds, in a daze I entered a forest.
The people here told me they use leaves for clothes.
This is a world of nakedness, should I reject it
or should I bow my head in shame to look for leaves at my feet.
I decided to leave this place and go home.
But I had forgotten how I came here, didn't know how to go back.
At that moment a stranger was hastily passing by.
Hey! I asked him with a sense of urgency,
who was it that brought me here, brought me here.
He told me that if I wanted to go back, it would take the rest of my life,
but that was still a great many years.
Don't tell me that if I want to go back, it will take the rest of my life,
because that will still be a great many years.[11]

After leaving Asian or primitive collectivity, the protagonist of the song perceives his nakedness. Undeciding whether to stay or leave, he realizes there is no way back. These lyrics articulate the culture shock Xie must have experienced in the USA. His difficulty in securing a place in (or in relation to) the developed world is recognizable by large Chinese audiences.

The aporia performed in "Who Brought Me Here" goes beyond the clichéd teenager angst. It also resonates with postmodern global culture that is itself ridden by a profound feeling of unhomeliness and a confusing abundance of desires and forces. Xie addresses these insecurities by combining national musical traditions with grunge sounds without arriving at stable conclusions. He fans anxiety and simultaneously offers an outlet to vent it, all with the most powerful symbols and sounds at hand. Ultimately, this outburst of energy overrides any discourse of authenticity. Rock performances consist of compositions and choreographies whose constructed and rehearsed nature does not prevent, but enables the transfer of effects.

Beijing Punk Rock Showdown: CH+INDIE "Wrath of Khan" Festival at Dos Kolegas, July 7 and 8, 2007

Like discos or raves, rock festivals offer the audience an "otherworldly" experience, taking them away from the trials and tribulations of contemporary life, whilst also challenging some of the mainstream norms and values of society. The CH+INDIE Festival held on July 7 and July 8, 2007, provides an excellent opportunity for both wide-angle and close-up views of the performer-audience nexus in Beijing. A close analysis of this Beijing rock festival provides a panoramic view of performance styles and band-audience interactions in the punk rock scene, while also allowing us to zoom in on several of the top performers in that scene, including the new band, Hedgehog, and some older more established bands, Joyside, Lonely China Day, and SUBS.

[10] The guzheng is an ancient Chinese stringed instrument, akin to the zither.

[11] All translations by the authors unless otherwise indicated.

In the hot, sultry afternoon of July 7, 2007, I rock up to the front entrance of Dos Kolegas, a small rock pub located off the Liangmaqiao Road in the eastern Chaoyang District, in the ample grounds of a public park featuring a drive-in movie theater.[12] For the two day event known as CH+INDIE, the local indie record labels, Tag Team and Modern Sky,[13] have assembled some of their best acts and some other independent bands – punk bands, mostly, but also some more "experimental" bands such as Lonely China Day. The plan is for the bands to perform on an outdoor stage set up on the far side of a grassy lawn outside the venue. Stands are set up around the perimeter touting different music labels and band-oriented products. Soon after I arrive, The No Name, a punk band hailing from Xi'an, performs on the outdoor stage, all punked up in black outfits with body tattoos and punk hairdos, with their hair either spiked up with gel like the lead guitarist, or worn long and partially obscuring the face like the lead singer, Yao Rui. Their in-your-face music and attitude looks and sounds a lot like early Clash. A few dozen rockers, marked by their own punk hairdos, face and body piercings, and "alternative" clothes have gathered on the lawn when the anticipated rain arrives. Lead singer, Yao Rui, belts his song into the microphone as a powerful windstorm hits, tearing down the giant poster backing the stage, which gives the full name of the festival: "Wrath of Khan" (a pop culture reference to a Star Trek film) and forcing the band and the audience to run across the lawn and inside the crowded club, as the organizers struggle to get the equipment inside before it is drenched by the rain. Given the unseasonably bad weather, the crowd is more modest than expected, but nevertheless it packs the sweaty, smoke-filled club to capacity.

As the festival enters into the evening program, the crowd grows larger, spilling out into the grassy courtyard where tables with umbrellas are set up. Overall, around 400 people show up for the event on each day (Andrew Field interview with Matt Kagler, July 8, 2007). Copious amounts of beer are flowing - predominantly into foreigners - from the bar, which is set up to cover both the indoor and outdoor crowds, A British DJ spins tunes on a stereo system set up outside the club. People representing the two sponsoring labels have set up stands both outside and just inside the door of the club to sell CDs, T-shirts and other band-related paraphernalia. Other than a small number of shops dedicated to indie rock music, live performances are often the only occasion to purchase recordings by Beijing's local bands. Although the band is inside the small club there is no real barrier between them and their audience. The stage is only around one meter high, and people gather right at the base, where they can literally touch the band members.

Day two starts off badly with a long delay owing to technical problems with the sound se-tup – a common issue in Beijing clubs, where experienced professional sound technicians are few and far between. The afternoon begins with a low attended set by Nuclear, which is the band of the club owner and drummer, Liu Miao. Hedgehog, a young, dynamic, and popular Beijing-based band, brings up the energy levels and gets audience heads rolling and feet moving to the band's jumpy, upbeat sound. By this time around 50 to 100 people are walking in and out of the small club. Hedgehog's Atom is remarkable for her tiny size and

12 Andrew Field reports on this event. Liu Miao and Gao Feng chose the small, secluded venue to set up Dos Kolegas because of its relative cheapness and also because it is located far from any residential neighborhood.

13 A jovial, red-bearded American named Matt Kagler, who owns Tag Team Records, is organizing the event, along with Jin Hui, a local Beijinger who represents Modern Sky.

her powerful drumming. Lead singer/guitarist Zi Jian erupts into mad strumming sessions as he waves his guitar violently about. During a break in their session, Zi Jian says (in English) "this place is so hot!" From the audience a Chinese guy retorts—also in English—"you guys are so hot!" which elicits a round of laughter from the crowd. The band's next song "Noise Hit World" from their forthcoming album of the same name elicits head-shaking, and applause.

Joyside then hits the stage to deliver a few old-style songs, and the energy levels of the crowd rises in reaction to the heavy drumming and strumming of the band. As Joyside launches into a Ramones-like tune, a small crowd at the stage front erupts into a fiesta of moshing, slamdancing, and pogoing. The playful pushing, jostling, and bumping of bodies, male, female, Chinese and foreign, in a whirlpool of energy that gathers near the front of the stage, as lead singer Bian Yuan sings in his trademark lethargic, inebriated style. Joyside are an older, more established band, known for their hedonistic lifestyles and songs that celebrate the pleasures of beer, cigarettes, urination, and sex.[14] They are also more rooted in 1960s British rock music than most other punk bands in the city – on other occasions, we have heard Bian Yuan perform songs by the Beatles, Rolling Stones, and David Bowie, to name but a few. Other band members who have finished their set now drink, mingle, and dance with the audience. The three young members of Hedgehog are now deep in the mosh pit, bodies jostling and banging, sweat dripping down their faces, brimming with excited smiles.

Veteran punk rock band Joyside, led by stylish lead singer Bian Yuan (front and center), perform at Dos Kolegas, July 8 2007. Photo by Andrew Field.

The crowd at Dos Kolegas watching the performance by Joyside, July 8 2007. Note the predominance of foreigners and the signs of belonging to the punk rock scene. Photo by Andrew Field.

With few exceptions, there is no attempt by bands to isolate themselves from or elevate themselves to a higher status than their audience. Neither does any band cultivate an image of distancing rock stardom of the sort of Xie Tianxiao, nor do they present themselves as an intellectual or political vanguard or model (*bangyang*), as more idealist rockers such as Cui Jian might have done. Bands and audience members alike hang out together, smoking the same cigarettes and sometimes drinking from the same bottle of beer. The internal equality of the crowd in front of the stage could hardly be more perfect.

---

[14] Joyside have also been the subjects of two video rockumentaries, *Wasted Orient* (dir. Kevin Fritz, Plexifilm DVD 2007) and a German independent production, *Beijing Bubbles* (http://www.beijing-bubbles.com).

The penultimate act of the two-day event is a psychedelic set by Lonely China Day, whose dual guitars, drums, and electronica are enhanced by the projection of a multicolored light show onto the band. Though often grouped with other punk bands, this is a more experimental band that aims to build melodic soundscapes rather than waves of dissonance. Guitarist/lead singer Deng Pei and co-guitarist Wang Dongtao face each other on stage as the pixilated lights turn their faces, bodies, and guitars different shades of red, white, blue, purple, and green. The hard-driving rhythmic pulse of music from two heavily distorted electric guitars and the pulsing effect of the light show puts us all into a sort of trance. Bodies and heads sway back and forth like a sea of anemones as we engage with the band onstage in a collective "oceanic" experience reminiscent of the ecstasy club scene in the UK (Malbon 1999). At this point, the majority of the crowd are foreigners – ironic since Lonely China Day is the only band in the final lineup that sings in Chinese. Their songs are known to draw inspiration from lyrical poems of the Song Dynasty (960-1279). For a non-native speaker of Mandarin, the lyrics can be difficult to follow even on paper let alone in a live act, so instead the focus of most foreign audience members (and probably most Chinese as well) is on the hypnotic, repetitive guitarwork of Wang Dongtao, which alternates hard strumming and arpeggios, carrying the audience up and down in waves of emotion in line with the emotive highs and lows of Deng Pei's vocalizing. At this point it matters little what Deng is actually saying—the audience gets it nonetheless.

While the lyrics (which are always translated into English in their album liners) may enhance the music for those "in the know," the music itself is central to the communion between audience and performer. Some fans might be familiar with the albums of Lonely China Day, which is arguably one of the most popular Chinese indie rock acts outside China, but only in a live venue such as Dos Kolegas can the audience experience the "magical" and "shamanistic" qualities of the music enhanced by the close proximity of the performers, the aural intensity of the amplifiers, and the visual intensity of the psychedelic projection. The collective experience of listening to the band live carries the aura of a religious rite, far different from the personal act of listening to a CD or MP3 player. It is no coincidence that Dos Kolegas, with its intimate stage setup, is one of Lonely China Day's favorite performance venues and that the band usually asks to perform alone. And unlike most other bands, LCD members rarely stick around before or after their show, seeming to prefer the status of mystics, prophets, or shamans, rather than that of punk rockers.

SUBS hit the stage for the final act on Sunday night, bringing the two-day festival to an end with a deafening roar. By this time the crowd is beginning to disperse. Around forty people, mostly foreigners, are intensely following the band's act. The female lead singer, Kang Mao, alternately screams and squeals out her English-language lyrics, while prancing, jumping, jogging, and moaning onstage.

SUBS lead singer Kang Mao performing onstage at Dos Kolegas, July 8, 2007. Kang Mao pours intense energy and passion into her performances. Photo by Andrew Field.

As Public Enemy play onstage, fans in the general area are blocked from the stage by a VIP section and by the highly visible presence of a squad of *bao'an* security officers. A few foreigners are trying to jump the barrier and are being pushed back by the guards. One foreigner is trying to win over an officer with jokes. From this angle, you can see how far away the band is from the main crowd, compared with bands at the local clubs.

Kang Mao paces the floor, commanding the show. Her black dress – really just a miniskirt and tank top – white-laced black Converse High-tops, black cat tattooed on her shoulder, and long curly hair partially covering her eyes reinforces her status as a punk rocker. She delivers her songs with enormous energy and passion, while Zhu Lei and Wu Hao back her in an aggressively masculine call-and-response mode, belting out short rejoinders to her vocals. The music is hard driving, melodically simple and rhythmically intricate. At one point in the act, Kang Mao kneels down at the front of the stage and bows her head and arms down onto the floor, as if kow-towing to the audience. At other points, she twirls the microphone around her neck, mimicking the act of a self-hanging, or curls herself into a fetal position onstage and writhes on the floor. In spaces between her lyrics she pumps her body back and forth in a primordial, sexualized motion. All of these acts, while seemingly spontaneous, are in fact carefully staged to coincide with the music, and as I discover later when viewing other SUBS concerts, they are part of a physical repertoire that Kang Mao uses in every performance.

The sexual energy of the audience is palpable as well. As SUBS begins "The Man," a song that starts with a slow, sexy bass line, one young woman who appears to be Eurasian is dancing by herself at the center of the floor, close to the stage. She flirtatiously entices a foreign man by lifting her shirt to reveal her bare belly. He responds with great excitement by coming together to dance behind her as if miming the sexual act. This performative, sexual interpretation of the violent music of SUBS is entirely legitimate, but not supported by the lyrical content of this particular song, which centers around the repeated demand to "tell the truth." This song, "Brother," conveys the anguish that Kang Mao felt after the crackdown on the Tiananmen protestors in 1989, of which her own brother was one of the victims. Whether the "truth" should be about this event, or more generally about political events in China that the government has whitewashed, is not certain. Towards the end of the song, Kang Mao kow-tows to the audience, banging her head repeatedly at the front of the stage, as if beseeching them to spread the word and "tell the truth." Following the song,

Kang Mao breaks to deliver a short speech in Chinese about the importance of rock music in China (ironic since most of the crowd by now is foreign). "If only we can increase the audience of this concert by a thousandfold, if only China can be more open, if only people can learn to think more, if only, if only..."

In their performance of "Brother" and other songs from their latest self-produced album *Down* (2006), SUBS are acting out a deep trauma sustained by the violent crackdown of 1989. The violence of the music and performance is simultaneously the reenactment of an experience of loss that exceeds conscious signification and a conscious and significant exhortation to act up and "tell the truth." Such political consciousness is not the norm in the Chinese punk scene. Furthermore, the topic is addressed only in general terms in English lyrics that are hardly understandable in a live setting although they printed in the booklet of their album. Thus, it is doubtful whether the lyric's full semantic potential is consciously understood by the bulk of the audience, though it is likely that most of the audience still "gets" that a violent trauma is being exorcized on stage.

Joining the Game: Punk Rockers at the Beijing Pop Festival, September 8 and 9, 2007[15]

While we wish to draw attention away from an exclusive focus on the politics of rock music in China, we nevertheless acknowledge in this paper that politics is definitely an important part of the legacy of rock and punk rock music in China. In May 1989, Cui Jian's song, "I Have Nothing" (*Yi wu suo you*), performed publicly during the Tiananmen protest movement, became an anthem of the student protest movement that converged on Tiananmen Square. This was the last time in the People's Republic of China that rock music was so brazenly associated with organized youthful rebellion against the Chinese state (Brace et al 1992; Jones 1992, 1994; Huang 2003; Baranovitch 2003). The brutal military crackdown that ended the Tiananmen Crisis from May to June 1989 fundamentally altered the political and social space in which the political intentions of rock music in China can realistically maneuver, compelling most of the musicians to refrain from political outspokenness, and a number of them from politics altogether.

The Beijing Pop Festival, held in early September (in 2007) at Chaoyang Park in Beijing, offers an opportunity to examine the dynamics of punk rock and its relationship to Chinese state power and authority in a much larger, more public and open setting than the rock club. For this particular event, which attracts several thousand music fans over two days,[16] a large number of bands come to China from abroad to perform, including the punk legends, The New York Dolls, and The Ramones' drummer, Marky Ramone, and headliners, Public Enemy, whom the Chinese state has decided can only be publicly referred to as P.E. given the controversial name, and the industrial rock band, the Nine Inch Nails – all with anti-establishment credentials. A number of Beijing-based bands, including punk bands, also appear on stage.

There are two stages for the festival, both well ensconced in spacious Chaoyang Park.[17] The first stage, sponsored by local radio station HIT FM, is the teaser stage – people can

---

[15] Both authors attended this event in its entirety, although we saw different shows on the two separate stages. The title also refers to P.K.14's song "Against Those Who Join the Game (*Jujue canjia youxi de ren*)."

[16] According to the official website, http://www.beijingpopfestival.com, the event sold 15,000 tickets per day.

[17] The following section draws from a blog of the event recorded by Andrew Field soon after on his blogsite, http://shanghaijournal.squarespace.com. See the entry: "Hang the Police, We're here to Rock."

enter for free. The main stage is located further north beyond a hillock that keeps the two stages from interfering with each other. After paying 200 RMB in advance or 250 at the gate (or less if you wanted to risk buying from a local "yellow cow" (*huangniu*) or scalper) you walk in and make your way onto the grass field. Between this large field and the stage is a fenced-off "VIP" area with reserved seating. A team of uniformed Beijing *bao'an* security officers is arrayed along the inner side of the metal fence to keep the masses from jumping over into the VIP section.[18]

The physical and psychological rift between audience and performers created by the VIP area and security cordon is challenged repeatedly by the more raucous members of the crowd – mostly foreign men, but also some Chinese men. The challenge starts playful, and both the security officers and the crowd interact with smiles, though a strong tension underlies the interaction. A crowd of young punks, both men and women, Chinese and foreign, gathers just behind the fence near center stage, sporting their mohawks and baring their chests in defiance of the fence. When the more energetic bands come on stage, some members of the crowd near the fence mosh violently and crowd-surf, occasionally sending a crowd-surfer over the fence, only to be repelled back by the hands of policemen. This happens repeatedly during the Public Enemy concert on Saturday night, and again during the Marky Ramone concert on Sunday afternoon. At one point, a young punk must have grabbed a security officer's hat off his head, which the crowd then flings repeatedly in the air in a ritual taunting gesture against the authorities. Some people in the audience – foreigners mainly – even try to talk with the police and get them on their side. But the rockers, even the most notoriously anti-establishment ones, are conspicuously cautious. At one point, Marky Ramone asks the audience to calm down so that they can hold the event again next year. At the end of the second night, Trent Reznor, lead singer of the Nine Inch Nails, humbly thanks the Chinese and the city of Beijing for allowing them to perform. The message is relayed to the Chinese through an onstage interpreter.

The main stage program on the second day begins with a series of Beijing-based punk bands, including Hedgehog, Scoff, and Brain Failure. One of the older and most established punk rock bands, Brain Failure has enjoyed unparalleled success both at home and abroad, and has toured the USA. Lead singer Xiao Rong has successfully cultivated an aura of punk rocker stardom, and is known for his slender, cut figure (a sign of pure energy), his rapid guitar-playing and playful antics (he jumps around a lot on stage), and above all, his leopard-skin crew-cut, which features on the album (his short-cropped hair is dyed blond with black spots). Their song, "Coming Down to Beijing," with its ska rhythm reminiscent of some Clash or English Beat tunes, can be read doubly as a celebration of the newfound vitality of the city in the post-Mao era and as a critique of the extraordinarily rapid development that the city has undergone over the past two decades. The band uses sarcasm and humor to express a sense of bewilderment and dissatisfaction with the modernizing agenda of the Beijing government:[19]

---

[18] It should be noted that the concert was organized by an American rock promoter, Jason Magnus, owner of the company and promotional vehicle rockinchina.com. Magnus was at that time engaged to the granddaughter of the former Chinese leader, Deng Xiaoping, which apparently helped him to get the connections to vet the concert with local authorities. This was the third annual Beijing Pop Festival, held since 2005.

[19] These lyrics appear in the liner to Brain Failure's CD *Coming Down to Beijing* (Bad New Records, 2007).

How it's so funny, it's so lovely
How it's so pretty, it's so junky
All these things're happening in this city
How did they build all the building.
It could survive only a second.
Hey (you've) went away for two weeks come back.
Can't find your home!
We're coming down.
Coming down. Coming down.
B.E.I.J.I.N.G!

During Brain Failure's performance of "Coming Down to Beijing" the crowd sings along and raises their fists in unison (note that most of the fist-raising is done by Chinese, not foreigners). Beijing Pop Festival, September 10, 2007. Photo by Andrew Field.

P.K.14 lead singer Yang Haisong performing at Mao Livehouse, November 9, 2007. Photo by Andrew Field.

Although the use of English distances the band from its Chinese audience, which may not possess proficient English skills, savvy listeners still ought to be able to read into the lyrics a criticism of how the city's recent modernization has displaced countless thousands of residents, seemingly considering them to be emotionless objects that can be moved at will. Despite rumored ease with censorship (the album Coming Down to Beijing is distributed in China by Modern Sky Records), the most common rationale bands give is that the sounds of the English language suit punk music better. When performed live, it is not apparent that the audience understands the import of the lyrics. The chorus line "Coming Down, coming down, coming down to B. E. I. J. I. N. G!" provokes a strong response; audience members repeat the lines, raising their fists in the air. The lines are easy to sing along with, even if one's English skills are minimal. The result is more of a collective celebration of the city than an ironic commentary on its recent development. In other words, more knowledgeable members of the audience may appreciate the band's critical message, yet most probably see it as a rather simple paean to the city. Brain Faillure plugs into mainstream culture's buzz that pushes Beijing in the direction of a cosmopolitan, global city. Additionally, featuring "authentic" Chinese rock bands as well as high-stature international acts to play as equals on the public stage, the Beijing Pop Festival as a whole coincides with a broader image of the city promoted by the vigorous modernization campaign leading up the 2008 Olympics.

Punk bands thus play an ironic role in supporting the city in its bid to go global. While not necessarily supportive of the current regime, the hedonistic stance of many punk bands in Beijing, including Brain Failure, Joyside and the mock punk of New Pants (*Xin kuzi*), but also of a host of younger bands such as Hedgehog and Queen Sea Big Shark (*Houhai da shayu*), is also not in conflict with the state's planned market economy (Davis 2000, Steen 1996). Rather than opposing the Communist state and the capitalist market on principle, they ask to join in and even define its benefits, which to them mean partying with friends and indulging in alcohol, cigarettes, and sex.[20]

Our taxonomy of explosive acts in the Beijing punk scene so far consists of the redirection of frustration by Xie Tianxiao, the shamanistic trance of Lonely China Day, the traumatic explosion of SUBS and the cynical, hedonistic partying of Brain Failure, amongst others. Yet there are other, more self-reflective strategies present at the Beijing Pop Festival.

A few hours later, the rays of the setting sun reflect in singer Yang Haisong's glasses as he performs with his band P.K.14 (Public Kingdom 14) at the HIT FM stage. This band, along with several others that work the Beijing scene (such as Re-TROS, Snapline, and Carsick Cars)[21] are often labeled post-punk, since their musical style is more poetic, more complex, and more sonically experimental. Yang Haisong, with his "nerdy" appearance – collared shirt, black-rimmed glasses – fits the mold of the post-punk rocker. The large glasses on his slender face stress his intellectual credentials as he delivers his oration of existentialist self-doubt with a typical high-pitched and unstable voice. The lyrics appeal directly to the audience, both because they are in Chinese and because the second person pronoun appears frequently – in contrast to Xie Tianxiao's 'I' and Brain Failure's pronoun-less slogans. The use of this pronoun is illustrative also because it is singular: during most part of the performance audience members are somewhat dispersed over the field and do not engage in collective dances. In the course of the concert as the audience becomes more and more immersed in the music, some dance and create space around themselves, while others seem to be awestruck.

and don't easily believe
and don't easily press forward
and don't easily believe
on this gently warm evening
the angered sage has been on the road, traveled too far
so you say
tell the children, why there exists, this dying city
tell the children, why there exists, this dying city

The vocals build up the tension, supported by the reverberating bass line played by Zhang Xudong – ex-bass player of Brain Failure and ex-drummer and founding member of SUBS. The tension releases with the distortion guitar of Xu Bo and the continuous drum fill of Swedish-born Lei Tantan (Jonathan Leijonhufvud). More individual audience members enter into a trancelike dance.

---

[20] Xiao Rong even chants "suck my dick in a KTV" repeatedly in one song on the Brain Failure album Coming Down to Beijing. The lyrics are obvious when listened to, but they are not present on the lyric sheet – perhaps intentionally in a bid to get past the government censors.

[21] The latter two published their debut albums on Maybe Mars records, a new indie label established by D22's Michael Pettis and P.K.14's Yang Haisong.

The city is a place of decay, but it's the only home we have. The song "Tell the Children (*Gaosu haizimen*)" performs existentialism's "being-thrown-into-this-world" by combining the up-beat energy of punk and even more danceable ska and bossanova rhythms and bass lines with the overtones and near-dissonant fragility of emo-rock and noisy guitar riffs. The individual is an unstable pulsar on the verge of dispersing into dust:

the star-houses desire rediscovery again
and the dust during treatment gradually ages
so you say, don't stop, let the sound continue
even if the fountainhead has been lost
even if the privileges are quietly sinking [into oblivion]
tell the children, don't stop, let the sound continue
tell the children, don't stop, let the sound continue
tell them, don't stop, let the sound continue

The repetition in the lyrics stresses the insecurity, and depletes the words of their semantic content. The band gives everything, and the audience of a few hundred appreciates actively. The greater the shock when the unthinkable happens: the band stops, the show is over. Despite desperate shouts and ceaseless applause, they do not return.

Conclusion: Punk Rock in the Postmodern Age

"The desire of the consumer age has finally become the new main theme of Chinese rock music" concludes the prominent rock critic, Zhang Xiaozhou, in his review of the latest generation of bands (Zhang 2008). We agree that much of punk (and post-punk) rock performance culture in Beijing is properly situated within the largely apathetic, depoliticized culture of urban consumption that has arisen in China in the wake of 1989, which many Chinese intellectuals have dubbed "postmodern" (Dirlik 2000). Whereas the dominant Chinese popular music from Hong Kong and Taiwan caters to the market and thus self-censors its space for negotiation, punk rock is relatively marginal and offers an important playground for alternative styles and attitudes within government-directed consumer culture.

In his landmark book, *Crowds and Power*, Elias Canetti argues that carrying out orders leaves "stings" that must eventually be discharged either through flight, by passing them on to others, by killing or by challenging authority (Canetti 1962:358-361, 380-382). Canetti rallies a rich variety of examples from the military to the religious and from the ethologic to the cultural for his argument, and we argue that its basic tenets are viable for punk rock audiences in contemporary China too. Through inevitable, repetitive complicity to their immediate environment, members of Chinese punk rock audiences bring along constellations of stings, and acts appeal to this potential energy. The different but interconnected energetic strategies of the punk rock bands discussed in this paper can be described in the following terms. The macho rock hero, Xie Tianxiao, consciously performs a role that absorbs and directs anger, presenting representatives of sting-sources in stage personnel and his guitar. Lonely China Day's shamanism invites the audience to escape into a sting-transcending trance. Young bands like Hedgehog sing songs in English that are, on the surface, purely nonsensical and fun, but their powerful performances on their instruments suggest an undercurrent of frustration beneath the fun of contemporary life and a way to "get it out." SUBS combine punk and heavier music styles to perform a traumatic explosion – a cathartic restaging of sting-inflicting events.

Conversely, punk bands such as Brain Failure and Joyside are more cynical about the political significance of rock music and celebrate hedonistic mosh parties, dissolving potential political energy into a kaleidoscopic whirlpool of clashing bodies, but also encouraging collective first-raising formations through anthems such as "Coming Down to Beijing."[22] Finally, P.K.14 explores a strategy also picked up on by other post-punk bands, such as Snapline and Carsick Cars, which consists of performing a Kafkaesque inability to contain the stings injected by society and the world, resulting in the imminent breakdown of harmonic songs into dissonant sounds, crowds into individuals and even threats to dissolve individuals themselves. These bands' performances are thus an ironic commentary on the hollowness of contemporary Chinese nationalism in the wake of the reform era, in which individuals bent on gain are ruthlessly taking advantage of others in a mad dash to gain money, sex, and power – a situation that many contemporary Chinese novelists also satirize.

The performances are over, and the audience departs. Chinese and foreigners, performers and audience members alike have gained a collective sense of identity and community through the sonic, visual, and physical experience of the Beijing rock concert. This points to the other purpose of the rock scene: ritualized interactions and the diffusion of tensions between Chinese and foreigners in a rapidly globalizing environment.[23]

References[24]

Anonymous (2005) *Xie Tianxiao: Ziran he zhenshi zui zhongyao* 谢天笑：自然和真实最重要 [Xie Tianxiao: natural and genuine is most important] <http://www.musicchina.com/starface/show.php?id=42&sort=>, accessed 12 March 2008.

Baranovitch, Nimrod (2003) *Chin'as New Voices: Popular Music, Ethnicity, Gender and Politics, 1978-1997*. Berkeley: University of California Press.

Barmé, Geremie R. (1999*) In the Red: On Contemporary Chinese Culture*. New York/ Chichester: Columbia University Press.

Brace, Timothy and Paul Friedlander (1992). "Rock and Roll on the New Long March: Popular Music, Cultural Identity, and Political Opposition in the People's Republic of China" in Reebee Garofalo (ed.) *Rockin' the Boat: Mass Music and Mass Movements*. Boston: South End Press, pp. 115-28.

Canetti, Elias (1962) *Crowds and Power*. Translated by Carol Steward. London: Penguin Books.

Cheng, Qijin 程绮瑾 (2006) *Xie Tianxiao: Ni bu hui juede wo fandui shangye ba?* 谢天笑：你不会觉得我反对商业吧？[Xie Tianxiao: you didn't assume I oppose commercialism, did

22 Elaborating on this strand, the New Pants (*Xin Kuzi*), a Beijing-based band firmly rooted in punk rock, have more recently incorporated disco and even Cantopop elements in their increasingly self-mocking and campy music (De Kloet 2001:92-95, New Pants 2006) and have thus paved the way for Queen Sea Big Shark, Hedgehog (*Ciwei*) and other upcoming bands that assemble party-crowds.

23 Canetti ends the section "Liberation of Stings" with the remark that even when an uprising fails, its participants will always long for the time they were a mob because only then they were free of stings. In this sense the rock club functions as a powerful site for "muscular bonding." See McNeill (1995) for a study of the importance of muscular bonding through dance and drill in human history.

24 Online musical examples of the artists mentioned in this paper can be found on their homepages and myspace pages. Links are listed in the Japanese language Chinese Rock Database (www.yaogun.com) and in the pages of the English language Chaile and Rock in China Wiki (wiki.chaile.org).

you?] In *South China Weekly* 南方周末 <http://www.nanfangdaily.com.cn/zm/20061102/wh/dyyy/200611020046.asp>, accessed 25 March 2008.

Condry, Ian (2006). *Hip-Hop Japan: Rap and the Paths of Cultural Globalization.* Durham: Duke University Press.

Davies, Jude (1996) "The Future of "No Future": Punk Rock and Postmodern Theory," in *Journal of Popular Culture*, (Spring) 29/4, pp. 3-25.

De Kloet, Jeroen (2001) *Red Sonic Trajectories: Popular Music and Youth in Urban China.* Amsterdam: Phd dissertation, University of Amsterdam.

Dirlik, Arif (ed.) (2000) *Postmodernism and China*, Durham: Duke University Press.

Field, Andrew (2008) "From D.D's to Y.Y. to Park 97 to Muse: Dance Club Spaces and the Construction of Class in Shanghai, 1997-2007," in *China: an International Journal* 6/1, pp. 18-43.

Fritz, Kevin (2007) *Wasted Orient*, Plexifilm: DVD.

Gilbert, Jeremy (2004) "Signifying Nothing: 'Culture', 'Discourse' and the Sociality of Affect, in *Culture Machine* 6 <http://www.culturemachine.net/index.php/cm/article/viewArticle/8>.

Hebdige, Dick (1978) *Subculture: The Meaning of Style*, London: Routledge.

Huang, Hao (2003) "Voices from Chinese Rock, Past and Present Tense: Social Commentary and Construction of Identity in Yaogun Yinyue, from Tiananmen to the Present," in *Popular Music and Society* 26/2 (June), pp. 1-17.

Jones, Andrew F. (1992) *Like a Knife: Ideology and Genre in Contemporary Chinese Popular Music*, Ithaca: Cornell University Press.

Jones, Andrew F. (1994) "The Politics of Popular Music in Post-Tiananmen China" in Jeffrey N. Wasserstrom and Elizabeth J. Perry (eds) *Popular Protest and Political Culture in Modern China*, Boulder: Westview Press, pp. 148-165.

McNeill, William (1995) *Keeping Together in Time: Dance and Drill in Human History*, Cambridge, MA: Harvard University Press.

Malbon, Ben (1999) *Clubbing: Dancing, Ecstasy, and Vitality*, London: Routledge.

Steen, Andreas (1996) *Der Lange Marsch des Rock'n'roll: Pop- und Rockmusik in der Volksrepublik China*, Münster: LIT.

Steen, Andreas (2000) "Sound, Protest and Business. Modern Sky Co. And the New Ideology of Chinese Rock" in *Berliner China Hefte* 19, pp. 40-64.

Tsitsos, William (1999) "Rules of Rebellion: Slamdancing, Moshing, and the American Alternative Scene" in *Popular Music* 18/3 (Oct), pp. 397-414.

Selected Discography

Brain Failure (2007) *Coming Down to Beijing*. Bad News Records.

Hedgehog (2007) *Noise Hit World.* Modern Sky Entertainment Co.

Joyside (2004) *I AM L.A.Z.Y.* Modern Sky Entertainment Co.

Joyside (2006) *Joyside*. Modern Sky Entertainment Co.

Joyside (2007) *Booze at Neptune's Dawn*. Maybe Mars.

Lonely China Day (2007) *Sorrow*. Tagteam Records.

New Pants (2006) *Dragon Tiger Panacea*. Modern Sky Entertainment Co.

P.K.14 (2004) *shei shei shei he shei shei shei 谁谁谁和谁谁谁* [who who who and who who who] Badhead/Modern Sky Entertainment Co.

P.K.14 (2005) *baipishu 白皮书* [white paper]. Modern Sky Entertainment Co.

Snapline (2007) *Party Is over, Pornostar*. Beijing: Maybe Mars.

SUBS (2006) *Down*. Beijing: Beijing beiying luyinxiang gongsi 北京北影録音録像公司.

Xie Tianxiao (2005) *X.T.X.* Beijing jingwen 北京京文

Andreas Steen

Postsocialist Creativity and Confusion: CD-Covers and the Visual Presentation of Chinese Popular Music

The music market of the People's Republic of China (PRC) and the advertising industry have undergone tremendous changes over the past three decades. When the PRC moved from the New Era (1976-1989) to the post-socialist era in the 1990s, the production and availability of different music forms increased, as did the diversity of promotional images. So far, however, only little has been said about the "Art of Selling Songs", to borrow the title of Kevin Edge's book (1991).[1] This "art" includes various aspects and considerations, both cultural and economic, carried out by an (inter)national musical industry that is constantly refining its promotion strategies. Far from covering all these processes, this article will single out one particular item: the design of CD-covers. Kevin Edge stresses the importance of the cover design in the following words:

A new piece of music is often seen as a song-sheet, poster or record sleeve before it is heard. The immediately apprehended words and imagery in that case perform an informing, promissory, encapsulatory role, seeking to signify, by means of readily understood visual terms, the likely idiom, origin, atmosphere, and qualitative nature of the music within. Once the music has been heard, the same words and images begin to operate as a specific mnemonic; a frozen visual analogy of the music which in some way conveys the aural, temporal nature of the represented piece to the mind of the consumer (Edge 1991: 5-6).

Today, one may hesitate to agree that "a new piece of music is often seen as a ... record sleeve before it is heard." Music can first be seen on a music video/DVD, on one of the TV channels (e.g. MTV) or on one of the many Internet web-pages related to various music styles. This development notwithstanding, CDs are offered for sale, circulate in large quantities and are easily identifiable with their covers and leaflets containing the song lyrics and other information. CD-covers are found in a culturally prominent position because they combine economic interests with artistic considerations, design, the idea of music, the personality of the artist, popular mass culture and trade calculations. In other words, the CD-cover is directly linked to the artist and his/her or the company's idea of successfully presenting the product on the market. It is intended to attract audiences and is often the first item to be taken home, privately possessed and identified with. Since record sleeves, tape-covers and CD-covers are deeply embedded in their cultural and economic contexts, we can also accept them as eyewitnesses, commentators and/or active participants in the PRC's cultural transformation. Before doing so, however, it is necessary to comment briefly on some general aspects related to the production and distribution of CDs in the PRC.

In the late 1990s, most of China's musical repertoire produced during the turbulent twentieth century appeared side by side on the shelves in the music stores for the first time. It was a decisive moment in modern Chinese history, enriched by an increasing creativity in musical expression, lyrical content, style and visual design. Like so many other aspects of cultural production, this development has in one way or another been shaped and formed by

[1] On the return of advertising after 1979, see Hong 1994. More recent works on advertising concentrate on foreign firms' strategies of "becoming global and becoming local" in China, e.g. Wang Jian (2000), and may also include aspects of the music industry, e.g. Wang Jing (2007).

the effects of globalization and China's move "into a postrevolutionary, postsocialist, and postmodern (but not postcolonial) society" (Lu 2001a: 66), especially by the country's consumer revolution and the commercialization of Chinese culture. (Davies 2000, Dirlik 2001) As a matter of fact, we can argue with Frith and Horne (1989: 189) that – also in China – "pop songs are the soundtrack of postmodern daily life, inescapable in lifts and airports, pubs and restaurants, streets and shopping centers and sports grounds."

From an international perspective, the PRC's music market is still relatively small, but the big international major labels are optimistic and see "China Packed with Potential" (McClure 2001).[2] The sound recordings circulating in the PRC are produced by foreign and state-owned companies, by private and individual studios. All record companies have to release their products through one of the 250-300 approved publishing houses, which are usually state-owned firms (de Kloet 2002: 97). Since the cover-designs are also examined, we can expect them to be carefully designed and well-calculated in order to pass censorship boundaries and attract the highest possible number of consumers. Yet domestically produced Chinese sound recordings are not usually censored. The system is more complicated, as censorship takes place after, not before, the appearance of a work. Curt Kraus (2004: 117) rightly observed that "Postproduction censorship effectively turns political risk into economic risks." This also affects large numbers of pirate copies, which are still estimated to make up between 80 and 95 percent of the market share (Montgomery/Fitzgerald 2006: 410). Generally speaking, CD/DVD piracy in the world of music concentrates on popular and already "approved" cultural products. To avoid economic losses, the publication sector tends towards self-censorship, but for the same reason and because of its sheer size, the quantity of musical products and competition, it steadily pushes the boundaries even further.

Under these circumstances, "the structure of the music industry in China is not conducive to financial success" (de Kloet 2002: 96), censorship is partly ineffective or arbitrary, and banned recordings do not ever totally disappear. They may be sold individually, together with privately recorded and designed CDs during concerts, on the streets and in specialized CD-shops, sometimes with a new CD-cover. Disputes over the design are rarely reported outside the music industry, although some prominent exceptions illustrate the importance of visual images: an international conflict arose with Dadawa's recording "Sister Drum" (1995), when Tibetans criticized her Han-Chinese representation of Tibetan clothing and culture on the CD-cover. Another example is the inaugural issue of the Chinese edition of the American *Rolling Stone* magazine in spring 2006. The content and the title page, featuring an image of China's No. 1 rock star, Cui Jian, gave rise to a temporary ban on the journal after three weeks.[3]

In this article, I do not intend to cover the whole variety of music styles available on China's music market, but will focus on CD-covers in the field of pop and rock music that have been circulating in the PRC since 1989.[4]. I am concerned with the interplay of CD-

---

2 D. Rushe (2004) writes: "The Chinese [music] market is small. Last year [2003], legitimate sales were $198m (£110m) compared with $3.2 billion in Britain, according to the International Federation of the Phonographic Industry (IFPI). But China's sales grew 22% last year while sales in the developed world were flat at best." On China's music industry, see also de Kloet 2002

3 For the dispute on "The Politics and Poetics of Sister Drum," see Upton 2002: 99-224. About the *Rolling Stone* cover, see articles by Fowler 2006 and Helmore 2006.

4 Pop music is certainly is the biggest segment in the music business, followed by the category instrumen-

covers and nostalgia, "a clever instrument of the merchandiser's toolbox" (Appadurai 1996: 77). More specifically, I will concentrate on what Wu Jing (2006: 362) identified as the three main key historical objects for nostalgic appropriation during the 1990s: "the revolutionary past, imperial China – particularly the dynasties of supposed prosperity and national strength – and the short experience of colonial modernity in Shanghai during the early 20th century." For obvious reasons, I will not talk about Shanghai-related images, which despite their popularity are more of a local phenomenon in the realm of music.[5] The other two "nostalgia" have appealed to many cultural products, also to pop and rock music. The case of rock music is particular interesting, because the globalizing force identified by Jeroen de Kloet as the "rock mythology" makes Beijing musicians want to localize rock music's sound and image. As he puts it: "In order to become and remain authentic, the hard force of rock – a force with a strong imagined sense of origins in the West – demands localization when the sound travels to places outside the West" (de Kloet 2005: 322).

By analyzing the commercial packaging of China's pop and rock music from the perspective of nostalgia and localization, I intend to look behind the seemingly free and random use of visual images under the conditions of postsocialism in order to unravel the ongoing struggle in the contested field of popular culture.[6] CD-covers may act as visually active components in a highly symbolic battle over meaning and power in the PRC. The visual design is inspired by individual creativity and the commercial exploitation of populist trends such as nationalism and patriotism; it is also reflected in its appropriation or absorption of the main features of Chinese postmodern culture, namely "hybridity, unevenness, nonsynchronicity, and pastiche" (Lu 2001: 14). Therefore, what you see is not necessarily what you get: similar images of Chinas' history represent different music styles, genre distinctions are blurred and images possess either specifically coded meanings or none at all regarding the music they represent.

The Revolution Goes Pop, 1989-1997

At the end of the Cultural Revolution, the New Period began, which saw the rapid decline of the "poster power" that celebrated Mao Zedong as an "icon of power" (Benewick 1999). Simultaneously, both internal and external factors began to challenge the CCP's monopoly and political control over the contested field of musical production. One important aspect was that economic self-sufficiency was a goal declared by the new cultural policy (Kraus 2004: 56). Equally important were musical imports from Taiwan and Hong Kong, later also from Western countries, and the influx of cheap tape-recorders from Japan. The PRC's national music industry enjoyed an unprecedented period of political relaxation, seen in the

---

tal/music. Regarding the production of CDs, the statistics (2002) demonstrate that 45,43% of domestic CD-production concentrate on "songs" (total units = 51,21%). In addition, pop music determines 70,65% (total units = 80,30%) of the international music imports. See German Sounds AG 2005.

5 Since the early 1990s, many popular songs of Old Shanghai and the Republican period have been re-released in different styles and thereby actively supported the Shanghai Nostalgia. The topic itself is too large to be addressed here: it has already been dealt with in many articles and its influence on images of Chinese rock is, in any case, marginal. On the Shanghai Nostalgia, see Lu Hanchao 2002, Steen 2000a.

6 I agree with Shelden H. Lu, that postsocialism is "rather best understood as a totality encompassing the economic, the social, the political, the cultural, and the ideological." Understood in this way, postsocialism "pertains to perception and affects," "is everyday life," and "a battlefield of intellectual and ideological contention between different persuasions," among others. In: Sheldon H. Lu 2007: 204-210.

fact that the number of audio-and visual companies grew from one in 1978 to more than 200 in the early 1990s. As a result, music production entered a period of competition and negotiation, determined by commercial incentives and characterized by an increasing diversity of (conflicting) styles, sounds and ideologies, all of which began to influence the packaging and selling of music as a product. For the year 1999, de Kloet (2002: 96), for example, speaks of 69.9 million cassette tapes and 8.4 million CDs being sold officially in Mainland China.

Cui Jian: Hero on the New Long March

With the political relaxation of the 1980s and the new competitive environment, advertising practices changed and previous images of revolutionary icons were replaced by an increasingly global design. The official media criticized this trend towards "Americanization" (Hong 1994: 338). Meanwhile, new constructions of femininity and female eroticism began to appear on CD-covers, whereas on the male side, popular culture is said to have expressed a "post-revolutionary search for masculinity."[7] Inspired by the roots-seeking movement of the 1980s, rock music first fulfilled these promises for masculine power and identity through a new, northern and rhythm-oriented music style called Northwest-Wind (*xibeifeng*, 1984-87).[8] China's rock music was born in this context and first made available in 1988, when Cui Jian released his often discussed album "Rock 'n' Roll on the New Long March" (*xin changzheng lushang de yaogun*). The cover provides interesting insights into political and commercial calculations for album design at that time.

The original tape/CD, published by a state-owned company in the PRC, features the image of a strong-willed, determined and forward-looking Cui Jian on a red background, with the title of the CD printed below. Both the color and the title were highly symbolic. The red color stands for happiness and marriage in traditional China, and for the CCP in modern China. The Chinese characters "*changzheng*" refer to the famous and heroic Long March led by the Red Army (1934-35), which signified the beginning of both Mao Zedong's and the Chinese Communist Party's (CCP) rise to power. The phrase "New Long March," however, was a recent creation of Deng Xiaoping to prepare the people for the hardships to be faced during the reform policy. Thus, rock music is promoted as being part of that New Long March, and Cui Jian, inspired by the PRC's (historical) revolutionary spirit, playfully used its rhetoric and even distributed flyers that denoted places where his band already had performed as "liberated areas" (*jiefangqu*).[9] Cui Jian's album included some of the most popular songs of that period; most of them were circulated amongst students and were sung during the democracy movement in 1989. It is surely no exaggeration to regard this album as the soundtrack of the movement (Jones 1994). The cover design, although symbolic and easily understood, obviously proved to be not revolutionary and challenging enough outside the PRC. The Hong Kong and overseas edition therefore employed another combination of images when it was released in 1989. Here, the title was changed to "Having Nothing" (*Yiwu suoyou*), which was his most popular song. Cui Jian himself appeared on the cover blindfolded by a red cloth, clearly singing one of his, by then, most controversial songs, "A Piece of Red Cloth" (*Yi kuai hong bu*). The album did not contain that song, and the

---

7 See Baranovitch, 2003: 114-189.

8 *Xibeifang*-songs are basically adaptations or imitations of northern Shaanxi folksongs. See Steen 1996, Dujunco 2002, Baranovitch 2003.

9 One of the flyers is reprinted in de Kloet, 2001: 11.

provocative visual message of a young musician on the Long March had been changed into one of severe criticism. As an album title, "Having Nothing" turned out to be the main message of this record. It directly addressed the lack of material needs, political and individual freedom, and thereby confirmed the image of the PRC among overseas consumers in Hong Kong and Taiwan.[10] The Chinese characters, in addition, were deep red and dried out, as if they had been written long ago with thick blood. Overemphasizing revolutionary sentiment, suffering and anti-government protest with reference to the events of June 1989 were intended to boost CD-sales outside the PRC.

Fig. 1: *Rock 'n' Roll on the …*, 1988

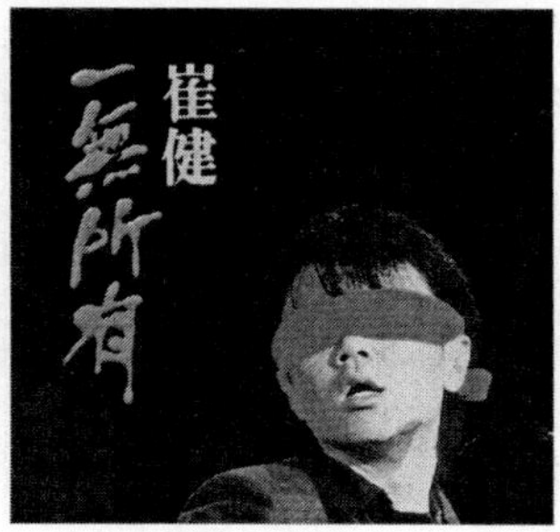

Fig. 2: *I have Nothing*, 1989

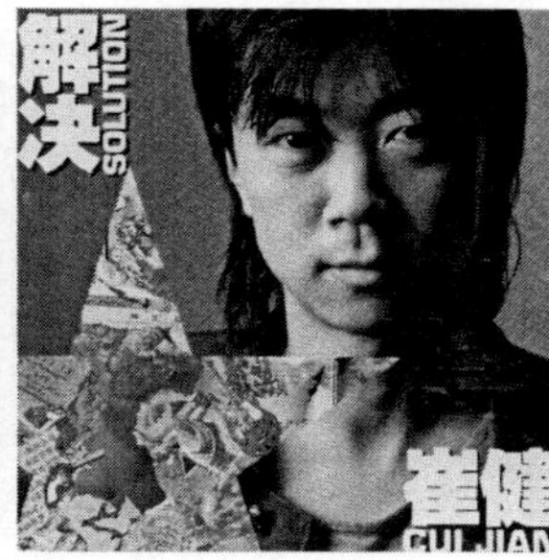

Fig. 3*: Solution*, 1990

Both covers contained subversive political messages and referred directly to the conditions in the PRC. These were the first representations of a new and challenging "rebellious spirit" (*fanpan jingshen*) in the field of music that had begun to emerge from Beijing's urban grey culture (*huise wenhua*).[11] The design was certainly innovative, depicting revolutionary energy and demonstrating that resistance can also be sexy and commercially attractive. Western album covers and those of popular *Gangtai* rock stars like Luo Dayou, Qi Qin, Zhao Chuan and the band "Beyond" might have broadened this creativity. In most cases, however, they featured individualism and rebellious gestures, but lacked the political message included in Cui Jian's covers.[12] However, when "Rock 'n' Roll on the New Long March" was officially re-released to commemorate the 10th anniversary of the PRC's most popular rock recording, its former rebellious image had itself become a symbol of another revolutionary nostalgia.

Nostalgia and Localization: The Revolution Sells

After "June 1989", China entered a period that is usually referred to as Post-1989, post-Tiananmen, and post-New Period – all these are terms that cover the postmodern moment (Lu 2001: 11). In this post-New Era, political idealism and the modernist-humanist paradigm of the previous New Era collapsed and were "thoroughly dismantled […] by the conjoint forces of the market and the ideological apparatus of the state, as well as by a rising populism and nationalism, and, above all, by the thoroughgoing commodification of culture" (Zhang Xudong 1999: 80). Generally speaking, this decade saw rock music incorporated into popular culture and the PRC's musical industry, and ended with the publication of the

10 The lyrical content and meaning of this album are discussed in Jones 1992 and Steen 1996.

11 On the emergence and early period of "huise wenhua", see Barmé 1992.

12 A detailed list of the images used in this article is provided at the end.

heavily promoted best-seller "China can say No!" (*Zhongguo keyi shuo bu!* 1996), which "sparked what happened to be a return of nationalist favor in urban China" (Dai Jinhua 2001: 161).

The beginning of China's so-called "Second Cultural Revolution" is often associated with a new set of images.[13] In terms of the visual arts, this decade began with the international success of the 5th Generation of Chinese filmmakers (e.g. Zhang Yimou, Chen Kaige) and China's avant-garde art. Inside China, people were affected in various ways by a "Mao Zedong Fever", inspired by the fact that the Chairman's image had turned into a "floating sign," that is "a vehicle for nostalgic reinterpretation, unstated opposition to the status quo, and even satire" (Barmé 1996: 16). Thus, on the one hand, Mao was part of people's nostalgia for a strong leader and a simple but stable life, but, on the other hand, his images became objects of deconstruction in avant-garde art circles, either inspired by cynical realism (*wanshi xianshi zhuyi*) and/or by political pop (*zhengzhi bopu*).[14] Both styles exerted an influence on the design of CD-covers, which now came to express the earlier mentioned "three main nostalgic trends." However, it must be remembered that the most widespread album covers were self-portraits, usually photographs.

As I have already pointed out, Cui Jian was the first to use images of the PRC's revolutionary past on his Long March of Rock 'n' Roll in order to subvert and ridicule official Chinese history. Part of his visual symbolism was the use of the "Five-Cornered-Star" or pentagram, an old religious symbol that, since the early 20th century, has been associated with the socialist and communist revolution. The "Red Star" became widely known as a symbol of socialism after the Russian Revolution and the founding of the Soviet Union. It also became the symbol of the People's Liberation Army (PLA) on the Long March, gained nationwide popularity in China after 1949, and is *the* signifier for the CCP and socialism in the PRC.

Cui Jian's public use of the "Red Star" was certainly a provocation. In the early 1990s, this image appeared on his recording "Solution" (*Jiejue*, 1990), and one year later on a compilation entitled "Beijing Reggae", produced and released by the Chinese-American producer, Jeffrey Cheen. The two messages could not have been more different. Cui Jian filled the pentagram with a collage that included images of a pistol, a guitar, the Great Wall and roses, amongst others. Even more provocatively, the album offered an altered version of a song from the War of Liberation, entitled *Nanniwan* (Lit.: Southern Muddy Bay), which later resulted in a ban on his performances. By simply omitting the last stanza of the song, which dealt with the arrival of the Liberation Army in *Nanniwan*, he managed to deprive the song of his original political message and turned it into a peaceful landscape description. Cui's creative efforts to deconstruct the revolution became obsolete with the arrival on the market of the album, "Beijing Reggae." The cover showed a guitar player jumping off a Red Star. The star marked the center of Beijing, as the city wall surrounding it was marked by the four gates and the Chinese characters for East-West-North-South. Obviously enough, the image pointed at Beijing as China's new center of musical revolution. It was, nevertheless, an officially sanctioned revolution from above, as the phrase "Thanks to Zheng Liangcheng of the Chinese Ministry of Culture …," printed in English and in red within the leaflet, revealed. This cooperation was also reflected in the fact that the recording

13 On aspects of the "Second Cultural Revolution," see Dirlik 2001.

14 See Andrews/Gao 1995, Lin Xiaopin 1997, Sheldon Lu 2001: 146ff.

contained a complete version of *Nanniwan* in reggae style. Gregory Lee (1995: 107) is right in concluding that "Beijing Reggae" was arranged "with the full and open cooperation of Chinese communist officials in charge of the music industry." According to Lee, it was with this album that "reggae and rhythm and blues cover versions of revolutionary classics" exchanged subversion for popular consumption (ibid.). In other words, the album reflected the "official" incorporation of revolutionary songs and the "Red Star" into popular entertainment culture.

Fig. 4: *Beijing Reggae*, 1991

Fig. 5: *The Red Sun* (tape), ~ 1992

Fig: 6: *Red Rock*, 1992

In the following year, this trend gained even more popular momentum. In 1992, the state-owned music industry took the initiative to benefit financially from two outstanding campaigns, namely the 50th anniversary of Mao's "Yan'an Talks on Literature and Art" (1942) and Chairman Mao's 100th birthday in 1993. Already in late 1991, the PRC's cultural world had come to be shaken by the "Red Sun Phenomenon" (*Hong taiyang xianxiang*), providing "Odes to Mao Zedong. Uninterrupted Songs in New Rhythm." The recording had been carefully planned and sold four million copies in the first two months.[15] The instant success of danceable Mao-tunes came as a surprise and did not only lead to a large number of pirate copies, but also inspired critical debates on the preservation and/or popularization of the PRC's revolutionary musical heritage.[16] Also in 1992, an album entitled "Red Rock" (*hongse yaogun*) appeared on the market, recorded by the musician, Hou Muren, and the band "Modern People" (*xiandairen yuedui*). The front cover showed singer Hou in front of a PLA-soldier with a Red Star helmet. The motivation for their releasing, for example, a distorted rock-version of the revolutionary classic "Socialism is good" (*shehuizhuyi hao*) is difficult to explain; perhaps it was a synthesis of irony, patriotism, provocation and commercial incentives.

The "Red Sun" was a phenomenon, heard in every corner of the country in 1992 and nourished by more than 15 similar tapes/CDs and pirate copies over the following years. Suddenly, images of the Forbidden City and Tiananmen Square as the center of state power had entered the realm of popular culture, together with a growing number of revolutionary songs in dancing-style. Tiananmen Square and/or Mao Zedong appeared on almost all "Red Sun" editions, as could be seen in Geremie Barmé's *Shades of Mao* (1996), sometimes even together with dancing legs in sports boots.[17]

15 See Steen 1996: 151, Wu Jing 2006: 363, and Barmé 1996, who also translated some lyrics, pp. 192-194.

16 See Audio and Video World (*yinxiang shijie*), 1992.

17 Barmé (1996) offers many pictures of consumer items related to the "Mao Fever," including one of the first edition of "The Red Sun." See also Dujunco 2002.

These images were clearly meant to convey security and happiness, since "dancing under the Red Sun" was part of the Mao-Fever in the early nineties, which also saw the commodification of "Mao-Kitsch" and organized travel tours to his hometown.[18] Meanwhile, the other side of the coin was reworked in the realm of avant-garde Chinese art, depicting a distorted and cynical Mao-image in a style referred to as political pop. In short, while different sounds and images of "floating" Chairman Mao were circulating in the early nineties, the former "poster power" had clearly evaporated in different commercial directions. As Gregory Lee (1996: 158) recalls: "On the street stalls selling music cassettes and compact discs, Mao is on sale alongside a subversive rock star, Cui Jian. In late twentieth century capitalist China, the market has established a consumerist and mythic equivalency between Mao and Madonna and Cui Jian."

The mid-1990s saw releases which added other aspects to this atmosphere. Cui Jian's album "Balls under the Red Flag" (*hongqi xia de dan*), for example, showed an embryo in an egg-shaped amniotic sack below a red flag, the eyes covered with a red scarf. The English translation of the title appeared on the left and right sides of the cover, arranged on a red background that resembles China's traditional practice of hanging a pair of antithetical couplets written on scrolls on both sides of the entrance door during the Chinese New Year festivities. Inside, the leaflet contained images of a computer-made stone-relief revealing a group of young boys, a female Red Guardist and one of Cui & Band enclosed in an egg, the background filled with Chinese *Renminbi* bank notes. The Chinese album title suggested two translations or interpretations, that is, "eggs" laid by the red flag or "eggs" lying under the red flag. Both metaphors were intended to describe the Chinese people, who were to be seen as fragile eggs: already alive but not yet born, thrown into life but breeding and dozing under the red flag, the CCP. The rather unusual album combined rock with jazz and Chinese sounds of *guzheng* and percussion, it criticised hypocrisy, the loss of feeling and commercialization – a society that had turned from one revolution into another.

Fig. 7: Cui Jian, 1994

Fig. 8: *Shenzhou Yaobai*, 1994

Fig. 9: *Popular Rock*, 1997

Cui Jian's use of "red elements" contrasted with other CD-covers that now began to show the influence of political pop, thereby producing atmospheres of irony, sarcasm and humor. One sample of rock from Mainland China, entitled "Rocking Holy Land/China" (*Shenzhou yaobai*), released 1994 in Hong Kong, depicted the painted image of a PLA soldier with a guitar hanging round his neck. He stands without moving, but looks straight ahead through

[18] On the "Mao Fever" see Barmé 1996.

his spectacles into the eyes of the consumer. His thoughtful, hesitating and rather unemotional appearance contrasts with the background of the cover, where people are ecstatically dancing.[19] Various interpretations of this picture are possible. Are Mainland Chinese musicians insiders or outsiders? Are they not relaxed (or technically not good) enough to enjoy good plain fun? Or is Mainland China, here poetically addressed with the old expression "Holy Land" (*Shenzhou*), rocking and shaking, while the PLA-soldier hesitates to join in? Or is the Mainland musician depicted as the cool revolutionary who will soon start to "rock China"?

It should be mentioned that musicians and critics in the PRC regard those years as heralding the decline of rock music. Rock had not fulfilled people's expectations. Intrigued by a new commercial culture and more concerned about their future prospects, audiences had shifted to the less problematic lyrics and sounds of soft pop music. Rock music, it was feared, had lost its former political power and threatened to be absorbed into popular consumer culture (Jones 1994). How actively foreign companies tried to explore the PRC market can also be seen in the initiatives of the Taiwanese company "Rock Records and Tapes" (*gunshi,* discussed below) and in the fact that, by 1994, a record company called "Red Star" (*hongxing*) had been founded in Hong Kong, promoting also Mainland China's rock and pop songs as "Red Star Music" (*hongxing yinyue*).[20] By 1995, rock music's rebellious gestures, individualism, and sound had obviously reached a new stage of official acceptance in the PRC. The state-owned music industry was already speaking of "rock classics" (*yaogun jingdian*) and released a sampler under the same name to commemorate "10 years of hardship", as the leaflet put it. This chapter can be closed with a double CD entitled "Popular Rock" (*liuxing yaogun*, 1997), which resembled the above mentioned "Chinese Rock Classics" and underlined rock music's arrival in the world of pop. On the cover, the PRC was depicted as orange-red as on most of the "Red Sun" recordings, and the only city that needed to be mentioned was Beijing. To identify (popular) rock with the capital is a form of localization that is also intended to function as a trademark. This, however, depicted a new form of local patriotism, inspired by a rather nationalist spirit that fitted well into the discourse of this period, "the years of "China saying no" (Dai Jinhua 2001: 166).

It is certainly an exaggeration to speak of the "decline" of rock music, since a number of innovative records were produced during this period, some of which will be mentioned later. Yet the expected profits had failed to materialize, and companies like Rock Records/Magic Stone (Taiwan) and Red Star (Hong Kong) "did gradually pull out of the Chinese rock market" (de Kloet 2002: 100). However, it was also the period of He Yong and his album "Garbage Dump" (*lajichang*, 1994), the beginning of Punk in Beijing. Similarly to the West, Chinese punk introduced a new form of musical expression as well as a new aesthetic quality regarding the design of CD-covers.[21] Meanwhile, these years also saw the emergence of a new nationalism and a younger generation that lacked personal experience with the Cultural Revolution. Related topics, images and vocabulary became difficult to communicate, but were not dismissed as outdated. They were, rather, retranslated, modified and filled with new meanings. Probably also for these reasons, Cui Jian

---

19 See Steen 1996.

20 To commemorate the 10th anniversary of the label, Beijing's Taihe Rye Music Co. (*Taihe Maitian*) released a special CD, covering songs from the period 1994-2004. See http://www.trmusic.com.cn/disc.html.

21 On the visual impact of Western punk on record cover design, see Edge 1991: 95ff.

stopped using these images, except for the Red Star, which had become his "trademark" and was also shown prominently on the cover of his recording, "Show your Color" (*gei ni yidian yanse*, 2005).

New Sounds, Visual Tactics: The Underground and the State, 1997-2007

The year 1997 is remembered as being historically very important for the PRC: in February, Deng Xiaoping died. Meanwhile, a large clock on Tiananmen Square was counting the days-hours-minutes-seconds until the return of Hong Kong to Mainland China. The actual ceremony was broadcast as a major nationalist event. In addition, the PRC's most expensive film production, a movie entitled "The Opium War" (*Yapian zhanzheng*, 1997), delivered the necessary historical information for those who had already forgotten the colonial past. Patriotism and the new nationalism were widespread sentiments, and not without effect on the musical scene in Beijing. In the same year, the musician, Shen Lihui, managed to start the PRC's first independent record label, "Modern Sky" (*modeng tiankong*).[22] Meanwhile, Hao Fang published his translation of the biography of Curt Cobain (1967-1994), whose suicide had caused a crisis in Beijing rock circles. After the publication of this book, playing in an underground band became respectable if not "hip". This new spirit and local initiatives of record production encouraged a new production boom (Yan Jun 2002: 15). The underground, a space that was already seeing the rise of punk music in Beijing, became the platform of a new creativity, visible also in the fields of art and the design of CD-covers.

Fig. 10: Modern Sky Records, Vol. 2, 1998

Modern Sky promoted the movement as the "New Sound of Beijing" (*Beijing xinsheng yundong*) and deliberately made use of the term "underground," while stressing the central importance of Beijing. Shortly afterwards, record labels like Jingwen, Scream and Newbees were founded in Beijing. The movement relied on musicians of the post-Cultural Revolution generation, whose background and intentions resembled their Western models and counterparts. They stemmed from urban well-off families, fulfilled different duties and jobs during the daytime or were society drop-outs who earned their livings as self-trained but

22 On Modern Sky, see Steen 2000 and www.modernsky.com.

professional musicians. "New Sound" was advertised as a revolution, global and international in sound and design. Thus, two Chinese observers concluded in 1999 that "Modern Sky" is what can be termed "a typical post-modern PRC paradox" (Guo/Su 1999). The crucial aspect is that the work space and subject matter of the company are underground, but the music and magazine it publishes are commercially successful. Modern Sky's early advertisements stressed the company's urgent message to spread Chinese rock in the Western world, and indeed, over time, more and more bands of that label began to incorporate English translations of titles or song lyrics in the leaflet; later they even sang in English. Today, the company can offer about one hundred records, various sub-labels included, and enjoys a fairly good standing in China's (underground) music community. It organizes festivals and signed bands who work with foreign musicians. The website includes a map of Mainland China's Modern Sky stores and information in English about overseas/international mail order conditions. "Ironically", as de Kloet (2002: 102) rightly remarks, "the local turn signifies a desire to become global."

"New Sound" strengthened the self-consciousness of Beijing's underground scene, the commercial potential of which Modern Sky and other companies were eager to exploit. With its combination of art and music, the movement also affected the design of CD-covers, which now reached a new stage of artistic expression. The artist, Feng Jiangzhou is an interesting example: he is the singer, composer and lyricist of the band "The Fly" (*cangying*), and also creates the cover designs. The band released its first album in Taiwan (1997); two years later it was released in the PRC on the Modern Sky label. The Fly is famous for vulgar lyrics, dissonant sounds and its negation of daily life; the music combines avant-garde, techno and different hardcore genres. Feng's collage-style surrealist paintings combine various images from China's revolutionary history. The CD-cover of "The Fly: Fallen Love" (1999) carried 1960s propaganda paintings of well-nourished boys and girls with red cheeks.[23] They were surrounded by healthy colorful vegetables of all sorts, with the character "feng", in the center, meaning rich and plentiful. It is also the family name of Feng Jiangzhou. These posters are, then, interwoven with and attached to microscopic, biological, anatomical illustrations of a fly's leg, wing, etc. and photographs of band members. It is a rather daring collage of images, especially considering the meanings attached to "flies". A set of oil paintings that illustrate the CD-cover and leaflet of "The Fly II" provides some other mocking situations: imagine an empty restaurant and a couple apparently waiting for the wedding ceremony. On the front, you see two policemen offering water melons, and two persons with unclear identities; maybe they are simply guests. On the back, there is a PLA soldier with a machine gun inspecting the empty tables and chair, while two women-fighters from the famous opera ballet "The Red Detachment of Women" (*hongse niangzijun*) fly over the top of him straight through the room. The chosen cover for the Mainland China edition is taken from another painting that shows an elderly ballerina, easily identified as the "White Haired Girl," dancing in one of the washing rooms of the food-chain Spaghetti House.[24] Feng's visual exposure to China's revolutionary history and his deconstruction of formerly holy icons are linked to his work in the avant-garde arts sector. It is rather unique for such paintings are used for the design of rock music's underground

23 This first album was recorded with the Taiwanese band, 3rd Nova. On The Fly, see also Steen 2000 and de Kloet 2001: 56ff.

24 Released by Hardcore Pop Co., Taiwan, later Jingwen Records, Beijing.

CD-covers. It should be mentioned that these are almost the only "revolutionary" images in the Modern Sky repertoire.

Fig. 11: The Fly, 2000

Fig. 12: Li Xiaolong, 2000

Between 2000 and 2005, this artistic playfulness, these provocative gestures and this critical reworking of the PRC's revolutionary heritage reached a new height, one that revealed the competing ideas and the various options for visualizing China's revolutionary history in the battlefield of popular culture. First, we shall take a brief look at hip-hop, which had become an increasingly popular music style in urban centers by the late 1990s. Li Xiaolong was one of the most important figures, and, in 2000, he reminded us of the pentagram with which we started this article. Speaking for a new generation, however, the "Red Star" does not denote a provocation or "patriotic" revolution similar to that of Cui Jian. Here, the symbol functions as a popular icon of resistance and/or rebellion. Its provocation has already been absorbed by postmodern consumer culture.

The emergence of Red Jazz (*hongse jueshi*), by contrast, was initiated by the most powerful players in the music industry, the state-owned companies. Red Jazz was released as a set of three CDs by the Shanghai Record Corporation (2000-2003), featuring the genre as "Chinese Jazz" (*Zhongguo jueshi*) and "Memorable Jazz" (*nanwang jueshi*). All the songs are related to China's revolutionary history and are performed in an instrumental smooth-jazz format, with the piano at its center. The style was definitely innovative, though only the melodies were "memorable." In 2001, the Taiwanese record company, Rock Records & Tapes also released a recording entitled "Red Jazz", featuring songs such as, "I love Beijing Tiananmen," "Our Chairman Mao Zedong" and "Revolutionary Soldiers are most honored." The CD-cover shows a detailed image of a group of heroes and revolutionaries, taken from the Monument to the People's Heroes at Tiananmen Square in Beijing. The leaflet contains pictures of the Great Wall, Tiananmen Square, Mao Zedong and peasant-workers, and their arrangement leaves it to the reader to decide whether the "masses" are listening to Mao or to Red Jazz.

The production of these CDs suggests that there was an audience interested in this innovative refreshment of old popular songs, yet it remains difficult to gauge the popularity of this genre amongst patriots and/or jazz enthusiasts. Not only Mao Zedong himself, but also the cultural workers who composed the songs would have been astonished to listen to these interpretations of their compositions. However, as has already been pointed out, Red Jazz was not without its predecessors. Generally speaking, these images lacked the playfulness of the other styles and came with a clearly formulated message: remember the War of Resistance (1937-45) and do not forget the Rise of China under the leadership of the PRC. This message was inscribed on the CD-covers, which showed a collage made of images from the war period, the Rising Red Sun symbolizing Mao Zedong and the CCP. The synthesis of revolutionary music and jazz was unthinkable throughout the 20th century. At the turn of the century, the birth of this new genre suggested both creative freedom and indifference. Shanghai, being famous for its "jazz age" in the Republican period, chose to go beyond its legacy of formerly criticized "yellow" jazz songs and finally produced a set of "Red Jazz". Despite these efforts, the popularity of Red Jazz remains questionable. It is not heard very often (today), nor is it a topic which fills the columns of music journals as did the "Red Sun" ten years ago.

Fig. 13: *Red Jazz*, PRC 2000

Fig. 14: *Red Jazz*, Taiwan 2001

"Red Jazz" underlined the fact that formerly unimaginable expressions of "red culture" were allowed to be produced and distributed by state-owned companies. It also demonstrated the state's willingness to actively raise its voice in the field of music and popular culture. This was further emphasized in 2002 through the "Songs Collection of China" (*Zhongguo gedian*), which were released on ten CDs to commemorate the fiftieth anniversary of the PRC. The selection of songs was, of course, officially approved and included none of the songs that were popular in the realm of rock music. Cui Jian's "I have Nothing" was not included, and the only song with a certain affiliation to rock circles was Zang Tianshuo's notorious pop-ballad "Friend" (*pengyou*), which was circulated widely. Leaving aside the musical content, each decade was covered and represented by two CDs, whose cover-images were designed to illustrate the collective efforts towards the progress and rise of the PRC.

The images were painted in a combination of Soviet style socialist realism, earlier propaganda posters and modern pop art. The CD-box proposed a convenient historical arrangement in five decades, which focused on socialist advancement and strength, thereby eliminating discontinuities and periods of crisis or protest. Thus, the 1950s and the building of a New China were symbolized by a train carrying the image of Mao Zedong and his "Thoughts" through the country. The 1960s were shown as a period of Red Book-culture, depicted through a huge fist carrying the Little Red Book and years of mutual instruction and of constant reading and learning. The 1970s showed a group of three happy revolutionaries – peasant, worker, soldier – in a field of sun flowers, carrying the "Collected Works of Mao Zedong," and the opening of China towards the end of the decade, depicting equally happy foreigners. The 1980s were represented by a group of students who were welcoming Deng Xiaoping and the reform policy, and – on the second cover – technical and military advancement. The 1990s, finally, were covered by a group of energetic businessmen and intellectuals, eagerly marching forward. Economic success was also the main message of the second image: the building of the Bank of China in Hong Kong, the Shanghai TV-Tower, the Jin Mao building in Shanghai and various skyscrapers shining under the light of an illuminating firework display.

Fig. 15: Song Collection of China,
2002

It is not surprising that this CD-box was accompanied by images which conveyed a positive and progressive image of the PRC's success story. Yet it is not entirely clear, why each CD-cover should bear the name of the same popular song, both in Chinese and English: "I love Beijing Tiananmen." The square at the center of Beijing is, of course, loaded with different meanings, reaching from the center of power and patriotic demonstrations to June 4th and resistance. Here, we may interpret it as a hint to love the national center, the CCP and the Motherland. Altogether, this CD-set provided the official canon of PRC-Pop. It played with sentimental feelings for the past, with nostalgia, and stimulated a historically positive and uncritical listening habit among consumers. Yet the number of potential consumers and buyers for a 10 CD-set is difficult to estimate. In this context, it is worth mentioning a CD entitled "My Homeland" (*wo de zuguo*, Dec. 2005),
produced by Taihe Rye Music Co., Beijing.[25] This CD featured a selection of ten songs from different periods after 1949. All the songs were re-recorded with new accompaniment and new sound, sung and played by various popular singers and musicians, which were united under the heading "*Sanlitun yinyue*" – obviously a reference to the well-known entertainment district in Beijing. However, the recording promoted patriotism (*aiguo zhuyi*), as the cover showed, and the design served as a reminder of the propaganda posters from the Great Leap Forward period, except for the satellite antennas at the top left and right.

A search on the Internet reveals that the CD was released to commemorate the successful victory over Fascism and Japanese imperialism sixty years earlier.[26] The product was aimed at both older and younger consumers, a nostalgic and patriotic audience, but did not seem to be very sought after. China's Amazon homepage originally offered the product for 28 yuan, but the price has now been reduced to 15 yuan. Another Internet shop offered the CD for 15 yuan, now reduced to 6 yuan.[27] Taihe Rye Music still promotes the recording on its homepage. An explanation for this obviously low demand can be found in a letter from a person called "Toutou" (2006), who may be in his forties and who published a lengthy review on the homepage of Taihe Rye Music. He commented that such a compilation does not "only result in a rustic yearning for the past among the majority of listeners, but it is

[25] Chin. *Taihe maitian yinyue wenhua fazhan youxian gongsi.* Taihe Rye Music is a devision of one of China's biggest entertainment companies. See Montgomery/Fitzgerald 2006, and: http://www.trmusic.com.cn.

[26] http://www.trmusic.com.cn/disc.html, accessed in May 2008.

[27] See www.amazon.cn and www.dangdang.com, accessed in May 2008.

absolutely not the *style* [orig. in English] that young people need today. Have a look at the cover, and (you want to) put it back into the shelf. And then continue to choose (another) one of those East-West-combinations, foreign music (*yang yinyue*) combined with Peking opera and storytelling." The author suspects that the company made the recording for its own enjoyment, not for audiences, because "today's main consumers are young people, who seem to have lost the slightest sense of curiosity, not to mention love for one's mother country. Apart from [romantic] love, all other topics and emotions that are in some way related to love have already greatly faded from memory." With reference to the songs in the compilation, the author prefers listening to the original versions, which are simple songs, sometimes only accompanied by mouthorgan and guitar, and convey a beautiful feeling (*meigan*), e.g. "The Open Sea, ah" (*Dahai, ah!*) and "Hometown" (*guxiang*).
The story of "My Homeland" is an interesting case because it illustrates the fact that private companies try to benefit from the popular wave of patriotism and nationalism. The first two recordings of "Sanlitun Music" were a double-CD compilation called "Collection of Bar Singers: Boys and Girls" (*jiuba geshou heji: nanhai nühai*, Dec. 2004) and "Boys & Girls' Valentines Day" (*nanhai nühai de qingrenjie*, Feb. 2005). Since these are closer to the area of Sanlitun than to patriotic songs, this might indicate a trail-and-error marketing experiment. The example also shows that private companies may be more open, more receptive to criticism. The Managing Director, Michael Song, who studied in the USA for six years, is working on new business models for the music industry in China, and also established one of the now popular dialogue forums on the company's homepage which encouraged Toutou to write a review and criticize both the cover and the content. Yet this single criticism does not allow for a larger estimation of "My Homeland's" popularity: it only suggests that re-arranged old songs and this package attract neither the elder nor the younger generation.

Fig. 16: *My Homeland* 2005

Fig. 17: Scream 2003

Fig. 18: Punk Party: *Rock & Frog* 2005

A closer look at the PRC's music repertoire actually reveals that the use of old images from the revolutionary past is not restricted to compilations of propaganda and patriotic music. Consumers can easily be misled if they only look at the CD-cover, because the counter culture makes use of the same visual heritage. Images of socialist and revolutionary China appear on different CDs, with different companies and in different costumes. One example would be the front cover of a recording released by the company "Scream". "Nahan," again, is the title of a famous collection of essays by Lu Xun, published in 1918. In this case, however, the message is inscribed in the title and says: "SCREAM for the Chinese Rock 'n' Roll Yesterday." Here, the image of Red Guards was chosen to promote the rock 'n' roll revolution on two CDs: a recording that includes Chinese rock music of the early period and a documentary on VCD. Another example offers the Punk-CD "Punk Party: Rock & Frog" (*Yaogun qingwa*), released by a band called "Workers & Soldiers" (*Gongbing yuedui*, 2005) which plays with the image of a Red Guard who is holding a little Red Book.

History, Tradition and Signifying Chineseness

Although images of revolutionary nostalgia were eye-catching and prominent in the realm of popular culture during this period, they were hardly the only ones. Another set of "nostalgic" images referred to the discourse on China's history and tradition that had attracted a wide range of artists and intellectuals since the mid-1980s. The heavy metal band "Tang Dynasty" (*Tang Chao*), founded in 1988, reflected this trend even in its name and is probably the earliest and most well-known example. The band's lyrics suggested a "Dream Return to the Tang Dynasty", and offered a playful confrontation with China's historically most prosperous and international period. The band created a popular image of the glorious past, spoke favorably of this in interviews and adhered to a masculine heavy metal performance style. Their on-stage posing and attitude could easily be linked to popular knight-errant novels (*wuxia xiaoshuo*), a genre that inspired the cover design and was also exploited for the cover of the Beijing rock-compilation "Chinese Fire" (*Zhongguo huo*). Both records were released in late 1992 on the Magic-Stone label of the Taiwanese company, Rock Records & Tapes, which promoted Mainland China's new rock music as a distinguished art form rooted in and emerging from China's long tradition.

Heavy Metal à la *Tang Dynasty* was provocative, not only as a new musical form in the PRC, but also because it stressed a vague return to feudal values and to tolerance of China's culturally most glorified dynasty. It can, however, also be read as an act against globalization, as patriotic admiration of Chinese culture, and as a signifier of Chineseness in a period when exactly these values were threatened. Tang Dynasty's heavy metal release of "The Internationale" (*guoji ge*) should be perceived in a similar way, as both innovative and mainstream. Finally, Tang Dynasty is also the name of a rock band and a foreign-sponsored commercial product, which, despite a provocative attitude, was part of a larger discourse and followed the general trend of those years. This patriotic spirit even gained them official praise (Hao Huang 2001). Political relaxation and an officially more tolerant attitude towards rock music led to an increase in initiatives within the music industry and helped many bands to sign contracts. References to China's past, either in music, lyrical content, visual images or band names were not uncommon. One example for this localization was the band "Zi Yue", a name that is translated as "Confucius Speaks" or "The Master Speaks". Founded around 1993, the band plays a combination of "(Peking) opera rock" and experimental funk, and released its first album in 1997. The name was perhaps inspired by the then popular discourse on "Asian values", and the economic success of the "Four little Tigers", all of which resulted in the promotion of Confucian values. The band name was creatively designed on the cover: it depicted the image of a head, the eyes and nose of which were formed by the character "zi", with the mouth consisting of the character "yue". Later, however, the band discussed changing its name because the singer, Qiu Ye, felt "it was too arrogant, as though his music was telling the truth [...]" (de Kloet 2001: 62). If "Confucius Speaks" was at one extreme of possible designs, the stylish image of Tiananmen Square on the cover of "Red Sun No. 5" (1996) would be at the other. Between these two extremes, some Beijing-centered images could be placed, for example, the second recording of "Beijing Reggae" (1997), this time without revolutionary images on the cover, but with an actor from the Peking opera, equipped with guitar, microphone and keyboard.

Fig: 19: Tang Dynasty, 1992

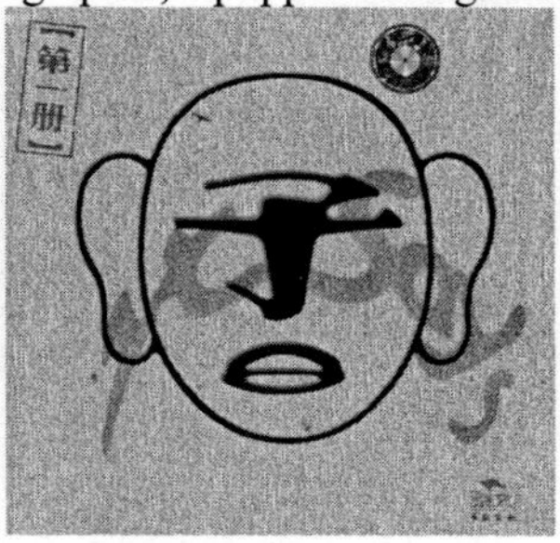

Fig. 20: *Zi Yue*, 1997

Fig. 21: *Beijing Reggae*, 1997

Another creative collage was designed by Zuoxiao Zuzhou (= Wu Hongjin), an artist and the singer, composer and lyric writer of the band "No", who later also released several solo recordings. His music includes styles such as punk, trash metal, rock, soft blues, elements of acoustic guitar and traditional, but distorted Asian-sounding melodies. The highly symbolic cover of "No's" album "The Missing Master" (*zuoshi de zhuren*, 1999), released on the Modern Sky label, gives a special touch, as it features a slightly altered painting by the Tang dynasty (618-907) painter, Zhou Fang, who became famous for his paintings of beautiful, elite women. A concubine is represented here, holding a stick in her left hand, with a red collar fixed around the neck of a little dog. The dog's head appears to be the head of Zuzhou, smiling and sticking out his tongue. A large measure of irony and sarcasm can be read into the scene: the concubine, representing the old traditions and the glorious times of the Tang dynasty, serves as a cultural background for the power of the "red collar", which can be interpreted as the CCP, and is wrapped around the neck of a little dog. The dog itself might symbolize the masses and the younger generation, which despite all this appears strong enough to laugh and mock the whole situation.

A similar image, although less ironic, could be found on the cover of "Lonely China Day" (*jimo xiari*). The band was promoted as one of the leading voices of "Chinese Indie Rock", also worked with lyrics from the Song Dynasty (960-1279) and featured a newly- painted well-known image on its cover: the old and wise scholar, passing his zither on (*qin*) to the young generation. On the back cover, there is another classical image, that of the student playing the instrument under willow trees by a lake.[28] There are, of course, different levels of "classicism" in cover design and localization. The Peking opera mask, for example, is a very popular cultural signifier. The pop-rock band, Point Zero (*lingdian*), placed a mask next to the guitar on its front cover, and a privately released foreign recording entitled "Beijing Band" (2001) also used a distorted and bleary picture of Peking opera actors on its cover.[29]

---

[28] See www.tagteamrecords.com.

[29] Aside from many Chinese recordings that make use of Peking Opera images, we can also mention foreign initiatives, e.g. the privately released recording "Beijing Band 2001", produced by Mathew Corbin Clark, Kemaxiu Music 2003. This recording features ten songs of different underground bands. See www.beijingband.com.

Fig. 22: No, 1999

Fig. 23: *Lonely China Day*, 2005

The cover design of the band, P.K.14 (= "Public Kingdom Fourteen"), explored other possibilities on the recording "White Paper" (*baipishu*, 2005): the front cover showed a sexless human body with legs and arms, painted in stickman-style. In place of the head, there was a long neck that seemed to transform into a hand at the end. A woman's face was painted on chest and belly. This rather absurd image corresponded to the fragmented and postmodern content of the lyrics, but not with the lyric's design. The lyrics were found inside the leaflet, stylishly printed in the form of popular Ming-Dynasty, Qing-Dynasty woodblock prints, written from top to bottom, and from right to left.

Three further examples will serve to illustrate the creative use of historical images: the members of the band, "Autumn Mosquitoes" (*qiutian de chongzi*, 1999), appeared with white painted faces, blond dyed, strange-looking hair styles and rather dull facial expressions which could be interpreted as a synthesis of Beijing opera and gothic rock style. The title of the recording allows various interpretations: "Diary of a Madman" (*kuangren riji*). It is, of course, a familiar name to every literary person in China, with reference to Lu Xun's short story with the same title (1918), being the first written in colloquial Chinese. However, in this context, it is more likely that the recording related to the very successful rock album released by Ozzy Osborne (1981). The title was the same, the design was similar and it was re-released in 1995.[30] The second example played with images of old Shanghai, combining its fashion, flowers and references to the underworld. The cover of "Happy Avenue" (*xinfu dajie*) depicted a woman in a cheongsam (*qipao*) holding a knife in her hand; the pictures inside the leaflet further elaborated on this image, which stressed aspects of violence, femininity, seduction and romantic flowers. It promoted the female lead-singer, Wu Hongfei, and her band, which adhered to quick tempo folk rock style rock music.[31] Images of femininity in the realm of rock music tend to credit women with power, in other words: seduction is provoked and controlled by women. The final example would be the cover design of recordings by the first generation rock musician, Dou Wei, and his music formation, "Not Sure Yet" (*buyiding*). The idea for the project was based on music being in motion, always changing, never static and unfinished. Thus the music was not rehearsed in a conventional way, and each performance and recording was a unique moment. The music style could be defined as a synthesis of elements from rock, jazz and improvisation. The CD-

---

[30] Ozzy Osborne released "Diary of a Madman" in November 1981. Byl October 1994, three million copies of the recording had been sold (Triple Platinum). In August 1995, the album was re-released.

[31] Wu Hongfei (b. 1978), graduated from Beijing's Qinghua University with Bachelor's degrees in environmental engineering and the editing of scientific books, and an M.A. in modern Chinese literature. She works as a journalist and novelist. See http://en.wikipedia.org/wiki/Happy_Avenue.

covers often (but not always) related to traditional images, for example, landscapes, calligraphy, bamboo, etc. One double CD recording especially underlined this connection with the past: "Journey to the East" (*dong youji*, 2006). The title itself reminded everybody familiar with Chinese culture of the famous novel "Journey to the West" (*Xi youji*). Thus, "Journey to the East" can easily be understood as a journey back to China and to oneself, underlined by a particularly quiet and meditative music and sound. The design of the CD cover was as simple as it was eye-catching: it resembled an old book, bound together by a specific technique, with a simple blue cover and the title written in the right-hand corner.

Fig. 24: Point Zero, 2004

Fig. 25: Happy Avenue, 2004

Fig. 26: Dou Wei, 2006

Postsocialist Nostalgia and Creativity

The aim of this article is to provide a preliminary insight into one particular aspect of advertising and popular culture in the PRC, namely the evolution and design of CD-covers. I began with the decline of Maoist "poster power," discussed Cui Jian's rock revolution, the post-Mao nostalgia and deconstruction, and also the utilization of revolutionary and historical signs and images. Throughout the post-New Era, CD-covers accompanied, critically commented on or otherwise reflected China's transformation as "frozen visual analogies of music" (Edge 1991). This article ends with examples that reveal an ongoing competition between political propaganda and (unofficial) popular culture, both of which are characterized by their visual dissolution in the age of global postmodernity.

The CD-covers discussed here were deliberately "made" to address issues of Chinese history and society, yet they also reveal the absorption of general trends and discourses, be they the question of Chineseness, nationalism, patriotism or the three expressions of nostalgia mentioned at the beginning. Their existence is based on the cultural logic of postsocialism, "in accordance with which artists, filmmakers, and writers negotiate the residual socialist past and the emergent capitalist present to concoct new imaginaries of a transitional society" (S. H. Lu 2007: 208). However, many images and design forms have not been mentioned, and many more topics are possible, for example, femininity and masculinity, beauty, sexuality, boredom and violence, to mention only a few. Analysis of these images is, with some exceptions, complicated by the fact that often less is said about the artists and the music, than about advertising strategies and consumer preferences. As early as 1995, Gregory Lee discovered that images of Madonna, for example, were being used to promote a music magazine which contained a selection of nationalistic and party songs (Lee 1995: 99). In addition to this practice, women's participation in the creation of their representations can be seen as rather limited. Baranovitch (2003: 148ff) showed how men literally control the production of the "neotraditional image of womanhood" and the definition and representations of womanhood in general in the popular music scene. The male-dominated arena of rock music is no exception, although the few women associated with it seem to be equipped with more power.

Amidst the variety of images, those that refer to the PRC's socialist and revolutionary past are certainly commercially attractive in art circles as well as in the music business. The latter employs them both for official propaganda and for underground rock/punk styles, often inspired by political pop art. The reason for and the success of this nostalgia might be considered to reside in the search for an image that combines the quest for stability and simplicity with revolution, power and Chineseness, yet there is again a big difference. While official propaganda uses these popular images to visually "update" its product for the market, rock circles may see them as a means to strongly localize their product. With regard to the younger generation, however, both practices cater to an "armchair nostalgia", that is, "nostalgia without lived experience or collective historical memory" (Appadurai 1996: 78). China's younger generation shares this lack of experience with foreign audiences, who, in many instances, are equally obsessed with these images. Both consumer groups ignore the PRC's past history and propaganda, and are free to establish "revolutionary China" as the signifier of Chinese avant-garde/underground culture and postmodern Chinese resistance. That this concept is internationally appealing can be seen by two underground/indie/rock-compilations that were recorded in Beijing, produced in Chicago and are now available on the international market via amazon.com and other homepages.[32] Both records were produced by the drummer, Martin Atkins, who is also the owner of Invisible Records in Chicago. As is said in the *Press Release*, "Atkins set out to create an album that reflected what he was seeing and hearing in Beijing." Thus, the two records offer a subjective selection of present Beijing underground music, combining punk, post-punk, dub and experimentation with "traditional Chinese musicians and instruments and Tibetan singers for a fuller picture" (ibid.). To attract foreign consumers to this musical "hot pot," Atkins chose two images that are particularly popular and easily identifiable with the Chinese underground. The cover of one features Red Guards with the Little Red Book and, in the second case, two steel workers hitting a drum, painted in the style of socialist realism.

Reviews of the two albums were generally positive, if not enthusiastic; critics also spoke of the music's historical "backwardness" and future perspectives. The *Rolling Stone* wrote about "Look Directly into the Sun:" "Venture into a city to record unsigned bands, and what you get is a whole lot of nothing in no particular order. [...] The reason is the city: Beijing, 15 million strong, a hub of the kind of thrilling, contradictory, upward mobility that gets kids rocking. Most of the songs are by English-singing guys with guitars whom we'll call garage punk because that can mean almost anything cheap and catchy. [...] These eighteen bands are too excited to explore their contradictions yet. But that too will come."[33] The *Chicago Reader* is more positive. "There's only been a native scene for maybe a decade," it is said, and a "Beijing sound" has yet to develop." Nevertheless, underground rock in China is "surprisingly good overall," and: "*Look Directly Into the Sun* makes me wonder

[32] See "Look Directly into the Sun. China Pop 2007," and "Made in China. By Martin Atkins' China Dub Sound System," 2007. See http://www.bloodshotrecords.com/artists/invisiblechina, accessed May 2008.

[33] See Christgau, 2007.

if a Chinese Invasion is imminent."[34] Does Chinese rock have to be sung in English to amount to a Chinese invasion?

Fig. 27: Martin Atkins 2007

Fig. 28: Martin Atkins 2007

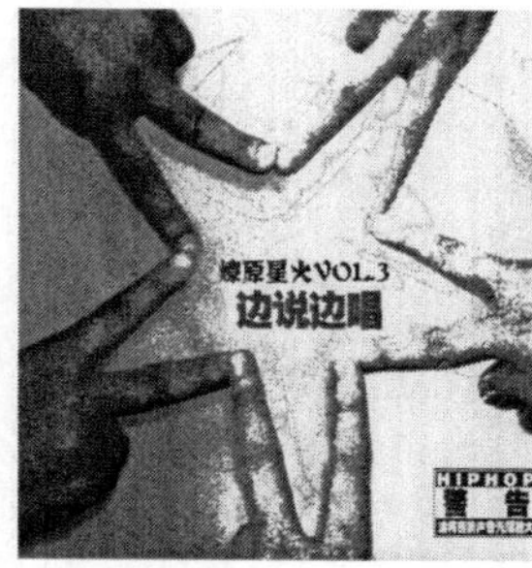

Fig. 29: Hip-Hop 2007

Answers to these questions may be found later; for the moment, an analysis of CD-covers can be seen to provide a specific perspective on strategies of cultural production and consumption in (and with) postsocialist China. Images relate in different ways to the products they represent and advertise, yet their creative designs are not necessarily connected to a certain music style or ideological intention. Although this transformation of the visual was not initiated by CD-covers, these products are still part of an ongoing process, in which they openly operate between art and music, commerce and politics, popular culture and everyday life. Among the latest examples combining visual creativity and revolutionary symbolism is the hip-hip compilation "Setting the Fields on Fire, Vol. 3" (*liao yuan xing huo*, Vol 3), 2007. Here, we see the "Red Star" being formed of five hands that are performing the victory sign. Images like this are global, though we may also regard them as bearing traces of nostalgia and other national discourses, so-called Chinese characteristics and different forms or stages of localization techniques. This approach appeals to Chinese musicians and producers as it does to foreign companies, although it is, by far, not the only strategy for promoting pop and rock music.

Today, the PRC's revolutionary images of the past help to promote Chinese propaganda songs; they are also useful for advertising and identifying with Red Jazz and underground rock – not only in China. In other words, the transfer of the "Little Red Book" appears to symbolize the arrival of a new moment in Sino-foreign cultural interaction, characterized by the simultaneous appearance of red jazz in China and Chinese rock in the western world. Yet there is a fundamental difference between these two forms: Red Jazz builds on a specific group of popular songs and follows a general pattern, namely, that "Pop music continually recycles its own history: remakes, revivals, cover versions and comebacks" (Frith/Horne 1989: 189). Chinese rock, by contrast, has only just begun to "recycle" and its acceptance though orientalized entrance into rock music's international arena is a fairly young phenomenon. Ironically, images of the Mao period represent Chinese rock in the West at a time when many musicians and bands regard these images as backward and non-international. Some of them, like Hang on the Box, Re-establish the Right of Statue (*zhongsu diaoxiang de quanli*) and Joyside, sing only in English and the latter released albums entitled "Drunk is Beautiful" (2004) and "Bitches of Rock & Roll" (2006). Although

[34] See Raymer, 2007.

these albums are very international, both in sound and design, global recognition and success are, of course, not only a matter of packaging.

References

Andrews, Julia F. and Gao Minglu (1995) "The Avant-garde's Challenge to Official Art," in Deborah S. Davis, Richard Kraus, Barry Naughton and Elizabeth J. Perry (eds) *Urban Spaces in Contemporary China. The Potential for Autonomy and Community in post-Mao China,* New York: Woodrow Wilson Center Press/Cambridge University Press 1995, pp. 221-278.

Appadurai, Arjun (1996) *Modernity at Large. Cultural Dimensions of Globalization*, Minneapolis: University of Minnesota Press.

Arac, Jonathan (1997) "Chinese Postmodernism: Toward a Global Context," in *boundary 2*, 24/3, pp. 261-275.

Baranovitch, Nimrod (2003) *China's New Voices. Popular Music, Ethnicity, Gender and Politics, 1978-1997*, Berkeley: University of California Press.

Barmé, Geremie (1996) *Shades of Mao. The Posthumous Cult of the Great Leader*, Armonk/New York: M. E. Sharpe.

Barmé, Geremie (1992) "The Greying of Chinese Culture," in Kuan Hsin-chi and Maurice Brosseau .(eds) *China Review,* chapter 13, Hongkong, pp. 1-52.

Benewick, Robert (1999) "Icons of Power: Mao Zedong and the Cultural Revolution," in Harriet Evans and Donald Stephanie (eds) *Picturing Power in the People's Republic of China. Posters of the Cultural Revolution*, Lanham: Rowman & Littlefield, pp. 123-137.

Christgau, Robert (2007) Review: "Look directly into the Sun. China Pop 2007," 29.11.2007, in *Rolling Stone Magazine* (online) <http://www.rollingstone.com/reviews> accessed 21 March 2008.

Dai Jinhua (2001) "Behind Global Spectacle and National Image Making. The Tide of Nationalism," in *positions*, 9/1, pp. 161-186.

Dai Jinhua (2002) "Redemption and Consumption: Depicting Culture in the 1990s." in Tani E. Barlow (ed.) *New Asian Marxisms*, Duke University Press, pp. 89-105.

Davis, Deborah S. (ed.) (2000) *The Consumer Revolution in Urban China*, Berkeley: California University Press.

de Kloet, Jeroen (2005) "Sonic Sturdiness: The Globalization of 'Chinese' Rock and Pop," in *Critical Studies in Media Communication* 22/4, pp. 321-338.

de Kloet, Jeroen (2002) "Rock in the Hard Place: Commercial Fantasies in China's Music Industry," in Stephanie Hemelryk Donald, Michael Keane and Yin Hong (eds) *Media in China. Consumption, Content and Crisis*, London: Routledge Curzon 2002, pp. 93-104.

de Kloet, Jeroen (2001) *Red Sonic Trajectories – Popular Music and Youth in Urban China,* Ipskamp: Enschede.

de Kloet, Jeroen (2000) "Let him Fucking See the Green Smoke Beneath my Groin: The Mythology of Chinese Rock," in Arif Dirlik and Zhang Xudong (eds) *Postmodernism & China*, Durham/London: Duke University Press, pp. 239-274.

Dirlik, Arif (2001) "Markets, Culture, Power: The Making of a 'Second Cultural Revolution' in China," in *Asian Studies Review*, 25/1, pp. 1-33.

Dirlik, Arif and Zhang Xudong (1997) "Introduction: Postmodernism and China," in: *boundary 2*, 24/3, pp. 1-18.

Dujunco, Mercedes M. (2002) "Hybridity and Disjuncture in Mainland Chinese Popular Music," in Timothy Craig and Richard King (eds) *Global Goes Local: Popular Culture in Asia*, University of Vancouver: British Columbia Press 2002, pp. 25-39.

Edge, Kevin (1991) *The Art of Selling Songs. Graphics for the Music Business 1690-1990*, London.
Frith, Simon and Howard Horne (1989) *Art into Pop*, London: Routledge.
Fowler, G. A. (2006) "Rock 'n' Rolling into China: Rolling Stone has launched a Chinese Edition – Minus the Sex, Drugs and Politics," in *Wall Street Journal*, 10.03.2006, p. B1.
Fung, Anthony and Curtin, Michael (2002) "The Anomalies of being Faye (Wong): Gender Politics in Chinese Popular Music," in *International Journal of Cultural Studies*, 5/3, pp. 263-290.
Gao Minglu (2003) "Post-Utopian Avant-Garde in China," in Aleš Erjavec (ed.) *Postmodernism and the Postsocialist Condition. Politicised Art under Late Socialism*, Berkeley/Los Angeles: University of California Press, pp. 247-283.
German Sounds AG (ed.) (2005) *Information on the Chinese Music Market and a Chinese Press Review*, Source: Bureau des Musiques Actuelles (BMA) / European Music Platform.
Gold, Thomas B. (1993) "Go with your feelings – Hongkong and Taiwan popular culture in Greater China," in *The China Quarterly* 136, pp. 907-925.
Guo Jieming and Su Fei (1999) "Modern Sky Empire," in *Beijing Scene* 6/8 (Dec. 1999), pp. 4-6.
Hao Huang (2001) "Yaogun yinyue: Rething Mainland Chinese Rock 'n' Roll," in *Popular Music*, 20/1, pp. 1-11.
Helmore, Edward (2006) "Banned by Beijing – but Rolling Stone gathers no kudos," in *The Guardian*, 02.04.2006.
Ho, Wai-Chung (2006) "Social Change and Nationalism in China's Popular Songs", in *Social History*, 31/4, pp. 435-453.
Hong, Junhao (1994) "The Resurrection of Advertising in China. Developments, Problems and Trends," in *Asian Survey*, 34/3 (April), pp. 326-342.
Jones, Andrew F. (1992) *Like a Knife – Ideology and Genre in Contemporary Chinese Popular Music*, New York: Ithaka.
Jones, Andrew F. (1994) "The Politics of Popular Music in Post-Tiananmen China," in Jeffrey N. Wasserstrom and Elizabeth J. Perry (eds) *Popular Protest and Political Culture in Modern China* (Second Edition), Boulder/Colorado, pp. 148-165.
Kraus, Richard Curt (2004) *The Party and the Arty in China. The New Politics of Culture*, Lanham: Rowman & Littlefield.
Lee, Gregory (1996) *Troubadours, Trumpeters, Troubled Makers. Lyricism, Nationalism, and Hybridity in China and its Others*, Durham: Duke University Press.
Lee, Gregory (1995) "The 'East is Red' goes Pop: Commodification, Hybridity and Nationalism in Chinese Popular song and Its Televisual Performance," in *Popular Music*, 14/1, pp. 95-110.
Lin, Xiaoping (1997) "Parodic Images: A Glimpse of Contemporary Chinese Art," in *Leonardo*, 30/2, pp. 113-122.
Liu, Kang (1997) "Popular Culture and the Culture of the Masses in Contemporary China," in *boundary 2*,. 24/ 3, pp. 99-122.
Lu Hanchao (2002) "Nostalgia for the Future: The Resurgence of an Alienated Culture in China," in *Pacific Affairs*, 75/ 2 (Summer 2002), pp- 169-186.
Lu, Sheldon H. (1996) "Postmodernity, Popular Culture, and the Intellectual: A Report on Post-Tiananmen China," in *boundary 2*, 23/2, pp. 139-169.
Lu, Sheldon H. (2001a) *China, Transnational Visuality, Global Postmodernity*, California: Stanford University Press.

Lu, Sheldon H. (2001b) "Global Post Modernization: The Intellectual, The Artist, and China's Condition," in *boundary 2*, Vol. 24, No. 3, pp. 65-97.

Lu, Sheldon H. (2007) *Chinese Modernity and Global Biopolitics. Studies in Literature and Visual Culture*, Honolulu: University of Hawaii Press.

McClure, Steve (2001) "China Packed with Potential. Battling Pirates and Finding Raw Talent, Major Labels are optimistic about the Future Role of the Emerging Chinese Market," in *Billboard*, 113/47 (Nov. 24, 2001) (Asia Pacific Quarterly), p. 1, 2, 4.

Montgomery, Lucy and Fitzgerald, Brian (2006) "Copyright and the creative industries in China," in *International Journal of Cultural Studies*, 9/3, pp. 407-418.

Raymer, Miles (2007) "He's Givin' us Chinese Rock. Industrial Legend Martin Atkins goes to Beijing and brings back two albums of eye-opening Music," in *Chicago Reader*, <http://www.chicagoreader.com/features/stories/sharpdarts/071108/> accessed May 21, 2008.

Rushe, Dominic (2004) "China could top the Music industry charts," in *The Sunday Times* (Business), repr. in: German Sounds AG (ed.) 2005, pp. 17-18.

Steen, Andreas (2000a) "Tradition, Politics and Meaning in 20th Century China's Popular Music. Zhou Xuan: 'When will the Gentleman come back again?'" in *CHIME – Journal of the European Foundation for Chinese Music Research*, No. 14/15, 1999/2000, pp. 124-153.

Steen, Andreas (2000b) "Sound, Protest and Business. Modern Sky Co. and the New Ideology of Chinese Rock," in *Berliner China-Hefte* 18, pp. 40-64.

Steen, Andreas (1996) *Der Lange Marsch des Rock 'n' Roll. Pop- und Rockmusik in der Volksrepublik China*, Münster: LIT..

Toutou (2006) "Sanlitun yinyue zhi wo de zuguo – Ni zai yule shei?" in: *http://www.trmusic.com.cn/news/news_view.asp?newsid=105*, accessed May 2008.

Upton, Janet L. (2002) "The Politics and Poetics of Sister Drum: 'Tibetan' Music in the Global Marketplace," in Timothy Craig and Richard King (ed.) *Global Goes Local: Popular Culture in Asia*, University of Vancouver: British Columbia Press 2002, pp. 99-129.

Wang, Jian (2000) *Foreign Advertising in China: Becoming Global, Becoming Local*, Ames: Iowa State University Press.

Wang, Jing (2007) *Brand New China. Advertising, Media, and Commercial Culture*, Cambridge, Mass.: Harvard University Press.

Wu, Jing (2006) "Nostalgia as content creativity: Cultural industries and popular sentiment," in: *International Journal of Cultural Studies*, 9/3, pp. 359-368.

Xu, Ben (2001) "Postmodern-Postcolonial Criticism and Pro-Democracy Enlightenment," in *Modern China*, 27/1, pp. 117-147.

Yan Jun (2002) *Didixia* [Undergroundground], Beijing: Wenhua yishu chubanshe.

Yang, Xiaobin (2002) "Postscript. Answering the Question. What is Postmodern/Post-Mao-Deng?" in Xiaobin Yang (ed.) *The Chinese Postmodern, Trauma and Irony in Chinese Avant-Garde Fiction*, Ann Arbor: University of Michigan Press, pp. 230-246.

Yinxiang shijie [Audio & Video World] (1992) *Hong taiyang weihe chaoxiao?* [Why does the Red Sun Enjoy this Popularity?], No. 3, pp. 2-3.

Zhang, Xudong (1999) "Postmodernism and Post-Socialist Society: Cultural Politics in China After the 'New Era,'" in *New Left Review* 237, pp. 77-105.

Images

1 Cui Jian: Xin Changzheng lushang de yaogun (Rock 'n' Roll on the New Long March), prod. by Zhongguo lüyou shengxiang chubanshe (China Tourist Sound Co.), TAV9-5, Cover Design: Song Xiaohong, Cui Jian, Zhang Wei, Liang Jiewei; Beijing 1988.

2 Cui Jian: Yiwu suoyou (I have Nothing) EMI Music Publishing (S. E. Asia), LTD, Made in Japan 1989.

3 Cui Jian: Jiejue (Solution), EMI Music Publishing (S. E. Asia), LTD, FX 500762, Made in Japan 1990.

4 Beijing Reggae, Golden Pony Records, LTD, GLP 1003-2, Design: Rican Design Associates, Illustration: Maxim Tang, publ. by Jeffrey Cheen; Made in Japan, 1991.

5 The Red Sun – Sentimental Dance Tunes (Hong Taiyang – wubuqing), tape, Guangzhou yinxiang chubanshe, GH-179, ~1992.

6 Hou Muren & Xiandairen: Hongse yaogun (Red Rock), prod./distr. by Shenzhen jiguang jiemu, SC-92-035, Shenzhen 1992.

7 Cui Jian: Hongqi xia de dan (Balls under the Red Flag), Beijing East & West Art Prod. Co., marketed by EMI Music Publishing (S. E. Asia), LTD, 7-2438-30801-4-4, Beijing 1994.

8 Shenzhou Yaobai (China Rocks/Rocking China), Music Communications Limited, D.I.Y. 002-2, Hong Kong 1994.

9 Liuxing yaogun (Popular Rock), Production: Beijing Xingdie wenhua fazhan gongsi, Release: Baitian'e yinxiang chubanshe, ISRC CD-F23-97-442-00/A.J6; Distribution: Meika Records, MKCD-1149, Guangzhou 1997.

10 Modeng Tiankong (Modern Sky Records): Vol. 2, ISRC CN-A26-98-443-00/A.J6, Beijing 1998.

11 The Fly: "z", Jingwen Records, ISRC CN-A01-00-341-00/A.J6, Cover Design: Feng Jiangzhou, Beijing 2000.

12 Li Xiaolong: Li Shaolong, produced by Beijing Qilin tong wenhua chuanbo youxian zeren gongsi, distributed by Shanghai shengxiang chubanshe, ISRC CN-B04-00-389-00/A-J6, Shanghai 2000.

13 Hongse jueshi (Red Jazz), Shanghai Listen Audio & Video Co. LTD, ISRC CN-E03-00-443-00/A.J6, Shanghai 2000.

14 Hongse jueshi (Red Jazz), Rock Records (Taiwan) Co., LTD., ISRC CN-D07-00-337-00/A.J6, Taibei 2001.

15 Zhongguo gequ (Songs Collection of China), 10 CDs, China Record Corporation, ISRC CN-G01-02-324-00/A.J6, Beijing 2002.

16 Sanlitun yinyue: Wo de zuguo (Sanlitun Music: My Homeland), Taihe Rye Music Co. (Taihe maitian yinyue), Beijing, ISRC CN-C18-05-401-00/A.J6, Beijing 2007.

17 Nahan – weile Zhongguo cengjing de yaogun (Scream – For the Chinese Rock 'n' Roll Yesterday), Jingwen Records Co., LTD, ISRC CN-A51-03-387-00/A.J6, Beijing 2002.

18 Gong bing yuedui (Workers and Soldiers): Yaogun qingwa (Punk Party – Rock & Frog), Scream Records, ISCR CN-A51-05-304-00/A.J6, Beijing 2005.

19 Tang Chao (Tang Dynasty), Rock Records & Tapes (Magic Stone Co.), RD-1183, Taibei 1992.

20 Zi Yue: Zi Yue (The Master Speaks), Cover Idea: Qiu Ye, Cover Design: Xiao Hui, Beijing Jingwen Records, 1996, ISRC CN-A08-97-472.00/A.J6.

21 Beijing Reggae All Stars, Vol. 1, Cover Illustration: Ken Mok, Chinatown Music Co.,

CTCD-903, Hong Kong 1996.

22 No: The Missing Master (Zuoshi de zhuren), Design: Modern Sky Graphics Design Studio, Modern Sky Records 1999, ISRC CN A26-99-332-00/A.J6.

23 Jimo xiari (Lonely China Day), Tagteam Records, ISRC CN-A23-05-0111-1/A.J6., Beijing 2005.

24 Point Zero (Lingdian), Fenglei dong (Moving Storm), Graphic Design: Nod From Vapor Studio, released by Jiuzhou yinxiang chuban gongsi, distributed by Focus Music Dissemination Co., Guangzhou 2004, ISRC CN-A65-04-589-00/A.J6.

25 Xingfu dajie (Happy Avenue): Xiaolong fangjian limian de yu – When the Fish loves Xiaolong, So Rock! Records, Beijing 2004.

26 Dou Wei et. al: Dongyouji (Journey to the East), 2 CDs, Shanghai yinxiang gongsi, Shanghai 2006, ISRC CN-E02-06-0003-0/A.J6.

27 Look directly into the Sun. China Pop 2007, prod. by Martin Atkins, Invisible Records, Chicago 2007.

28 Made in China. Martin Atkins' China Dub Soundsystem, prod. by Martin Atkins, Invisible Records, Chicago 2007.

29 Liao yuan xing huo Vol 3, Hip-Hop. Bian shuo bian chang (Setting the Fields on Fire, Vol. 3, Hip-Hop. Talking and Singing), Jiuzhou Audio-Video Publishing Corp., Beijing 2007.

Yiu Fai Chow and Jeroen de Kloet

Building Memories - A Study of Pop Venues in Hong Kong

Changing cities produce many sights that are unfamiliar. But rapidly changing cities, cities without brakes like Hong Kong, produce something else as well: 'the unfamiliar in the familiar'; that is, the unfamiliar that is half-seen or seen subliminally behind the seen/scene of the familiar (Abbas 1997: 78).

Fluid Sounds

Indeed, for someone living in a fast-changing city, the landscape may resemble a war zone, where space is structured by a tug of war between disappearance and appearance, between the unfamiliar and the familiar. Ackbar Abbas' interest is essentially visual; his inquiry into ways of seeing a fast-changing city like Hong Kong is located in visual cultures such as architecture and photography. Our concern is to include the audio with the visual. Informed by the global importance of the local sound – Cantopop – in the 1970s and 1980s and its perceived disappearance by the end of the new millennium, and intrigued by the series of the so-called "comeback" Cantopop concerts around the year 2000, we find our unfamiliar in the familiar at the site of a music venue: the Hong Kong Coliseum. In this article, we will begin with a discussion of the "death of Cantopop" and some of its possible readings. Following a different approach to analyze and understand cultural consumption, we will zoom in on pop venues, which are prime sites for this emotive, audio-visual form of popular culture, to argue that one way of seeing, hearing and understanding the fast-changing city in the 21st century is to seek temporality – the passing of time, the memories, the emotions, the sounds, the fluidity – in stability, or in the buildings that stay.

What happened to the sound of Cantopop, which "in its heyday in the 1970s and 1980s [...] defined the look, feel and – with its lush, ultra-refined production values – even the sound of Chinese cool?" (Burpee in Chu 2007: 2) At a symposium on the development of Cantopop held in Hong Kong in March 2008, discussion was centered on the decline, if not the death of Cantopop. In his doctoral thesis, the veteran Cantopop lyricist and composer, James Wong, pinpointed 1997, the year Hong Kong was handed over to the Beijing authorities, as the end of the Cantopop era (Wong 2003). Figures are quoted to quantify its disappearance: in 1995, Cantopop sales amounted to HK$1.853 billion, while three years later sales had dropped to HK$ 0.916 billion (Wong 2003: 169). Cantopop itself and its over-commercialization are referred to as the reasons for its own sad fate. "People are getting tired of mainstream Cantopop because it rehashes the formula of big ballads and cheesy dance tunes year in, year out" (Lee 2002). Economy and technology are also cited as accomplices. According to Stephen Chu, "it is widely believed that the fall of Cantopop was caused by a combination of a bad economy, piracy and file sharing" (2007: 3). This gloomy narrative became even darker after the deaths of the Cantopop superstars, Leslie Cheung and Anita Mui, in April and December 2003.

According to the above accounts, a decade after the publication of Ackbar Abbas' acclaimed book, *Hong Kong – Culture and the Politics of Disappearance* (1997), Cantopop, which played such a pivotal role in the construction of a Hong Kong identity, is declining, dying, or at least, disappearing. It seems as if Hong Kong is haunted by the spirit of disappearance, as if the return to the "motherland" could only result in its erasure as the unique city so aptly described by Rey Chow: "What is unique to Hong Kong, however, is precisely an in-betweenness and an awareness of impure origins, or origins as impure" (Chow 1998: 157).

It is, however, precisely the disappearance of this in-betweenness, some would argue, that underwrites the perceived disappearance of Cantopop. Stephen Chu, for instance, asserts that "[t]he rise of a global Chinese music industry and media and the subsequent loss of the hybridity of Cantopop [...] is the major reason behind its recent decline" (2007: 13). In the globalization of Chinese music culture, Cantopop, performed in Cantonese, a regional language, is increasingly being superseded, at least in terms of sales figures and the number of stars, by Mandopop, sung in official, nation-wide Chinese. Such cultural development resonates with the general "re-nationalization" process in Hong Kong after the city joined the nation (Erni 2001) – it is no longer about "impure origins," but rather "pure origins."

In addition to placing the perceived disappearance of Cantopop in a wider political, cultural context, it is our wish to challenge such a reading and pose questions regarding the very "fact" of the disappearance itself. Anthony Fung and Michael Curtin, for instance, turn their gaze away from the traditional carriers of Cantopop, such as airplay and music release, to more recent forms of music consumption (Fung and Curtin 2002). Taking karaoke as their field of inquiry, Fung and Curtin argue for a different framing of the discussion. In addition to the disappearance narrative, which is largely framed by declining sales figures and dead stars, they urge to situate pop music consumption in general, and Cantopop in particular, also in the realm of the uncountable, the personal, and the emotive. We want to take this line of inquiry further. In proposing a counter narrative to the story of disappearance, we will show how the uncountable, personal and emotive consumption of music is grounded in solid buildings – the music venues – that help sustain a Hong Kong identity and defy disappearance, also in the post 1997 era.

Furthermore, to substantiate a story of disappearance by looking at sales figures and the number of stars is to fail to take into account, from our point of view, the changing landscape of popular music consumption. Even if the actual number of CDs being sold has declined rapidly, it does not necessarily mean that audiences are listening less to music. Apart from karaoke, there is a great deal of evidence to support the contention that there is continuing heavy emotive investment in popular music: ring tones as well as songs are frequently downloaded to individualize mobile phones; a quite astounding 34.8% of the 530 million mobile subscribers in China use their phones to listen to music, compared with 5.7% in the US.[1] YouTube is used to upload clips of subscribers either singing or mimicking songs, activities which turn the consumer into a producer. MySpace has opened up a space for bands to promote and share their music. Digital production techniques such as GarageBand have become accessible to many people, enabling the easy production of music.

Meanwhile, it seems that pop music consumption is becoming more and more personally oriented through the use of mobile audio devices, such as the mobile phone or the iPod, which enable users to fabricate their own soundtrack while traversing the city (Bull 2000). In short, there are signs that new modes of pop music consumption are not only challenging conventional producer versus consumer distinctions, but also subsuming the collapse of such distinctions into the realm of the personal and the emotive. In the following, we will continue our inquiry into Cantopop on the sites of pop venues, particularly the Hong Kong

1 From http://edpeto.com/the-next-generation/ accessed June 10, 2008.

Coliseum. We aim, through such an inquiry, to offer a different way of seeing, hearing and understanding music consumption in the city of Hong Kong. It is our contention that music venues, in particular, operate as emotive landmarks in the consumption of popular music. They allow citizens to feel that they belong to the city, as part of the city, of its citizenry and of a collective landscape of sight and sound. In short, they facilitate the construction of a collective emotive memory.

Monumental Buildings

Ten years after the handover of Hong Kong, a theme song entitled "Hong Kong always has you" (*Shi zhong you ni*) was commissioned and produced by the official authorities to commemorate the special occasion. Some of the lyrics run as follows:

Hong Kong always has you (Hong Kong always has you)
Let people applaud for a century
Hong Kong always has me (Hong Kong always has me)
A hundred thousand more surprises in this century
Thank you who have made a big world out of a small island
you never give up, you are so persevering, despite all the difficulties
that's why Hong Kong is so amazing, because Hong Kong always has you
the Lion Rock is connected to the Great Wall, we share the same blood
Hong Kong always has you (Hong Kong always has you) ......
you never give up, you are so persevering, despite all the difficulties
that's why Hong Kong is so amazing, because Hong Kong always has you
(Mandarin: Because you're here)
Let people applaud for a century
Hong Kong always has me(Mandarin: Because I'm here)(Translated by Vincent Zhu)

Lyrically, the song confirms the assumed link between Hong Kong and the mainland, while simultaneously stressing Hong Kong's alleged unique characteristics. The Han-centrism of such lines, as "the Lion Rock Hill is connected to the Great Wall, we share the same blood," is strengthened by the insertion of the Mandarin line "Because I am here." While we may wonder who the "I," "you" and "me" are referring to, or why certain lines have to be sung in Mandarin instead of Cantonese, the lyrics evoke a rosy image of post-handover Hong Kong. After applauding all the efforts and the perseverance of Hong Kong citizens who have made the city into a prosperous place, the lyrics claim that reversion to Beijing rule serves as a guarantee for an equally prosperous future.

Moving beyond the lyrics, we are confronted with the accompanying video clip showing the familiar images of the skyscrapers of Hong Kong. The clip starts with a rather unimaginative, postcard-like parade of skyscrapers, all the modern monuments of economic power, the images of Hong Kong as a city skylined by global capital. One scene includes a window cleaner at work. According to the writer of the lyrics, Chan Siu Kei, the producers deliberately included this window cleaning shot to emphasize the human element in the city's success story. At the end of the clip, we can see a parade of another sort, this time, a series of pop stars. This particular visual celebration of Hong Kong is primarily an act of collaboration between the government and pop music.

Yet, the venues where music is performed in Hong Kong are conspicuously absent in the clip. They never operate as landmarks of the city. Most if not all of the landmarks of Hong

Kong are either super-modern economic buildings pointing not only to the sky, but also to the future, or archaic, colonial architectures accommodating what would normally be called tradition or history. The latter draw our attention less frequently but none the less sharply when they are under threat, for instance, the case of the high profile campaign in 2007 to save the Queen's Pier in Hong Kong.[2] It seems that Hong Kong has to be imagined predominantly in terms of the future and occasionally in terms of the past; in other words, Hong Kong is largely imagined in terms of money and tradition, in terms of construction and destruction. And academics and activists privilege these two types of architectures, the economic ones and the heritage ones, as the prime site of their analytical concern or preservation efforts, of their understanding of contestation and resistance (Abbas 1997).

This article, however, is not about skyscrapers or colonial architectures, but about pop venues. It is about what Sophie Watson calls "mundane and commonplace spaces of the city where people simply muddle through or rub along" (2006: 16). Our concern is the relation between public space, in this case, pop venues, emotion and the possible production of identification and citizenry through the lens of collective memory. To paraphrase Saskia Sassen, this is an attempt to ground the soul of the city or a fragment of that soul in the materiality of the city, that is, pop venues (Sassen 2001). And among the venues, we are particularly interested in the Hong Kong Coliseum, which is generally considered the quintessential pop venue in Hong Kong. When the Hong Kong electronic duo, Pixel Toy, performed in Hong Kong at the Sheung Wan Civic Centre in July 2007, the band claimed on its leaflet "we may not be playing at the Coliseum, but we can still turn this into a big party." The Coliseum is the local temple of a global popular culture. The massive concerts that it has been hosting are a major source of collective emotion and memories for the people of the city.

In contrast to the dominant gloomy narrative surrounding Cantopop in the post-1997 decade, Hong Kong culture, particularly pop culture, was characterized not so much by the politics of disappearance but by the politics of reappearance. This reappearance was not only facilitated by new modes of music consumption as discussed earlier, but also embodied in a series of comeback/reunion concerts. Older pop stars who had retired or simply been fired by the culture industry reappeared in all their former glory. Bands which had broken up or become inactive, such as The Wynners and Tatming Pair, staged high-profiled reunion gigs. All these comeback or reunion concerts took place in the Hong Kong Coliseum.

The most talked about come-back concert series was probably the one by Sam Hui, the godfather of Cantopop. Sam Hui was the first to stage concerts at the Hong Kong Coliseum. That was in 1983. Twenty-one years later, he launched his series of comeback concerts. It became an instant hit, or as some would say, instant hype. In total, 38 concerts were staged, with almost half a million people witnessing Sam Hui's comeback. And the venue was of course the Hong Kong Coliseum. A local music critic attributed the success of his comeback to the local need for collective memory, which could be located in the context of fear. It was fear of disappearance, which hovered over the city before and after its handover to mainland China, a fear that could be relieved by the return of the legendary stars that helped to collectively remember the city called Hong Kong.

---

2 See http://www.nowpublic.com/hong_kong_heritage_site_queens_pier_about_be_demolish_hk_government, accessed June 10, 2008.

But then, if all these concerts had not been held in the Hong Kong Coliseum, would they still function in the same way? If all these comeback, reunion concerts symbolize certain articulations of a Hong Kong bygone but not quite, we may wonder whether these concerts might have become more a reminder of a Hong Kong bygone, totally and resolutely if they had not been held in the Hong Kong Coliseum. In a way, our questioning is not unlike Susan Fast's reflection on her experience with Live Aid in London, in 1985. For her, the best moments of that concert were during the performance by the band, Queen, but none of the written accounts she came across afterwards carried any reference to Queen at all. She started to ask the most fundamental question: "whose memory is it?" (Fast 2006: 138) And if this is a legitimate and relevant question, then our question would be: whose collective memory? And even: why is collective memory possible if our individual memories are so selective? We believe, as our analysis will show, that the answer, or part of the answer, lies in the venue, literally and figuratively.

The nostalgia, the emotive expression of collective memories and the articulation of cultural identity requires not only the software of pop music, but also the hardware; after all, it requires a space, a public space, a venue where people can gather, to confirm and affirm they share the same memories, to confirm and affirm their emotions, to confirm and affirm their collectivity, to confirm and affirm their sense of belonging, identification and citizenry. According to Abbas (1997: 65), "architecture [...] has the dangerous potential of turning all of us, locals and visitors alike, into *tourists* gazing at a stable and monumental image." But a massive and monumental venue like the Coliseum refuses, in its ordinariness, if not ugliness, to be turned into a tourist fetish. Instead, it turns Hong Kongers, indeed, into Hong Kongers. For the identity to be iterated and reiterated, the venue has to remain the same – far from disappearance, the venue may exude a strong sense of persistence, of defying disappearance. This is perhaps also why Hannah Arendt draws our attention to what she calls the "permanence of public space" (1958: 55). The permanence of certain public spaces, like the Hong Kong Coliseum, serves to comfort city dwellers with the feeling that something is staying, will stay essentially the same; in other words, that something will continue from some recent past into some near future. Pop venues are not only the embodiment of culture; they also help to construct and sustain a city and its culture.

Building Memories

In the following, we will distinguish among four stages in the development of pop venues in Hong Kong. In doing so, we will also try to connect the venues to the larger cultural formations of the city.

The first phase can be termed the pre-pop venue years, during which the British Hong Kong government, apart from pursuing predominantly economic and political interests, did make some effort to establish a cultural life in Hong Kong. The inauguration of the Hong Kong City Hall in 1962 was heralded as a major breakthrough in providing the city with cultural facilities. While opening the city hall, the governor at that time, Sir Robert Black, proclaimed: "We in Hong Kong are the beneficiaries of two great estates of culture [...]. This City Hall will bring light and pleasure to the people of Hong Kong, to the enrichment of their lives and the lives of their children!"[3] But how inclusive is the "we" really? The venue mainly followed the colonial logic and played host to cultural events and genres for the

[3] See: http://www.grs.gov.hk/PRO/srch/english/imgdisplay.jsp?RecordKey=799511&s=HKPRO_Archive_web&version=Internet&page=2.

privileged local elite and expatriate circles. During this phase, there seemed to be a dislocation of experience and identity. Dislocation, because the building itself, through colonial education, was branded for Hong Kongers as a marker or even an icon of the city, something the citizens identified, or should identify, Hong Kong with. Yet, most of the local population would never have stepped inside and experienced the space and its cultural activities. Typical old textbook of the 1960s presented an image of the City Hall being isolated, dominant and proud (see Fig. 1). Now, four decades later, it is dwarfed by its much more powerful neighbors (see Fig. 2), a visual account of the change in Hong Kong as a whole.

Fig. 1: The City Hall

Fig. 2: City Hall dwarfed amidst the Hong Kong skyline

Fig. 3: Academic Community hall

The second phase, in the late 1970s and early 1980s, saw the appearance of, first, the Academic Community Hall (1978, see Figure 3) and, then, the Queen Elizabeth Stadium (1980, see Figure 4). This was also the time when colonial elite culture was being contested, when local pop music, Cantopop, gradually established itself as a major musical genre and market in the colonial city. However, it was also a market characterized more strongly by a "workshop" logic, in the sense that pop stars as we know them later in the pop history of Hong Kong had not yet been produced. As these two pop venues were able to host audiences of 1,300 and 3,600 people respectively, they were perfect locations for smaller concerts. Subsequently, this phase also saw the emergence of the "collective" in terms of memory and emotion, when the local audience started to have a sense of gathering together to share some common experience. However, given the smaller venues and smaller gatherings, such experience remained fragmentary. Instead of privileging one dominant collective memory, there was a fragmented collection of collective memories. The venues and their concerts were not yet massive and monolithic enough to elevate the collective into collective identity, at least not in the sense of a Hong Kong culture and identity. If they were remembered, those venues would be more likely spoken of fondly as reminiscent of the days of folk songs, of the student era, but not of the city.

In the third phase, from the 1980s until now, the definitive venue was constructed, the Hong Kong Coliseum. It was opened on 27 April 1983. With an audience capacity of 12,500, it was much larger than any other performance venue built so far; it ushered in the experience of cultural activity at a different level of intensity and collectivity. According to 2007-2008 figures, more than 1,862,000 people attended activities held at the Hong Kong Coliseum, compared with 334,000 at the Queen Elizabeth Stadium.[4] This was the phase when local

4 See http://www.lcsd.gov.hk/CE/Entertainment/Stadia/HKC/en/about.php and http://www.lcsd.gov.hk/CE/Entertainment/Stadia/QE/index.html, accessed June 10, 2008.

pop music was maturing and canonizing into the genre of Cantopop, while the industry saw the full implementation of a more factory-like system when stars were largely seen to be manufactured, packaged and sold on a massive scale.

The Coliseum became the venue not only for performing stars, but also for producing stars. It was, and still is, *the* venue. Even today, new stars must pass through this temple of pop to be fully baptized into stardom. Collective memory is gradually changing from being experiential, even existential, into the expected. Audiences who go to a Coliseum concert these days are not only aware that they will collect memories; they expect to feel stirred emotionally and they also want to own records of their emotions and memories. For instance, DVD recordings of live concerts are one of the bestselling pop genres in Hong Kong. Guy Debord once described a spectacle as "capital accumulated to the point where it becomes image" (Debord 1995: 24). In this case, the image has also become another form of capital that circulates, to be owned by people who have seen the spectacle. The Hong Kong Coliseum's monopoly over audience expectations and therefore fulfillment of collective memory has turned this unique space into an important producer of Hong Kong culture and Hong Kong identity.

Fig. 4: Queen Elizabeth Stadium

Fig. 5: Hong Kong Coliseum

Fig. 6: Hong Kong Exhibition and Convention Centre

The fourth phase is more difficult to pin down. New venues have been built since the Coliseum, including the Hong Kong Exhibition and Convention Centre which was conceived and completed in conjunction with the Handover Ceremony in 1997; Star Hall, at the Hong Kong International Trade and Exhibition Centre; and Asia World Arena, close to Hong Kong's international airport. However, up to now, none has offered a serious challenge to the function of the Hong Kong Coliseum in the production of collective memory and identity. By the end of 2008, the Coliseum will be closed for large-scale renovation. At the same time, one new venue may arise as part of the West Kowloon Cultural District project, a government-initiated project that aims to promote Hong Kong as a creative city. The venue, referred to in the plan as a mega performance venue, will host up to 15,000 people, and thus a larger audience than the Coliseum. It remains to be seen whether the project will be actualized in this form, and whether such new venues will be able to replace the emotive power of the Coliseum.

The Coliseum

Given the central role the Coliseum has played in Hong Kong pop culture, it comes as a surprise that so little has been written about it. On the contrary, however significant the Hong Kong Coliseum might remain for the local people, Hong Kong is generally described by the Western media and local English media, most notably the South China Morning Post, as lacking venues for international stars. In particular, the lack of large outdoor venues presumably favored by Western mega stars or pop festivals is a recurring point of concern, although whether Hong Kong, given the heat and humidity, is a suitable location for outdoor events is another question altogether. This discourse sometimes conflates with the general shortfalls of Hong Kong, in terms of competitiveness, suggesting that it is in imminent danger of losing out to other Asian metropoles. Sometimes it conflates with the alleged lack in the ability of Hong Kong or the Chinese to party, to enjoy culture in an exuberant way. This criticism can partly be understood as eurocentric, as an attempt to impose certain Western experiences and values onto another locality, neglecting or ignoring local specificities.

It is clear that for the people of Hong Kong, the Coliseum is not only a public space; it is also a factory, literally, a production site, of collective memory, and a temple of experience and identity. Of all the venues, the Hong Kong Coliseum has not only the mechanics but also the magic to invest those collective memories with collective emotion and identity. To end our discussion on the Coliseum, we would like to pose a few questions for further deliberation in connection with the central inquiry of venues and memory. First of all, the Hong Kong Coliseum, being the canon of pop stardom, the temple of pop music, also hierarchizes, uniforms or even monopolizes the memories of Hong Kongers, while the Academic Community Hall and Queen Elisabeth Stadium, given their much smaller scale, would have more potential for multiplicity or collectivity in the plural. It remains to be seen how the dominant position of the Hong Kong Coliseum will impact on the writing of Hong Kong's cultural history. Another question concerns the Coliseum's "side effect" of facilitating a separation of space, emotion and identity. The Coliseum is an inside space, confined, forever connected to the city's entertainment, leisure, and fun. By and large, Hong Kong only has inside, confined pop venues, and no outside, public venues. Outside venues are always linked with major pop concerts/festivals such as Woodstock, Band Aid, Live8 in the West and the rest of the world, where pop and politics and activism form allies, being visible, being part of the public space in the city. There is, however, a clear line of demarcation in Hong Kong: outside venues, such as Victoria Park, can be used for political rallies but not for pop events. Inside venues, such as the Coliseum, are "only" for entertainment, rendered invisible, not directly part of the larger public space. This makes Saskia Sassen's question as to who has claims to the city more complicated. Sassen observes outdoor festivals, such as gay parades or Caribbean street walks, not only in terms of a moment of showing off, but also in terms of certain groups of people laying claim to the city. However, if a city has developed a habit of celebrating its pop events indoors, how are we to understand its public politics? If live performances staged in the confined space of the Coliseum help generate a collective memory, a Hong Kong identity, how are we to understand such essentially indoor, private moments, which seem to refuse to engage with Hong Kong's larger political landscape? Even more specifically, how are we to understand the identity politics embodied in the Coliseum during the political transition of the city from British to Beijing sovereignty? Would the Coliseum serve to erase a colonial capitalist history from the Hong Kong identity, producing nostalgia without melancholy, pain and a sense of struggle? Can we see the Hong Kong Coliseum, with its closed, massive and tomb-like monumental architecture, as a monument that seems to naturalize power – as monuments usually do?

Belonging and Temporality

These are some of the questions which we believe require further exploration. For the purpose of this article, we have argued that instead of thinking of Hong Kong and its sound, Cantopop, in terms of disappearance, we consider that the changing modes of music consumption and the related emotive investments signal a continuous negotiation of what it means to live in Hong Kong. In our view, music venues, the material, stable embodiment of sight and sound, operate as emotive landmarks that help to invest memory with emotion and therefore identity. The Coliseum has served, as we have shown, an important function in producing stars, creating collective memories and reinventing the stars from decades ago, precisely in the significant time-span during which Hong Kong became part of China.

This was also the time when Hong Kong was shocked by the untimely deaths of two of its stars. The suicide of Leslie Cheung and the death of cancer-stricken Anita Mui, robbed the city of its most celebrated legends, shocked it into an identity crisis, and ushered in the come-back phenomenon. The Hong Kong Coliseum has offered a space for the performance of a collective Hong Kong identity that refuses to disappear, helping to create a sense of belonging to a city that seems to be in constant flux.

Then what, to conclude, does this inquiry tell us about postmodernism and Hong Kong? At the beginning of the new millennium, the acclaimed volume on *Postmodernism and China*, edited by Arif Dirlik and Zhang Xudong (2000), was published. The idea of postmodernity is intricately linked to the issue of temporality. The constant state of in-betweenness, of being always in flux, makes it tempting to claim Hong Kong as a postmodern city. However, the "post" in postmodern produces an unjustified temporality, suggesting that the postmodern follows upon the modern. Based on our analysis, we believe it makes more sense to think of the postmodern in conjunction with the modern, in other words, to insist on the coevalness of the modern and the postmodern. If we translate these concepts into "temporality" (the "postmodern" idea of reality and identity being in constant flux) and "stability" (the "modern" idea of a stable, solid grounding of reality and identity), our study of popular music shows how the two can be considered mutually constitutive. Pop can be considered a temporal sound, it produces hits that make us think back to a specific summer; pop is a transient sound, with stars that come and go. "Pop is a performance of the artificial self; it is a spectacularization of the present. Pop's banality and artificiality render the music profoundly ambiguous, and it is this ambiguity that makes pop such a popular yet opaque musical form" (de Kloet 2005: 334). These reflections on the temporality of pop resonate with Chua Beng Huat's observation on the transience of consumer products: "the brevity of life of a consumer object and of a consumer trend makes it unavoidable that all published materials on consumer products and trends are by definition 'historical'" (Chua, 2003: vii).

Pop serves as a marker of time. Today, with the possibilities of new technologies and the arguable collapse of production and consumption, audiences have become producers, sharing and personifying sounds and images. Pop is intricately connected with temporality, memory and nostalgia. Drawing on Rey Chow, Helen Hok-sze Leung argues that "nostalgia is not simply a yearning for the past as though it were a definite, knowable object. Rather, nostalgia involves a 'sensitivity to the movements of temporality.' Understood in these terms, a nostalgic subject is someone who sits on the fence of time" (Leung 2001: 430).

However, pop is not only to be heard; it can also be seen. Sometimes, the sound needs material embodiment, a sight, to manifest itself. This is where the stable, gigantic and "modern" structure of the pop venue comes in. The Hong Kong Coliseum illustrates how a pop venue serves as a massive, monumental fence of time, producing collective emotive memories that are being recorded on DVD's, mobile phones, and cameras that are, in turn, being sold and shared with others on the Internet. Pop venues, as prime sites of this emotive, audio-visual form of popular culture, offer one way of seeing, hearing and understanding the fast-changing city in the 21st century: to seek temporality – the passing of time, the memory, the emotion, the sound, the fluid – in stability, or buildings that stay. Pop venues anchor pop, something which is temporal and in flux. Probably more than the skyscrapers that we see on all the postcards of Hong Kong, more than the monumental colonial buildings that ask for preservation, it is the Hong Kong Coliseum that helps the city to remember itself. It is a place, simply put, where you must have been, if you consider yourself a Hong Kong citizen.

References

Abbas, Ackbar (1997) *Hong Kong. Culture and the Politics of Disappearance*, Hong Kong: Hong Kong University Press.

Arendt, Hannah (1958) *The Human Condition*, Chicago: University of Chicago Press.

Bull, Michael (2000) *Sounding Out the City. Personal Stereos and the Management of Everyday Life*, Oxford: Berg.

Chow, Rey (1998) *Ethics after Idealisism. Theory - Culture - Ethnicity - Reading*, Bloomington: Indiana University Press.

Chu, Stephen Yiu Wai (2007) "Before and After the Fall: Mapping Hong Kong Cantopop in the Global Era," *LEWI Working Paper Series* 63.

Chua, Beng Huat (2003) *Life is not complete without shopping*, Singapore: Singapore University Press.

Debord, Guy (1995) *The Society of Spectacle*, New York: Zone Books.

Dirlik, Arif and Xudong Zhang (eds) (2000) *Postmodernism and China*, Durham: Duke University Press.

Erni, John Nguyet (2001) "Like a Postcolonial Culture: Hong Kong Re-Imagined," in *Cultural Studies* 15/3-4, pp. 389-418.

Fast, Susan (2006) "Popular Music Performance and Cultural Memory. Queen: Live Aid, Wembley Stadium, July 13, 1985," in *Performance and Popular Music: History, Place, and Time*, in Ian Inglis (ed.), London: Ashgate, pp. 138-54.

Fung, Anthony and Michael Curtin (2002) "The Anomalies of Being Faye (Wong): Gender Politics in Chinese Popular Music," in *International Journal of Cultural Studies* 5/3, pp. 263-90.

de Kloet, Jeroen (2005) "Sonic Sturdiness – The Globalization of 'Chinese' Pop and Rock," in *Critical Studies in Media Communication* 22/4, pp. 321-38.

Lee, Samuel (2002) "East Asia Is Crazy over Taiwanese Pop Stars Such As Jay Chou As Cantopop Fades Fades Away," in *The Strait Times Interactive* <http://www.asiawind.com/forums/read.php?f=2&i=1482&t=1482&v=t.> accessed June 8, 2008.

Leung, Helen Hok-Sze (2001) "Queerscapes in Hong Kong Cinema," in *Positions* 9/2, pp. 423-48.

Sassen, Saskia (2001) *The Global City. New York, London, Tokyo*, Princeton: Princeton University Press.

Watson, Sophie (2006) *City Publics: The (Dis) Enchantments of Urban Encounters*, London: Routledge.

Wong, James (2003) *The Rise and Decline of Cantopop: A Study of Hong Kong Popular Music*, PhD Thesis, University of Hong Kong.

Anne Wedell-Wedellsborg

Multiple Temporalities in the Literary Identity Space of Post-Socialist China: a Discussion of Yu Hua's Novel *Brothers* and Its Reception

Ever since the late 1980s and the emergence of so-called avant-garde or experimentalist (*xianfeng* or *shiyanxing*) literature, Chinese critics have debated whether or not such a thing as Chinese post-modernism already existed, could exist or might eventually exist at a later stage. Arguments in these discussions were largely connected to different conceptions of the degree of development of Chinese society at the time, and of the nature of Chinese modernity as compared to a western one, thus seeing literary post-modernism as only partially a question of mere literary technique. The most predominant lines of thought would also seem to basically continue the general idea (since May Fourth) of a chronologically progressing literary development, modeled on the West, presupposing a fully unfolded realism and modernism before genuine post-modernism might arise.[1]

Such focused theoretical discussions now seem to have abated, along with the near break-up of centralized discourse, rampant marketization, the general profusion of literary output and the dissolution of the almost symbiotic relationship and mutual influence between famous writers and prominent theorists or critics that existed during the literary waves of the 1980s. The vision of clearly defined, albeit partly overlapping, successive states of literary "isms" evaporated as the cultural scene was caught up in globalization at the same time as the increasing individualization and differentiation of society was reflected in a great variation of styles, themes and genres. Indeed, such a state of affairs, resulting in the dissolution and de-centering of hegemonic discourse, is what Sheldon Lu has described as the "post-modern turn" (Lu 1997: 130).

However, as also noted by Sheldon Lu, taken as a whole, it is probably more accurate to say that the cultural field of contemporary China – or post-socialist China – is characterized by the simultaneous existence of multiple temporalities (Lu 2001: 13): The pre-modern, the modern and the post-modern appear side by side in various configurations and combinations, and manifest themselves in almost every area of cultural production, one of them being literature. And furthermore, this confusion of temporal modes, along with conflicting attitudes to modernity as such, is not only reflected in different literary works or even within the texts themselves, but also in their reception, i.e. in literary criticism and in discussions about specific works in public fora such as the Internet. Here evaluations of and comments on a given work may sometimes appear to emanate from widely different time-epochs, evincing reader expectations ranging from those seemingly based on traditionalist or socialist-realist standards to those grounded in more or less sophisticated theories of western derivation. In the following, I discuss this phenomenon in connection with one very conspicuous and controversial bestseller published in the new millennium, Yu Hua's long novel, *Brothers* (*Xiongdi I-II* 2005-6).

One way of approaching this conception of multiple temporalities superimposed on one another is to view them, not as separate temporal modes, but as different paths of orientation available to the individual within the identity space of modernity. The sociologist, Jonathan Friedman, proposes a notion of modernity as an *identity space* which may offer a

[1] For discussions on postmodernism in China, see, for example, Yang 2002, Chen 2004 and Dirlik and Zhang 2000.

Berliner China-Hefte/Chinese History and Society 34 (2008), pp. 63-76

useful perspective on the situation in China in recent years. To Friedman, modernity is very broadly defined; it is not bound to any specific time or place but is rather "a kind of *identity space* or field of alternative identities that is structured by certain parameters such as individualization and developmentalism, which are themselves generated by the rise of a hegemonic power or zone in a system based on commercial reproduction" (Friedman 1998: 235).[2] Modernity as an identity space, or subjective consciousness, is then "a local product of global commercial systems, following the breakdown of holistic structures and fixed status" (Friedman 1994: 212). Friedman sets up *modernism* (culture and nature are to be overcome), *traditionalism* (valuing culture), *primitivism* (valuing nature) and *post-modernism* (culture and nature have relative value) as the four poles of potential identification that define a space of identity variation, i.e. paths of orientation available for the single individual according to the given situation. All four polarities are thus *within* the identity space of modernity. While the pole of forward-looking modernism will normally be the dominant one, the other three may be activated as ways of reacting against or criticizing the modernist pole (Friedman 1994: 91ff.).[3] With China as a rising power in today's globalized world, the subjective experience of its writers and intellectuals fits well with Friedman's description of modern identity and, as I shall try to show, not only literary works, but also the responses they create, may well be understood as relating to different poles of orientation within the identity space of modernity.

Literary output in China since the turn of the millennium has, to a great extent, been dominated by, on the one hand, works written specifically for mass consumption, such as crime stories or mysteries for popular entertainment, and on the other , novels and stories by an emergent group of very young, so-called individualized (*gerenhua*) or alternative (*linglei*) writers, including Han Han, Guo Jingming, Anni Baobei and many others, who write about themselves and their generation, their love and sex lives, loneliness, lack of purpose, search for meaning and desire for instant gratification. But the middle and older generations of established "serious" writers have also added to the variety of the literary scene with a number of widely-read novels, essays, memoires and short-stories. Among the conspicuous bestsellers of the last few years from the latter group of writers, Yu Hua's *Brothers* I-II stands out as especially interesting, both in terms of its sales figures and the contradictory reader response it has evoked. This novel deals with the Cultural Revolution and the reform period and has generated vehement controversy, with responses ranging from the highest praise to acid criticism. So while obviously appealing to large numbers of readers in "post-socialist" China, it has also provoked strong reactions that express not just different literary tastes but appear to be linked to the simultaneous existence of different temporalities, as observed by Sheldon Lu. Thus the widely differing opinions of critics and commentators of this book often seem rooted in interpretive preconceptions or literary prejudices that reflect separate temporal outlooks. Below, I analyze *Brothers* and its reception, bearing in mind Friedman's notion of modernity as an identity space, regarding the text itself and its interpretation by Chinese critics as paths of individual orientation in response to the

2 As such "it is tendentially present in all commercial civilizations to the extent that the social world is atomized into individuals who can neither conceive of nor experience themselves as part of a larger cosmological realm without the aid of drugs or oppositional movements of religious character" (Friedman 1994: 91).

3 Note that Friedman uses the concept of modernism as the dominant ethos of modern up-coming societies, not as a literary "ism".

predicament of modernity. The questions I ask are, what kind of identity space does this novel describe, how has this been interpreted by Chinese critics, and what can the critical reception tell us about the dynamics and tensions within the identity space of contemporary China.

Brothers

Yu Hua's novel *Brothers* is divided into two volumes, i.e. Part I and Part II. The first, dealing with the Cultural Revolution period, *wenge*, was published in 2005, the second and longer, covering the present reform period, *gaige*, came out in 2006. While the reception of Part I was mixed, but generally positive, Part II received quite a lot of negative reviews. However, as I shall show, evaluations were based on very different criteria, from moral objections or endorsements to arguments relating to questions of historical authenticity, to aesthetic judgments of style and narrative.

One considerable component in the general critical response is made up of the specific expectations with regard to Yu Hua, in view of his status as a celebrated, nationally renowned "avant-gardist-elitist-turned-popular-realist writer". The fact that his new novel was published a full ten years after his last success, *Chronicle of a Bloodseller* (*Xu Sanguan mai xue ji,* Yu 1996) set expectations even higher. Starting out as an experimentalist writer in the late 1980s, Yu published three novels, in the 1990s, which were written in an almost straightforwardly realist style; two of these, *To Live* (*Huozhe,* Yu 1993b) and *Chronicle of a Bloodseller* were highly acclaimed bestsellers. These two novels are both characterized by Yu Hua's special narrative style of combining sensitive irony and humor with a simple unadorned narrative which helps to subvert a sometimes lurking sentimentality. They both deal with ordinary people and their fates in the course of social upheaval, and strongly affirm the strength and perseverance of human dignity and the will to live, while, at the same time, underscoring the importance of the family as the primary unit of meaning for every single individual.

Indeed, the most consistent theme in all of Yu Hua's work has been the role of the family. In his early avant-gardist period, this was mostly viewed from its negative side, as in the story, *One Kind of Reality* (*Xianshi yizhong* 1988) which gave a chilling description of callous killings and revenge within a family of three generations, driven by the obsessive desire for male descendants. His first long novel, *Cries in the Drizzle* (*Zai xiyu zhong huhan,* Yu 1991b), is a psychological portrait of a lonely boy, an outcast, who, for unexplained reasons, is first mentally and then physically rejected by his own family. This novel, the most psychologically complex he has written so far, was met with disappointment and overly negative reviews by avant-garde critics when it was published back in 1991.[4]

In *Brothers,* Yu Hua continues the family theme, although in Part II, in the reduced form of the two brothers (who are not actually blood-related) of the title and one wife. The two main characters, Song Gang and Li Guangtou become brothers at age seven, when Li's mother, Li Lan and Song's father, Song Fanping marry. Part I deals with the fate of this nuclear family before and during the Cultural Revolution. Li Lan and Song Fanping's mar-

---

4 See, for example, the prominent avant-garde critic, Chen Xiaoming (1991). Interestingly, in 2007, in a different cultural climate, and after the publication of Brothers, Chen Xiaoming, wrote a highly laudatory re-evaluation and philosophical analysis of this 1991 novel which he had previously strongly criticized as old fashioned, now calling it Yu Hua's best. (Chen 2007) This kind of re-evaluation is another expression of the fluctuations in the social and spiritual climate and of changing paths of orientation in the identity space of modernity.

riage is a very happy one, and Song Fanping is described as an ideal husband and father, an upright honest person whose primary loyalty is to his family. This finally costs him his life, when he is beaten to death by red-guards, because he breaks out of house arrest in order to keep a promise to meet his wife when she leaves hospital. The madness and absurdity of political zeal is strongly contrasted with the warmth and integrity of family life and with the genuine feelings of love and respect between parents and children. [5] Part I ends with the death of Li Lan, after she has made Song Gang promise to look after his slightly younger foster brother, Li Guangtou, and share with him even the last bowl of rice and the last piece of clothing (Yu 2005: 251).

Li Guangtou can be regarded as the main character in the novel as a whole. In fact, Part I opens with the image of him, middle-aged, sitting on his gold-plated loo, a solitary billionaire with no relatives, and the rest of the novel is told in retrospect. We learn that he won early fame in Liuzhen by spying on women in the public toilet, where he managed to get a glimpse of the arse of Lin Hong, the prettiest girl in town. Two main components in the portrayal of this character, libido and business-talent, are thus hinted at from the start, since he manages to sell his graphic account of this view 56 times to the men of Liuzhen, each time getting a bowl of *sanxian* noodles in return. It turns out that his real father, Li Lan's first husband, died by drowning in the cesspool during a similar attempt.[6] Already in Part I, the differences in character of the two brothers are evident, with Song Gang as the more passive in character, weak and modest, tall, lean and bespectacled, and Li Guangtou as the more active in character, enterprising, crude, coarse, earthy and straightforward. This contrast is fully developed in Part II, which takes the narrative into the present reform-period. Here the relationship between the two brothers, who initially lived together harmoniously, disintegrates as Li Guangtou fails to win pretty Lin Hong for himself, despite giving persistent pursuit, and she instead marries Song Gang. In his frustration, Li Guangtou decides to have himself sterilized, and throws himself whole-heartedly into his already thriving business career as the "king of garbage." The story really takes off when Li, at the peak of his economic and entrepreneurial powers, arranges his nation-wide beauty contest for virgins (who turn out to be not that virginal after all) and Song Gang, by contrast, is lured into a disastrous business trip which takes him to southern China for a long period. His overall misfortune and humiliation culminates when he has a silicone breast implanted on his chest, as an advertisement for the fake breast-enlarging medicine he is trying to sell, in order to make a living and to secure a better life for his wife, Lin Hong. In his absence, Lin Hong falls into the arms of Li Guangtou and experiences great sexual fulfillment. When Song Gang, upon his return to Liuzhen, finds this out he commits suicide by lying on the rail-tracks. Li Guangtou and Lin Hong hear this news in the middle of hot sexual intercourse. Li consequently becomes impotent and also loses all interest in his business enterprise. In a kind of post-script, we learn that Lin Hong later became the successful owner of the local brothel, and we meet Li Guangtou for the last time as he prepares to go on a space trip carrying the ashes of Song Gang to be put in orbit around the Earth.

---

[5] This is further accentuated in the dramatic bi-episode where another young boy dies when the red guards try to cut his long hair, after which the father, originally himself a red guard, commits suicide in prison by hammering nails into his own skull.

[6] The image of someone drowning or dying in the cesspool also appears in Yu 1993a and Yu 1993b.

This novel, with its relatively straight story-line following the fates of the two brothers, also has a number of minor characters, mostly inhabitants of Liuzhen with characteristic nicknames, such as Liu Zuojia (Writer Liu) Zhao Shiren (Poet Zhao) Tong Tiejiang, (Blacksmith Tong) Yu Boya (Teeth-puller Yu, a reference to Yu Hua's past as a dentist) etc. It can be said of all the persons in the novel, including the brothers, that they are rather flat characters; there is no attempt at internal psychological descriptions, and most of the characterization is by way of dialogue, actions or events. Many key events take place in the public arena with the masses (*qunzhong*) as spectators on the sidelines, cheering or booing, and gossiping. Yu Hua's manner of telling the story is by focusing on episodes which are described in great detail, in between letting long periods of time pass in a few paragraphs. Scenes and episodes are mostly related through short-sentenced dialogue, but sometimes, as with the haunting description of Song Fanping's murder by the red-guards and Li Lan's grief, Yu Hua closes in on his characters and, through minute observations of their outward reactions, manages to convey deep psychological insights (Yu 2005: 173-181). The story is narrated by an omniscient narrator, who, by the recurring reference to "our Liuzhen" (*women Liuzhen*), points to his presence as a story-teller, and indicates that he himself is one of the inhabitants of Liuzhen. Obviously, behind this voice hides an implicit narrator who knows more than could possibly be known by any one person in Liuzhen.

All these traits – the one-dimensional characters, the explicit narrative voice, the repetition of stock phrases, the tying together of the plot by successions of events, the simple unadorned language, the atmosphere of small town gossip – provide the novel with a strong oral quality. Indeed, it is very much a *xiaoshuo* in the traditional sense of the word: a small story opposed to, but at the same time intertwined with, the grand narrative of history. As such, it can be read as a disrespectful and subjective comment on the official version of recent history, or (in Part II) even as a parody of government-sponsored pictures of economic reform and its social consequences. This recalls Sheldon Lu's discussion, through the lens of Lyotard's work on postmodernism, of the relationship between traditional Chinese historiography and fiction. Sheldon Lu distinguishes between "grand narratives" of legitimation and "small stories" of de-legitimation:

The fictional texts are small operations, guerrilla wars against the giants of historical narrative. The written texts, the acts of oral storytelling, or the extended novels, dislocate and deconstruct historical texts, produce heretical, apocryphal records, unofficial documents, and create ideological instabilities, moral vacuums and aporias in the vast inescapable meshes of Confucian society (Lu 2001: 65).

Although the structure of contemporary post-socialist Chinese society is hardly identical with the "inescapable meshes of Confucian society", it is nevertheless precisely the perceived ideological instabilities and moral vacuum in Yu Hua's novel which makes some readers of *Brothers* uncomfortable, while other readers see this aspect as a conscious act of deconstruction or de-legitimization of an officially recognized version of recent and contemporary history.

Perhaps the most conspicuous feature of *Brothers* is its humor and satire which ranges from the gross to the more subtle. Especially in Part II, this takes on surreal dimensions, as shown in the descriptions of the consequences of rampant economic reform. No one is spared as the frenzy of economic progress sweeps over Liuzhen, neither workers, writers, vendors, women, party-bosses, entrepreneurs, nor masses. The narrative does tend towards being exaggerated, parodic or just simplified – perhaps reflecting the overall atmosphere of gossip which would always tend to exaggerate or distort as an aspect of delightful *Hörensagen*. This tendency is also exemplified in the description of the lives of the two brothers. Li Guangtou, man of the times, active entrepreneur, becomes richer and richer, (we note a symbolic satire in his wealth being built on buying and selling second hand western clothing from the Japanese) and thus makes all of Liuzhen more prosperous. Song Gang, by contrast, is weak and lacks initiative, he loses his job, his health deteriorates, and with no money and no welfare, his fate represents the material dark side of reform.

Such dichotomies, epitomized by the personalities and fates of the two brothers, permeate the main themes of the novel: sex vs. love, masculine vs. feminine, active vs. passive, loyalty vs. betrayal, spiritual vs. material values. Li Guangtou's masculinity and sexual potency is prominent already in Part I, when as a young boy, he is seen peeping at women and masturbating in public. In Part II, he sleeps with hundreds of women without loving any of them, before finally giving Lin Hong total sexual fulfillment. Song Gang's relationship with Lin Hong, by contrast, is described as loving but almost asexual and his feminized nature is absurdly symbolized by the pathetic breast operation towards the end of the novel. Li Guangtou's affair with Lin Hong is certainly a betrayal of Song Gang, yet Song Gangs's marriage to Lin Hong is originally also a betrayal of Li Guangtou, since she is and remains Li's first and only love. Yet through his suicide and final letter to Li Guangtou and Lin Hong, Song Gang yields and fulfils his original promise to Li Lan (of sharing everything with his younger brother) by giving Lin Hong to Li Guangtou. Thus the underlying theme is that of brotherly loyalty, a Confucian moral code where the elder brother is supposed to care for the younger, and the younger, to respect the elder. While, in this novel, this ideal is either turned upside down or eroded by social and material forces, it is nevertheless constantly present as an implicit force and shown to be the true source of meaning, which by its absence ultimately invalidates the powers of sex and money. In Part I, the family love of Li Lan, Song Fanping and the two boys represents integrity and uprightness, amidst political madness, and in Part II, the brotherly bond between Li and Song is constantly referred to as part of their identity, even as their relationship falls apart. Li Guangtou's impotence and withdrawal from business is directly linked to Song Gang's suicide, and both the opening and the closing scenes of the novel underscore the fundamental importance of this relationship. *Brothers* can therefore certainly be read as a novel that celebrates classical family values. Yet, at the same time as he shows their importance, Yu Hua more or less declares them to be dead, or at least dysfunctional, in contemporary consumerist society: the two brothers are not even biologically related, and what is more, they have no descendants – the line is cut off, the familyline stops here. Could *Brothers* then be understood as a moral tale in a traditional vein, in which great disorder is shown to disrupt the harmony of family and society, with a Confucian morale of moderation, telling us that every virtue, if carried to extremes, becomes a vice (cf. the goodness of Song Fanping and Song Gang as well as the dynamism of Li Guangtou)? Or is it rather the other way round: an ironic comment on the obsolescence of traditional wisdom and values in post-socialist China? As I point out below, this kind of ambivalence and the contradictory messages seemed to disturb a great number of critics.

If we try to place *Brothers* somewhere within Sheldon Lu's diagnosis of the simultaneously co-existing multiple temporalities, it could – regarding both content and style – be shown to include traits of the pre-modern as well as the modern and postmodern. The traditional, *premodern* aspects could include the above-mentioned *xiaoshuo*-characteristics, the narration of the history of China in two crucial periods through a focus on "typical" characters in "typical" surroundings (typical here tending towards the extreme) and the thematical presence of classical values and obligations. The novel also evinces *modern* traits such as a focus on individual development, on the accumulation of wealth and control (in the figure of Li Guangtou), and perhaps also submerged humanist enlightenment ethics, if viewed as a critical text exposing the ills of contemporary society. Viewed in a *post-modern* light, the novel's lament over the loss of traditional values in consumerist society looks more like a parody or a pastiche, which amounts to a kind of carefree recognition of their dissolution. The heterogeneity and ambivalence of the message is underscored by what would, in this case, be viewed as a subversion of, or play on, established literary conventions (such as the family saga, the literature of scars, the *Bildungsroman*, popular stories of success and progress). Further, the technique of subjectively selecting and incorporating tropes and themes from other periods and genres is often seen as a defining trait of postmodern literature (Calinescu 1987: 296-309). Examples here could be the narrative voice of the story-teller, the role of the masses as a kind of "choir" (commenting on events as in Greek tragedies), Confucian ethics, and – as pointed out by one perceptive critic (see below) – even the use of Shakespeare's Hamlet as a subtext.

If, instead of different temporalities, we try to place *Brothers* within the framework of Jonathan Friedman's theory of modernity as an *identity space* and view the novel as a kind of fictional identity space, we arrive at a similarly ambiguous or heterogeneous result. The main difference is that where Sheldon Lu sees an expression of separate but co-existing temporalities, Friedman sees possible paths of orientation *within* the same identity space of modernity:

The four poles define a single space defined by modernist identity so that traditionalism, primitivism and postmodernism are included as logical markers of modernism, which is the dominant or 'normal' identity of capitalist civilization (Friedman 1994: 93-94).

Thus traditionalism and primitivism are not taken as pre-modern, residual left-overs from previous times, but are viewed as integrated parts of modernity, and ways of responding to or reacting against the predominant pole of forward-looking modernism.

Modernism, being the dominant ethos of up-coming societies, is characterized by Friedman as "the continuous process of accumulation of self, in the form of wealth, knowledge, experience." From this point of view, "the universe is thus the arena of expansion where the self-controlled ego can realize itself just as capital. The space of growth is the space of control, of nature and of self" (Friedman 1994: 91). Therefore "modernist identity depends on expanding horizons, the possibility of individual and social development, mobility and liberation from the fixed and concrete structures of non-capitalist forms: family, community, religion" (Friedman 1994: 94). In *Brothers,* the obvious representative of modernism is Li Guangtou, especially as he develops in Part II, where he almost epitomizes the extremes of this orientation. With his activity and entrepreneurship and his steady accumulation of wealth and his control over Liuzhen, he embodies the material side of modernism. And although his sexual prematurity and later promiscuity in the context of the (fake) virgin beauty contest may tend towards the *primitivist* pole, and his libido thus could be said to be out of control, he emotionally remains faithful to his first and only love, Lin Hong. Moreover, his vasectomy (voluntary sterilization) represents an act of control which, on the one hand, allows for free sexual indulgence, but on the other, prevents growth in terms of descendants. The primitivist pole is therefore an element in the character of Li Guangtou (but not the dominant one), and manifests itself further in the many descriptions of and references to body parts and bodily functions (genitals, arses, hymens, breasts, faeces, nose-bleed, snot, tears, etc.). It also shows itself in the madness of economic growth, with the people of Liuzhen caught in the grips of rampant marketization. The loving images of family life in Part I, and the underlying longing and nostalgia for Confucian values of loyalty in Part II represent, as also discussed above, the pole of *traditionalism.* Traditionalism, as noted by Friedman, is the aspect that is represented by culture, a system of concrete values pertaining to a world of personal relations. From this perspective, modernity is defined as a universe emptied of meaning (Friedman 1994: 241). As for *post-modernism*, Friedman describes it as the pole that "accentuates the opposition of nature, natural force, libido, unchained human creativity, to the fetters of modernity seen as a structure of power and control, the ego writ at large" (Friedman 1994: 92). Again we recall the figure of Li Guangtou. And as above, postmodernism is also a position from which to relativize the other poles, and one which focuses on the pastiche and parodic aspects of the ostensibly serious modernist, primitivist or traditionalist tendencies.

The Critical Reception of Brothers

How have Chinese critics reacted to this – as I read it – highly heterogeneous novel? Certainly, opinions have diverged widely – among the general public as well as among critics and literary scholars, and the Internet (blogs and literary sites) has been the forum of lively debates and countless comments. Here I shall concentrate on the intellectual response by looking at criticism and analyses published in printed literary or cultural magazines and in scholarly journals. Responses here do not only show varying opinions as to the literary quality of the novel, but also seem to reflect different preconceptions, grounded in literary expectations and interpretive codes linked to different temporalities or, in Friedman's words, to different polarities within the identity space of modernity. Generally speaking, the majority of critical articles, whether positive or negative, approach the novel from what, following Sheldon Lu and Jonathan Friedman, would be seen as a modernist (enlightenment) point of view, one which in the framework of Friedman's identity space, also includes more than a tinge of traditionalism.

The negative reviews all express great disappointment that the celebrated writer, Yu Hua, after ten years of fictional silence, could come up with such a bad novel. And wherein lies its failure? One recurrent complaint is its simplistic reproduction of black and white clichés from the two periods it describes, *wenge* and *gaige*. It is criticized for lacking authenticity, since it does not capture the real complexities and nuances of life, for its one-dimensional characters, for its unrealistic scenic descriptions, for its banal language and for its completely unconvincing plot. From an aesthetic point of view, critics object to the ugliness and cartoon-like figures and the coarseness of its language (Si 2007). Several critics consider it a serious flaw that Yu Hua does not seem to have any empathy with his characters, and since he never properly enters their minds, the reader has no way of understanding their choices, they simply appear as puppets manipulated by their author (Yuan 2007). This problem, according to several critics, is exacerbated by the ambiguity of the narrative voice, which purports to be both omniscient and belonging to one of Liuzhen's inhabitants (Wang 2006: 1).

In short, the novel does not reproduce a recognizable reality. This is indeed the underlying strand in most articles published in *Pulling out Yu Hua's Teeth* (*Gei Yu Hua bo ya* 2007), a book which is entirely dedicated to the negative criticism of *Brothers*. But there is also a strong moral criticism: How could Yu Hua allow such a shameless person as Li Guangtou to be successful, implying that treating other people as tools leads to success, while goodness (in the figure of Song Gang) leads to death (Si 2007). Several critics also see it as a fundamental problem that Yu Hua does not point to a way out of the predicament he describes (Yuan 2007).

So while the negative reviews may look divided as to the specific targets of their criticism, they nevertheless seem to rely on a common assumption that novels should somehow be "true to life", psychologically convincing, and evince a humanist outlook that is unambiguous. In other words, this kind of criticism works from a fundamental conception of literature as mimetic, realist and morally uplifting.

Now, the interesting thing is that the majority of the positive reviews seem to apply the very same criteria, and on that basis find in *Brothers* precisely what according to the above-mentioned critics is lacking. Viewed from this angle, *Brothers* succeeds precisely because it is carried by a deep sense of humanism (Sun 2007). Read as a work of critical realism, it reveals the dark side of consumer society, people driven by desire and greed, for money and sex – two things that were never valued in traditional culture (Luo 2007). It is to Yu Hua's merit that he is able to show how this greed destroys all that is good and lofty, first of all through the fate of Song Gang, but also through that of Li Guangtou and Lin Hong who, despite outward success, are left with spiritual and moral emptiness after the death of Song Gang. Some critics even stress, in contrast to those previously mentioned, that the main characters are real people caught in the grips of specific, tangible historical and social forces (Luo 2007), and the figure of Li Guangtou, in particular, is described with fullness (*fengfuxing*), depth (*shenkexing*) and symbolic significance (*fuhaoxing*); his final loss of interest in sex and money effectively demonstrates the meaninglessness of consumerist desire without the existence of honesty, love and empathy. And the book does not even exaggerate – worse things happened in reality (Zhu 2007).

Yang Songfang, writing in *Dangdai Zuojia Pinglun*, sees *Brothers* as a classical work of high literature, whose main theme is the powerlessness of the single individual vis-à-vis history. It is precisely Yu Hua's empathy with his characters, the hallmark of classical literature, which helps the reader understand the social roots of tragedy. His satire makes the reader laugh and weep at the same time. The simple style is Yu Hua's way of going straight to the core, cutting away anything superfluous and hence provoking the reader to reflect (Yang 2007).

To sum up, the readings outlined above either search in vain for, or actually find some highly cherished enlightenment values in Yu Hua's novel, which are normally embodied in the progressive modernist individual. While some find these values positively reflected in the novel's main characters, including Li Guangtou, some conversely find them implicitly present in the text through its critical approach to the impact of consumerism and loss of values on people's lives. And others again criticize Yu Hua precisely for neglecting the task of promoting the much needed enlightenment and social morality. Behind such conflicting analyses seems to lie a common concern with, in the words of Sheldon Lu, "the pursuit and reconstruction of the subject in Chinese humanism" (Lu 2001: 39). According to this view, the role of the writer is to contribute to this still uncompleted project. Such lines of thought should perhaps also be seen in the context of the ongoing debates – since the mid 1990s – about the general deterioration of the humanist spirit (*renwen jingshen*) and its possible revival in contemporary Chinese society (Lu 2001: 38). "Because the discourse of enlightenment still needs to be situated at the center of culture, intellectuals must resume their former positions as subjects of enlightenment and take up their roles as the guardians, transmitters and creators of high culture" (Lu 2001: 36) Thus Lu writes about the situation at the end of 20th century. The response to *Brothers* discussed above would indicate that, in the new millennium, this need is still acutely felt by many.

While the opinions and analyses presented above either acknowledge the novel's heterogeneity and see it as a shortcoming, or simply ignore it, there is another group of critics who point to this as its defining trait and foremost asset.[7] These critics see Yu Hua's novel from what we might call a postmodern perspective, and typically start out from Bakhtin's notion of the carnivalesque (*kuanghuanhua*) (Bakhtin 1984). They find in *Brothers* the same kind of grotesque realism that Bakhtin discussed in relation to Rabelais' *Gargantua*. Qi Fangfang, for example, praises Yu Hua for turning established values and social classes upside down and for, by way of the novel's grotesque realism and dialogic structure, absolving its readers from all that is strict, absolute and eternal. Thus the novel plays out a dialogue, not only thematically between two historical periods, between lust and love, money and respect, but also stylistically between Yu Hua's early avant-gardist work and his realist novels of the 1990s (Qi 2007).

By far the most detailed and thorough analysis from this angle was published by Chen Sihe, Professor of Literature at Fudan University (Chen Sihe 2007). He goes right to the point and diagnoses the whole debate about *Brothers* as being rooted in questions of different aesthetics. Taking Bakhtin's studies on Rabelais as his point of departure, Chen argues that Yu Hua's novel transgresses and offends all the usual aesthetic criteria, and can only be approached if the reader tears himself out of all traditional literary conceptions. Especially the character of Li Guangtou challenges all that Chinese intellectuals have been used to cherish since May Fourth. According to Chen, predominant aesthetic criteria in China today basically derive from a combination of post-renaissance early European bourgeois taste, Russian realism and a bit of western modernism (Chen 2007: 56).

Before presenting *Brothers* as a full-bodied example of grotesque realism in the tradition of the carnivalesque, Chen Sihe sets out to unravel what he calls the subtext, or shadow structure (*yinxing wenben jiegou*), hidden beneath the immediately visible structure of the novel. And here a *Hamlet*-like motif of revenge unfolds: the initial scene with young Li Guangtou lurking in the public toilet, which offended many readers who found it vulgar and unnecessary, in Chen's analysis turns out to play a central role in the dynamics of the entire plot.

Li Guangtou's real father drowned in the cesspool, because he lost his grip on the barrier when he was caught lurking by Song Fanping, who later married Li's mother. Thus Song Fanping, Li Guangtou's stepfather, is indirectly the one who killed his real father. According to Chen Sihe, Li Guangtou's early sexuality symbolizes his biological heritage and corresponds to the scene in Shakespeare's *Hamlet*, where Hamlet's father's ghost appears before him. His own lurking and being paraded through the streets of Liuzhen is to be understood as his public announcement of whose son he really is. He later avenges his father, by inadvertently being the cause of Song Fanping's death (by revealing his casual remarks to the red guards). In Part II, Song Gang represents his father and is also indirectly

7 Among them, there are also those who find that Yu Hua simply fails in his conscious attempt at the postmodern, see, for example, Bai (2007).

killed by Li (who is the cause of his suicide). In this scenario, Lin Hong represents at the same time Ophelia and the Queen. When Li Guangtou lets himself become sterilized, it is an indication that he refuses to continue this bloodline, and everything, his libido, energy, goals, is now concentrated in his present existence (from now on his sex life is disconnected from both love and procreation), but he still has the two sides, the biological inheritance from his real father and the spiritual one from Song Fanping (energy, activity, making people feel good). The virgin contest can be seen as an enlarged replica of or substitute for the lurking scene – re-enacting Li Guangtou's desire for the 14 year old Lin Hong – and as his attempt to make up for the loss of his original object of desire (Chen 2007: 57-59).

Chen Sihe finds this rather serious plot-line embedded in the world of the carnivalesque, characterized by ambivalent laughter and the profanation of all that is held sacred in official life, opposed to all hierarchy and dogma. Chen quotes Yu Hua as telling how, when working on Part II, he felt "his writing was controlled by the narrative" (*xushu tongzhile wode xiezuo*)[8] and takes this as proof that the novel somehow expresses the collective unconscious in present day society, corresponding with what Bakhtin termed "the collective ancestral body of all of the people" (Chen 2007: 56, Bakhtin 1984: 19). Thus, abusive language, the vulgarity and the obscenities that readers have criticized actually reflect the coarse narrative tropes of popular usage. And since the narrator seems to be part of the masses (cf. W*omen Liuzhen*), he naturally shares their original, more direct attitude to bodily fluids and functions. To Bakhtin, the sense of the grotesque, as in the carnivalesque body, incarnates the opposite of the established and the regulated:

The grotesque body is not separated from the rest of the world. It is not a closed completed unit; it is unfinished, outgrows itself, transgresses its own limits. The stress is laid on those parts of the body that are open to the outside world, that is the parts through which the world enters the body or emerges from it, or through which the body itself goes out to meet the world. This means that the emphasis is on the apertures or convexities, or on various ramifications or offshoots: the open mouth, the genital organs, the breast, the phallus, the potbelly, the nose. The body discloses its essence as a principle of growth which exceeds its own limits only in copulation, pregnancy, childbirth, the throes of death, eating, drinking, and defecation (Bakhtin 1984: 11, quoted by Chen 2007: 60).

In *Brothers,* we certainly find the same emphasis on the bodily parts that are open to the outside world, the essence of which, to Bakhtin, is a "principle of growth." And Bakhtin further states that:

The essence of the grotesque is precisely to present a contradictory and double-faced fullness of life. Negation and destruction (death of the old) are included as an essential phase, inseparable from affirmation, from the birth of something new and better. The very material bodily lower stratum of the grotesque image (food, wine, the genital force, the organs of the body) bears a deeply positive character. This principle is victorious, for the final result is always abundance, increase (Bakhtin 1984: 62).

In his article, Chen Sihe tries to make this same process of positive growth apply to Yu Hua's novel, through what I see as a rather far-fetched symbolic interpretation of the final/initial scene depicting Li Guangtou on his gold-plated loo: he considers the shape of the loo to be a symbolic representation of the female uterus, and thus an indirect reference to the principle of growth and fertility (Chen 2007: 64). He thereby attempts to save what, in

8 Yu Hua writes this on the back cover of Part II (Yu 2006).

my reading, tends more towards either a pessimistic, ironic or highly ambiguous ending, as a fundamentally optimistic and life-affirming expression of carnivalesque humor.
If indeed we see in *Brothers* the death of the old – which according to Bakhtin's theories based on medieval European literature, should be the necessary precondition for the birth of the new – as represented by the suicide of Song Gang and the dissolution of Confucian values, then the birth of the new, as well as abundance and increase, is conspicuously missing from the concluding chapters of the novel. Song Gang's death does not lead to renewal, but to the termination of the relationship between Li Guangtou and Lin Hong, and to the termination of the further expansion of Li's material prosperity. And the sterility of Li Guangtou ironically underscores the absence of birth and fertility. As for the last scene, what could be more lonely, unsocial and un-bodily in the Bakhtian sense, than orbiting the Earth in a spaceship together with the ashes of your last remaining relative.

Concluding Remarks

Yu Hua's novel *Brothers* I-II is certainly not the only literary work published in China during the last few years which has generated widely divergent responses.[9] But with its remarkable heterogeneity of style and content – its literary quality or lack thereof notwithstanding – it has probably acted as an especially strong catalyst for simultaneously bringing into play all of the multiple temporalities noted by Sheldon Lu, in the discussion of one single novel. As shown above, it is possible to identify pre-modern as well as modern and post-modern traits within the textual universe of the novel. Viewed as the expression of one Chinese writer's conception of a modern identity space, it demonstrates the interaction between the different ways of orientation available within this space (summarized by Friedman as four poles) and shows how forward-looking modernism (the usually predominant ethos of up-coming modern societies) is being challenged by, or complicated by, the interference of traditionalism, primitivism and postmodernism. Modern man (in the figure of Li Guangtou) for all his accumulation of wealth and control, is spiritually (and libidinally) lost without traditional values, but these values are themselves seriously threatened by the very forces of modernism. In Yu Hua's story, this well-known dilemma is relativized or made ambiguous by the special mixture of irony, exaggeration and pathos that permeates the text.
The fact that this novel has extracted and provoked such contradictory responses – and, notably, not just with regard to the question of its artistic value – reflects the composite picture that makes up the cultural scene in China today. It also shows that literature is still being viewed as an important point of reference for discussing issues of social and spiritual concern. Moreover, for quite a few critics, hopes for moral guidance and the upholding of ideals of enlightenment are seen as being placed in literary works, at the same time as these are seen to be under the obligation to reflect existing social reality, and hence subject to assessment according to their degree of perceived recognizability. At the other end of the spectrum, drawing explicitly on western theories, critics have focused on the literariness of Yu Hua's novel and seen it as an expression of the aesthetics of grotesque realism, or simply as a conscious (and more or less successful) attempt at post-modern writing. Altogether, the publication of *Brothers* and its contradictory reception attest to the liveliness and

9 One very conspicuous example is the heated debate around the immensely popular and best-selling novel, *Wolf Totem* (*Langtuteng* 2004) by Jiang Rong (pseud.)

multiplicity of the contemporary Chinese literary scene with all its crisscrossing currents of globalized and localized concerns.

References

Bai, Hao (2007) "Xianfeng de youhua meixue: 'Xiongdi' de yiyi" [The slick aesthetics of the avant-garde: the meaning of 'Brothers'] in *Xinan daxue xuebao* 7, pp. 149-152.

Bakhtin, Michael (1984) *Rabelais and His World*, transl. by Helene Iswolsky, Bloomington: Indiana University Press.

Calinescu, Matei (1987) *Five Faces of Modernity: Modernism, Avant-Garde, Decadence, Kitsch, Postmodernism*, Durham: Duke University Press.

Du Shiwei, Xu Mingfang, He Aiying (eds) (2006) *Gei Yu Hua bo ya: pandian Yu Hua de 'Xiongdi' dian* [Pulling out Yu Hua's teeth: taking stock of 'Brothers'] Beijing: Tongxin chubanshe.

Chen, Sihe (2007) "Wo dui 'Xiongdi' de jiedu" [My interpretation of 'Brothers'] in *Wenyi zhengming,* 2, pp. 55-64.

Chen, Xiaoming (1991) "Zui hou de yishi" [The last ritual] in *Wenxue pinglun* 5, pp. 30-61.

Chen, Xiaoming (2004) *Wu bian de tiaozhan: zhongguo xianfeng wenxue de houxiandaixing* [Boundless challenge: the postmodernism of Chinese avant-garde literature] Guilin: Guangxi shifan daxue chubanshe.

Chen, Xiaoming (2007) "Lun 'Zai xiyu zhong huhan'"[On 'Cries in the drizzle']in *Wenyi zhengming* 8, pp.117-132.

Dirlik, Arif and Zhang, Xudong (eds) (2000) *Postmodernism and China,* Durham and London: Duke University Press.

Friedman, Jonathan (1994) *Cultural Identity and Global Process*, London: Sage Publications.

Friedman, Jonathan (1998) "Transnationalization, Socio-Political Disorder, and Ethnification as Expressions of Declining Global Hegemony," in *International Political Science Review* 19/3, pp. 233-250.

Jiang, Rong (2004) *Lang tuteng* [Wolf totem] Wuhan: Changjiang wenyi chubanshe.

Lu, Sheldon Hsiao-peng (1997) "Art, Culture and Cultural Criticism in Post-New China," in *New Literary History* 28/1, pp. 111-133.

Lu, Sheldon Hsiao-peng (2001) *China, Transnational Visuality, Global Postmodernity,* Stanford: Stanford University Press.

Luo, Zhifang (2007) "'Xiongdi:' cong yuyan dao xie zhen" ['Brothers:' from allegory to writing the truth] in *Nanfang shifan xueyuan xuebao* 8, pp. 47-49.

Qi, Fangfang (2007) "Zhuixun 'kuanghuan:' 'Xiongdi'de xushu fengge fenxi" [In search of carnival: an analysis of the narrative style of 'Brothers'] in *Chongqing zhiye jishu xueyuan xuebao* 11, pp. 106-109.

Si Zhenlong (2007) "Mei chou shi heng: ping Yu Hua de xiaoshuo 'Xiongdi'"[Loss of balance between beauty and ugliness: a critique of Yu Hua's novel 'Brothers'] in *Jiangnan xueyuan xuebao*, 4, pp. 44-46.

Sun, Juan (2007) "Jiedu Yu Hua de 'Xiongdi' de daode mei" [An interpretation of the moral beauty of Yu Hua's 'Brothers'] in *Xiwang yuebao* 10, p. 18.

Wang, Xiaoyu (2006) "'Xiongdi:' Yu Hua de yici huali zhuanshen?" ['Brothers:' a magnificent turn around by Yu Hua ?] in *Zhonghua dushubao* 14, p. 1.

Yang, Songfang (2007) "'Xiongdi': yibu fu yu jingdian neihan de zuopin" [,Brothers:' a work rich in classical connotations] in *Dangdai zuojia pinglun* 6, pp. 141-146.

Yang, Xiaobin (2002) *The Chinese Postmodern: Trauma and Irony in Chinese Avant-Garde Fiction*, Ann Arbor: University of Michigan Press.

Yu, Hua (1989) "Xianshi yizhong" [One kind of reality] in *Shiba sui chu men yuan xing* [On the road at eighteen] Beijing: zuojia chubanshe, pp. 200-258.

Yu, Hua (1993a) *Zai xiyu zhong huhan* [Cries in the drizzle] Guangdong: Huacheng chubanshe.

Yu, Hua (1993b) *Huozhe* [To live] Changjiang wenyi chubanshe.

Yu, Hua (1996) *Xu Sanguan mai xue ji* [Chronicle of a blood-seller] Jiangsu wenyi chubanshe.

Yu, Hua (2005) *Xiongdi shangbu* [Brothers part one] Shanghai: Shanghai wenyi chubanshe.

Yu, Hua (2006) *Xiongdi xiabu* [Brothers part two] Shanghai: Shanghai wenyi chubanshe.

Yuan, Zheng (2007) "Yu Hua, 'Xiongdi' de ganga zhai men" [The akward narrow gate of Yu Hua's 'Brothers'] in *Wenxue jiaoyu* 5, pp. 70-71.

Zhu, Daxi (2007) "Xiaofei shehui de suoying" in *Shenyang daxue xuebao* 4, pp. 53-56.

Heather Inwood

Identity Politics in Online Chinese Poetry Groups

The East is black, the sun is bad
China has given rise to a School of Rubbish
You're black I'm even blacker than you
You're bad I'm even badder than you

Born as a Rubbish person
I'll die as a Rubbish ghost
I am the School of Rubbish
The School of Rubbish is me

In this self-satisfied world
Being degenerate is fantastic worshiping the high is exhausting
Black is School bad is also School
Rubbish, School is even more School

I am totally School of Rubbish
The School of Rubbish is totally me
If you want me to quit the School of Rubbish
The only way would be for me to quit me

Xu Xiangchou, Worshiping the High is Exhausting (崇高真累)[1]

Written in May 2003 as part of "Xu Xiangchou's Trample on the People Series" (Xu 2006), this poem is at once iconoclastic in its opening adulteration of that famous paeanto Mao, "The East is Red", and defiant in its declaration of loyalty to the poet's cause. That cause being, apparently, not a political leader nor party, nor even the Chinese nation, but a rather dubiously named Internet poetry group. The metamorphosis of the East from red to black (a morally suspect color in the Chinese vocabulary) would seem an ominous portent of what is to come. All hail the rise of the School of Rubbish (垃圾派), whose members compete to "blacker" and "badder" than the next, who are happy to be "degenerate," exhausted with "worshiping the high", and intent on being card-carrying members of the School until their eventual deaths as Rubbish ghosts. As the final stanza shows, not only is Xu Xiangchou loyal to this cause, he is the cause, his very existence inexorably tied to that of the School: "if you want me to quit the School of Rubbish/The only way would be for me to quit me."

Despite or perhaps as a result of poems such as this, the School of Rubbish experienced a growth in numbers and a rapid rise to fame in Chinese poetry circles in the first few years following their conception on the Internet forum Beijing Review (北京评论)[2] in 2003. By the end of that year the group had a total of 28 members, and although internal disputes have resulted on two occasions in several deciding to jointly quit the school, it has continued to attract new poets and is still active and accepting members in 2008. This article seeks to investigate the reasons behind the strong identification with the school exhibited by School

1 All translations in this article are the author's own.

2 URL: <http://my.clubhi.com/bbs/661473/>.

of Rubbish poets through an analysis of their approach to online literary production and reception. In particular, it examines issues of identity as played out in the three-way relationship between poets, the poetry community, and their immediate context of activity.

The association of identity politics with historically marginalized or socially oppressed groups is somewhat appropriate in this case, in so far as the School of Rubbish consists of poets who have been eschewed from participation in more conventional poetic channels, largely due largely to the extremely controversial nature of their writing. In this paper, however, it is less the intention to depict the school's struggle for recognition within a wider poetry scene, and more to focus on the implications of the poets' affinity with the poetry group. Referring to the notion of interpretive communities and the interpretive strategies that hold them together, the idea of group identity is built upon through examining the connections between the textual and metatextual output of the school, and considering how these connections may be influenced by the mode of production: the Internet, and online poetry forums (论坛 or BBS) in particular.

I shall begin by pointing to pseudonymity and the potential for multiple virtual identities as being among the more salient features of participation in an online environment, using School of Rubbish creator Lao Touzi (老头子) as an example. As the functioning of Internet poetry forums has been described elsewhere (Hockx 2005), I will keep technical explanation to a minimum. My analysis of the School of Rubbish falls into two sections. The first introduces the central poetics or interpretive strategies of the group and an early selection of poems produced by the school. The second looks at two examples of wannabe School of Rubbish poets attempting to join the group by posting their poetry on the school's main forum, *Beijing Review*. I conclude by suggesting that the approach to community membership demonstrated by the school is essential to understanding the overall functioning of the contemporary Chinese poetry scene.

Multiple "I"s to the Singular "Us"

Much has been written on the themes of virtual personality and subjectivity in the context of the Internet (for example Turkle 1995, Landow 1997, Ouyang 2003). Possibilities of anonymity, pseudonymity, multiple on-screen identities, gender performance and even identity deception have proved enticing topics for those interested in the relationships between online behavior, literary practice and critical theory. Scholars of the Internet appear collectively swayed by certain theoretical deconstructions for which online communication seems to allow, such as what Sherry Turkle terms the "eroding boundaries between the real and the virtual, the animate and the inanimate, the unitary and the multiple self" (Turkle 1995: 10). Differing theoretical approaches aside, it seems clear that the faceless anonymity intrinsic to online activity differs from "real life", face-to-face social interaction in that it puts identity construction directly into the hands of the individual concerned. Others' perceptions of one's identity, personality or self are governed almost entirely by how one chooses to portray oneself through various forms of technological mediation (digital text, images, sound and video recordings), and indeed how much one is inclined to reveal in the first instance. Furthermore, the level of overlap between this online, portrayed self and one's "real-life" identity can be as big or small as one likes.

Internet poets in Mainland China demonstrate a variety of approaches towards their online identity. At one end of the scale are those whose online identity wholly corresponds to their real life self, down to the use of their actual name (真实性名) and verifiable statements of profession, background and place of residence. At the other end are those poets who participate solely under the guise of a fictional web-name or ID (网名), and whose geographic whereabouts, IP address and legal name might only be accessible to forum moderators. The choice to operate under a pseudonym can in many cases be explained by the desire to reduce traceability, especially in cases when a politically sensitive or risqué style of writing could compromise the real-life situation of the poet.

A combination of one or more pseudonymous online identities with an intentionally provocative approach to writing can significantly increase the perceived popularity (人气) or symbolic capital of a writer, with ambiguity surrounding a poet's true identity adding to an air of mystique or a carefully manipulated sense of inaccessibility. One poet who knows the benefit of this is the creator and central figurehead of the School of Rubbish, Lao Touzi (老头子, literally "Old Man"). For two years after establishing the school in March 2003, Lao Touzi was an enigmatic figure, closely guarding the secret of his "true" identity and thus invoking much speculation as to who he really was. One result was that he found himself the frequent target of impersonation, to such an extent that in late 2003 one *Beijing Review* forum member even suggested holding open elections for the "post" of "Old Man." Resident poetry critic Zhang Jiayan called Lao Touzi's identity "an unbreakable riddle" (Lao Xiang 2003), and another poet suggested that perhaps he did not really exist at all.

Pidan (皮旦, a homophone of 皮蛋, thousand year-old egg) was the second poet to join the School of Rubbish, on March 18th 2003. He occasionally uses the alternative web-name Lao Tian (老天), is co-forum moderator of Beijing Review, editor of the School of Rubbish Webzine, and responsible for writing such important School of Rubbish texts as "On the School of Rubbish as a Movement" (Pidan 2003a) and the "School of Rubbish Synopsis" (Pidan 2003b). According to the group's official records, a third poet, Zhi Feng; joined the School of Rubbish on March 22nd 2003. Compared with Lao Touzi and Pidan, he kept a low profile, adopting a humble and self-effacing tone in his communications, and primarily spending his time engaging in poetic discussion on *Beijing Review* and contributing poetry to the group's webzine.

In March 2005, on the second anniversary of the School of Rubbish and the poetry forum *Beijing Review*, Lao Touzi ended speculation surrounding the person behind his web-name by posting a statement online admitting that he, Pidan and Zhi Feng were in fact one and the same person (Pidan 2005a). He explained that Zhi Feng is his real name, Lao Touzi the original name he used for posting theoretical writings, and Pidan his preferred web-name for poetry authorship and forum participation. He explained,

using the web-name "Lao Touzi" was originally meant to facilitate the writing of poetry criticism online. The only more complicated reason I could possibly give was that I had truly hoped to become a hidden [隐身] or virtual [虚拟] writer. Of course, I have now realized the difficulty of all of this.

Although here and elsewhere the poet seems to express a genuine (if now disillusioned) faith in the power of virtual identity on the Internet,[3] the general consensus amongst other School of Rubbish members and observers was that Lao Touzi had in fact been playing a tactical game, employing shrewd strategies of self-mythologizing and self-idolizing, and in doing so turning his ID into a symbol rather than a person or persona (Pidan and Li 2005b).

3 He has also stated that he sees the "virtuality" of the Internet as a powerful weapon in the fight against the "hypocrisy" (虚伪性) which he believes runs throughout Chinese history and culture. See Pidan 2003c.

Such image manipulation could be understood in light of the commodification of contemporary poethood (van Crevel 2005a), informed by China's increasingly powerful celebrity discourse, and boosted in this case by the relative liberties and flexibilities of anonymous online interaction. The example of Lao Touzi/Pidan/Zhi Feng also vividly demonstrates how the potential for multiple online identities can be exploited by both the individual poet and the poetry group to aid reputation building and the creation of communal myths: Lao Touzi's split personality is, in many ways, a key symbol in the creation and continued existence of the School of Rubbish. Pseudonymity itself may not be new to literature, having been practiced in print culture for centuries. What may be more unique to communication in online poetry forums, however, is the way it allows poets to maintain frequent contact (not just annually, monthly or weekly, but daily, hourly and instant) and thereby achieve a high level of intimacy with their readers and with other poets, often whilst preserving almost absolute anonymity as regards their offline existence. The Internet presents its participants with the opportunity to create for themselves new identities as poets, as literary thinkers and even as community leaders, opportunities that, due to practical limitations such as educational background, geographical location or social status, may not have been possible through more conventional channels.

Interpretive Communities

Pseudonymity and multiple personae allowed Lao Touzi to establish a poetry group, promote an unconventional style of poetic writing with no fear of personal backlash, then join it twice under different names, before distilling and expounding upon his own poetic views and putting them immediately into practice. This he did by both selecting and publicizing poetry of an appropriate style, and by writing such poetry himself under his other two pseudonyms.

In the section that follows I consider the School of Rubbish in light of Stanley Fish's theory of interpretive communities, looking at textual manifestations of communities on the poetry forum *Beijing Review*. Fish proposes that similarities and differences in textual interpretation can be explained by the existence of communities of individuals who share predispositions or habits and conventions of textual understanding – what he terms interpretive strategies. For example, readers of a more religious predisposition are more likely to read religious symbolism into texts where others might see none; those with a conservative attitude towards poetry may well perceive as nonsense what others view as a brilliant avant-garde work. The concept of the interpretive community not only functions as an explanation for the commonality of interpretation among different readers who belong to the same community and disagreement amongst readers who belong to different communities (Fish 1980: 15), it also accounts for the ability of individuals to employ different strategies at different times or under differing conditions, and thus "make" different texts from the same work – they simultaneously belong to different communities.

In Fish's hypothesis, the communities that share interpretive strategies are rather elusive and difficult to define. They can "grow larger and decline" – alignments are not necessarily permanent, but are always there. Access to community membership is no easy affair, as it is impossible to give an outsider a set of definitions to enable entry into the community, as "a system of intelligibility cannot be reduced to a list of the things it renders intelligible" (Fish 1980: 304). Likewise, if membership is achieved, it is equally difficult to prove, with the only evidence being "fellowship", or a "nod of recognition from someone in the same community" (Fish 1980: 173). This is because all acts of communication – even those that appear to suggest community membership – are subject to interpretation, and thus definite conclusions are hard to draw.

As we shall see, the elusiveness of interpretive communities formed and expressed on the Internet is open to some debate; nonetheless Fish's theory is helpful on several levels in understanding the functioning of the Chinese contemporary poetry scene. On the broadest level, contemporary writers of modern poetry (新诗 or 现代诗, as opposed to classical-style poetry 古体诗) can be seen as belonging to a wider interpretive community which views vernacular, free-verse poetry as a valid means of literary expression, and is not alarmed by ambiguity of meaning or unconventional use of language. This community could then be roughly divided into those who write state-approved verse that often upholds the current ideological guidelines of the CCP, and those whose writing is unashamedly individual, non-utilitarian and experimental, with the latter generally being classed – primarily for ideological and aesthetic reasons – as the contemporary avant-garde or unofficial poetry scene. Within this avant-garde are found smaller interpretive communities with their own understandings on the nature of poetic writing, linguistic style, thematic content, and so on. Individual poetry groups such as the School of Rubbish can be understood as one of these more defined interpretive communities, whose strategies for the reading and writing of poetic texts are distilled into specific poetic views and articulated in a variety of metatexts – anything they write *about* poetry, including slogans, manifestos, poetry criticism and theoretical essays.[4]

How to be Rubbish

The School of Rubbish is typical of Internet-based avant-garde poetry groups in that it demonstrates an organized, almost hierarchical structure within its ranks, is able to name with certainty the date of conception and major events that mark its development, and possesses a large volume of metatextual writings. The earliest and symbolically most important of these were all penned by Lao Touzi, of which the very first were his Poetry Epistles (Lao Touzi 2003a), posted on Beijing Review on March 15, 2003: this date was to become the official birthday of the school. They consist of a series of short commentaries on poets whose writings correspond to his own poetic views, the nature of which he explains in the course of discussing their work. Interspersed throughout are statements pronouncing the establishment and basic poetics of the School of Rubbish, which later form the basis of another text, the "School of Rubbish Manifesto" (Lao Touzi 2003b).

The *Epistles* commence with a declaration written in a quasi-classical, humorous style, explaining the potential benefits of participating on his forum:

Using Beijing Review as his headquarters, Lao Touzi will now come forward and play the lute. If you can stand it, then let me play; if you really can't stand it, then it's ok if you block [封] *me or kick* [踢][5] *me on Beijing Review.*

---

4 Van Crevel explains that "metatext simply means what people have to say *about* poetry, and denotes a discourse that includes one person's inability to name a single contemporary poet to someone else's ambitious, learned genealogy of the entire poetry scene – and, of course, the poets' own verse-external poetics", see van Crevel 2005b: 2.

5 This character *ti* 踢 (kick) is separated by one tone from the word *ti* 提 (bump), and is used as short-hand on forums to express the opposite meaning – strong disapproval.

To play the lute you need to have a score. Personally, I really don't know the score [一点谱儿也没有]. *So, Beijing Review has to lend me the score. Everything Lao Touzi relies upon when writing these poetry epistles is on Beijing Review. No matter who you are, as long as you come forward, there will be the possibility I will take you and use you as my score. If I play out of tune then shout; if it makes you happy, then shout; if I'm careless and hurt you, then shout too.*

This functions as an open invitation for interested poets to get involved in poetry writing on *Beijing Review*, with the tempting possibility of being noticed and studied from by the forum's creator and main moderator. The name of the poetry school created to uphold the poetic values promoted in these *Epistles* is not mentioned until the fourth section, which analyses a poem by Fa Qing (法清)[6] entitled "I Caught a Big Fish:"

Finish eating the fish, and turn it into faeces – this type of rubbish can only be transformed by going through the anus. If people who write this kind of poetry wanted to form a school, then that school would be the School of Rubbish. The USA has the Beat Generation [垮掉派, literally "Collapsed School"] *whose representative figure is Allen Ginsburg. After it has collapsed where does it go? The answer, of course, is rubbish. Therefore, if the Beat Generation walked a beat further forward it would become the School of Rubbish. If modernist poetry is to develop according to plan, it should have a School of Rubbish. Moreover, logically speaking, to compare the modernist School of Rubbish with the Beat Generation should be like comparing the philosophies of dialectical materialism and naïve materialism. In other words, the modernist poetry of the School of Rubbish should be one level higher than the Beat Generation.*

Here, Lao Touzi sets out the theoretical foundations and his personal ambitions for the School of Rubbish, complete with a rather idiosyncratic interpretation of Beat Generation poetics. This is likely owing to the mis-translation in Chinese of the word "beat", in which the adjective meaning "tired" or "worn out" becomes the past-tense verb "collapsed," but it nonetheless serves to position the School of Rubbish firmly on the side of the avant-garde, and alludes to sub-cultural tendencies. This position is further underlined through his use of explicit biological terms, effectively an endorsement of writing bodily functions into poetry. The desire to do one better than Beat Generation poets and make an important contribution to the larger goals of modernist poetry – not just Chinese modernist poetry – makes Lao Touzi's Rubbish Poetry an ambitious proposition.

The interpretive principles hinted at in this Epistle are further clarified in a later section, which contains of a culmination of Lao Touzi and Fa Qing's forum-based debate on the exact characteristics and definition of Rubbish Poetry. Here, Lao Touzi builds on his original suggestion of four principles ("return to the original, aim down, not soul, not flesh") to settle upon the following version of three sets of principles. They were to be known thereafter as the "Three Principles of the School of Rubbish" (垃圾派三原则), and still form the central theoretical precepts of the school.

> The first principle: return to the original, aim down, not soul, not flesh;
> [还原、向下；非灵、非肉]
> The second principle: separate and unified, contrary and common, no essence, no application;

6 Fa Qing was later to leave the School of Rubbish on May 18th of the same year, citing irrevocable differences with the group and its poetics. See Lao Touzi 2003c.

[离合、反常，无体、无用；]
The third principle: crude, unrestrained, both dead and alive.
[粗糙、放浪，方死、方生。][7]

He proceeds to elaborate on some of these principles by explaining that "not soul" separates the School of Rubbish from the Chinese tradition of poets taking agricultural civilization as the background to their writing, whilst "not flesh" distinguishes it from the Lower Body school (下半身), who primarily write about sex. As he states, "no essence" and "no application" cannot be satisfactorily explained from the words alone, as the characters 体 (body or essence) and 用 (use or application) represent complex philosophical ideas from China's classical tradition.[8] Although he does not explain the line "both dead and alive," poets might recognize it as a quote from Daoist philosopher Zhuangzi's text *On Leveling Things* (齐物论). According to Zhuangzi, life *is* death; birth marks the beginning of the end, and thus human existence is spent in constant contradiction between the two. Ultimately, this phrase emphasizes the transcendental nature of all things, which may form part of the philosophical grounding for the School's emphasis on the end result (waste, rubbish, decay) or futility of all human activity.

In an amended version of the Three Principles included in the prologue to *Poetry Epistle* no. 13, the "return to the original" (还原) of the first principle is replaced with "worship the low" (崇低) to take account of what was by that time considered the central poetic focus of the group. The phrase "worship the low" is created to directly oppose the phenomenon of "worshiping the high" (崇高, more commonly translated as lofty or sublime), which Xu Xiangchou finds so exhausting, and which is seen by many poets as one of the fatal weaknesses of much modern Chinese poetry. The School of Rubbish are by no means the first to emphasize contempt for this poetic tradition – "oppose the lofty" (反崇高) was a common battle cry amongst Third Generation poets in the 1980s, going hand in hand with a similar rejection of poetic heroicism (英雄主义).[9] This position was epitomized in the poetics of poetry school "Not-Not" (非非), whose name is composed of the two epithets "not-sublime" (非崇高) and "not-rational" (非理性) (Day 2006).

In *Poetry Epistle no. 10*, written about Xu Xiangchou, Lao Touzi summarizes the importance of worshiping the low to the School of Rubbish (Lao Touzi 2003a):

China is a country that has pursued spiritual "loftiness" for several thousand years – how many people can do a complete turn around and "worship the low" instead of "worshiping the high"? The School of Rubbish is a school that advocates worshiping the low, Rubbish poetry is a type of poetry that advocates worshiping the low, Rubbish culture is a culture that advocates worshiping the low, Rubbish spirit is a spirit that advocates worshiping the low, and Rubbish philosophy is a philosophy that advocates worshiping the low.

Such principles – or interpretive strategies – are referred to again and again, not just in the writings of Lao Touzi, but also in the large volumes of metatext written by and about School of Rubbish poets. The doctrine of "worshiping the low" in particular forms a recurring theme in School of Rubbish poetry criticism, with different poets expressing varying

7 Lao Touzi asks readers to pay particular attention to this use of punctuation in the Chinese version.

8 As in the phrase "Chinese essence, Western application" (中体西用). The origins and evolution of this particular concept are discussed in Li 2003: 310-321.

9 Han Dong's poem *Youguan Dayanta* 有关大雁塔 ("Of Wild Goose Pagoda") is often cited as a powerful example of anti-loftiness and anti-heroics in Third Generation poetry writing. See Lovell 2002, and Qin 2007.

understandings of exactly what this represents, both in their prose writings and in their poetry. Although Lao Touzi has his own definite ideas on this point, he suggests in his *Poetry Epistles* that the finer details of the "Three Principles" would be most effectively clarified through writing in the form of poetry, open discussion and debate on *Beijing Review*, thus indicating a certain willingness to share interpretive authority with other members of the community.

Being Rubbish

The first official collection of Rubbish Poetry selected to demonstrate these principles was posted by Lao Touzi on Beijing Review less than a week after he announced the founding of the school in his Poetry Epistles. The collection, entitled "Ten Representative Works and Commentary of China's School of Rubbish Poetry" (Lao Touzi 2003b), consists of ten poems or poem series written by individual poets with a commentary by Lao Touzi at the end of each. This text represents, according to the first edition of the *School of Rubbish Webzine*, an important milestone in the formation of the school. The poems and poets included in the collection, in order of appearance, are: "Poet 'i' Answers Questions from a Reporter from the Southern Weekend" by i; "Mama" by Ding Mu (丁目 *ding mu);* "What Have I Seen? My Heart Aches So!" by Little Moon (小月亮 *xiao yueliang*); "Madman" by Zhi Feng; "Beast" by Hong Chenzi (红尘子 *hong chenzi*); "No.1 Arse-Wiper" by Pidan; "Life" by Training Piglets to Fly in the Sky (训练小猪天上飞 *shunduan xiao zhu tianshang fei*); "Why Don't You Just Get Rid Of Me" by Xu Xiangchou; "Quotations of Qu Qiubai" by Blue Butterfly Lilac (蓝蝴蝶紫丁香 *lan hudie zi ding xiang*); and "Not a Rhinoceros Nor a Tiger: Why Insist on Roaming the Wilderness?" by Guan Dangsheng (管党生 *guan dansheng*).

As a set of texts these poems by no means represent a unified whole, demonstrating what appear at first to be divergent approaches towards the task of "Rubbish Poetry" writing. In general, however, most adopt a light-hearted, irreverent tone, are written in simple colloquial language and slang, and make frequent allusions to bodily functions, other famous poets and aspects of traditional Chinese culture, all features set to become hallmarks of School of Rubbish poetry writing. Lao Touzi's application of the interpretive strategies outlined in his "Three Principles" can be observed both in his choice of poems and in the commentaries which accompany them. The following two are typical examples of the style of interpretation adopted in this collection:

Poem no.5: Beast (畜牲) *by Hong Chenzi*[10]

> *The day this child was born*
> *His head came out first*
> *Then his hands and his feet came out*
> *But the child's cock was too long*
> *When it was finally pulled out of his mother's vagina*
> *Everybody said this child is a beast*

Comments on Hong Chenzi's "Beast":

[10] Hong Chenzi is one of the web-names of poet/critic Wang Feng 汪峰, the first group member after Lao Touzi to write theoretical criticism on School of Rubbish poetry.

This beast's cock must be at least one or two times longer than his legs, otherwise it wouldn't need to be pulled out; it must be a lot thicker than his legs too, otherwise it wouldn't need to be pulled out either. The single character "pull" really makes the poem great! My God, just think about it, what on earth will this beast be able to do in the future? Firstly, he will inevitably be ostracized to a certain extent by his family, because he will bring shame upon them; secondly, even those who seek able-bodied men won't want to seek him, because his disproportionate cock will have turned him into a totally useless piece of junk; furthermore, he is unlikely to get married, because he would need a suitable woman (at least as far as reproductive organs are concerned). I can guess that when this beast grows up the only thing for him is to join the School of Rubbish. The School of Rubbish is congenital; the Lower Body is doomed [垃圾派与生俱来，下半身在劫难逃].

Apparently this poem does not contain sufficient literary technique to allow for a detailed discussion of poetics, but does point to some of the predominant concerns of Rubbish Poetry (bodily functions and farcical situations) and inspires Lao Touzi to draw a cutting comparison between the School of Rubbish and its poetic predecessors and competitors, the Lower Body school. Following his analogy, Hong Chenzi's beast can be read as a metaphor for exaggerated sexual prowess gone awry, and the poem's overall effect is to make a mockery of the Lower Body group and its fixation with sex and the reproductive organs, as demonstrated in many poems written from 2000 to 2003 by Shen Haobo 沈浩波, Yin Lichuan 尹丽川, Li Hongqi 李红旗, Sheng Xing 盛兴, Nan Ren 南人 and others.[11] Thus: the Lower Body group is "doomed", just like the deformed child, but the School of Rubbish, in its acceptance of all that is twisted and useless, still has a future. Rubbish principles of "worship the low", "crude" and "unrestrained" are clearly on display in this poem, presumably explaining why Lao Touzi included it in this poetry collection.

Poem no.11: "Life" (生活)
By Training Piglets to Fly in the Sky

Training piglets to fly in the sky

Commentary on Training Piglets to Fly in the Sky's "Life":
Is "training piglets to fly in the sky" simply the name of a School of Rubbish poet? I've noticed that many heavyweight School of Rubbish poets have written poems of this name, why might this be? I maintain that it is not just the name of a School of Rubbish poet but, more importantly, a way of life; that so many poets have taken it as the title of their poems is also because it is not simply the name of a School of Rubbish poet, but symbolises a way of life. This life, in the eyes of School of Rubbish poets, is most definitely an extremely important life. "Obscure" poet Bei Dao [北岛] *once wrote a poem entitled "Life" which consisted of only one word: "net". Times, after all, have progressed. If even piglets can fly up into the sky, then what can that net, seen as so oppressing by Bei Dao, really count for! From this we can see the School of Rubbish's surpassing of the previous generation. Perhaps taking a poem only one line long as a representative work is rather risky, but Bei Dao's "Life" was*

[11] For an introduction to "Lower Body" writing and poetics see van Crevel 2003.

even shorter – only one character long; Gu Cheng's [顾城] *"Black Eyes" was not long either.*[12]

As Lao Touzi indicates, this short poem can be read as an alternative version of Bei Dao's canonical poem of the same name, and represents an attitude of jest on the part of the younger poet (born in 1982) towards both her poetic predecessors, and a poem which is often cited as a classic of the "Obscure poetry" (朦胧诗) era of the late 1970s and early 1980s. Like Bei Dao's single-word poem, the phrase "training piglets to fly in the sky" could possibly be read as an expression of the futility of life, but the imagery is more humorous than that of Bei Dao's poem, in which the "net" is usually taken as a metaphor for disillusionment or repression.[13] "Net" (网) also takes on new connotations in the context of the Internet (网络).

The poem is, furthermore, an example of reflexivity in poetry, as the phrase "training piglets to fly in the sky" – whether or not one takes this as a metaphor for life in general – is the web-name of the author. Referring to poets by name is a form of meta-poetry, and draws attention to the poem's constructed-ness. This is amongst the favorite devices of School of Rubbish poets, and can serve several functions. In some instances it is a blatant means of showing disrespect towards poetry foes or already canonized poets, as is the case in many of Little Moon's poems. In "What Have I Seen? My Heart Aches So!" from this collection, the narrator expresses disappointment towards former poet heroes Yi Sha (伊沙) and Shen Haobo, finding more to commend in the poetry of Rubbish poet Guan Dangsheng. She sighs: "Those great poets in my eyes […] How come they've turned into dog shit? How come they're so shameless and laughable?"

In other cases it can serve as a means of building up myths or creating a sense of intimacy within the group. Pidan's poem series "No.1 Arse-Wiper" (擦屁股的第一), also included in this collection, is a typical example of this, as it is set in a fictional village named after the poet, "Big Pi Village" (大皮庄), and features the poet himself as one of the main characters. The continued self-referencing in the poem helps blur the lines between fiction and reality as regards the facts surrounding Pidan (and thus Lao Touzi and Zhi Feng too): in his biographical introductions he even claims residence in "Big Pi Village". Blue Butterfly Lilac is another poet whose poetry frequently demonstrates meta-poetry characteristics – one poem of his written in February 2006 is entitled "Lao Touzi is King of Farts", in which he pokes fun at Lao Touzi and his attempts to become famous: "When Lao Touzi/had not yet become famous/he often said/if you want to be a poet/who is widely praised by all/the most reliable path/is mediocrity" (Blue Butterfly Lilac 2006).

Reflexivity or meta-poetry – whether demonstrated through name-calling, poetry about poetry or poetry written on the topic of the Internet – could also be considered a way of getting to grips with the materiality of the virtual world of the Internet: a form of engagement

---

12 I presume he is referring here to the poem "This Generation" (一代人), which includes the words "black eyes" (黑色的眼睛). Yeh's translation is as follows: "Dark night has given me dark eyes/With which I search for light," in Yeh 1991: 82.

13 McDougall and Louie point out that this not in fact a poem at all but a single stanza in Bei Dao's longer poem "Notes from the City of the Sun" (太阳城札记). They explain that the common reading of the character "net" as "a condemnation of the lack of freedom in Chinese life and the despair of those caught in its toils" is in fact a "creative misunderstanding", but do not suggest an alternative interpretation; cf. McDougall and Louie 1997: 433-434.

with the medium (Glazier 2002: 23). In this sense, faceless acquaintances made through virtual interaction are turned into more concrete realities by writing them into poetry – the community effectively "materializes" itself through writing. More than anything else though, it functions as a strong affirmation of community membership, and is a technique that, as we shall see in the following section, has not escaped the attention of would-be School of Rubbish poets.

Rubbish Wannabes

Beijing Review is not just the main location where the School of Rubbish post and discuss their own poetry and poetic ideas, it is also the website of choice for aspiring or wannabe Rubbish poets to display their work and get speedy feedback from already established group members. It provides access, through a series of drop-down and tabbed links at the top of the page, to other websites which act as a depository for "best-of" selections of Beijing Review postings – including the original follow-up posts (跟贴), School of Rubbish poetry criticism, "canonized" collections of poetry such as the *Ten Representative Works*, and all previous editions of the *School of Rubbish Webzine*. By reading through these texts, poets who wish to join the group can learn about Rubbish poetics and put them into immediate effect in their own writings.

Among the many Rubbish wannabes who have attempted to gain access to the group by writing poetry in what they believe to be a Rubbish style is a person going by the name Zhou Jun (周军). On November 14th 2003 he or she posted the following poem on *Beijing Review*, accompanied by a follow-up post asking, "Would each friend see if I'm Rubbish or not?" (Zhou 2006).

In order to be rubbish I am rubbish (为了垃圾我垃圾)

In order to take my seat I take my seat
in order to stand up I stand up
in order to stand up I take my seat
in order to take my seat I stand up

in order to die I die
in order to be born I am born
in order to be born I die
in order to die I am born

The immediate response by someone using the web-name The Poet Believes (诗人认为) was "not very rubbish" (不太垃圾). Another poet, Thirst Quenching (解渴), replied a few hours later that the poem was "forced" (做作), and another (School of Rubbish poet, later to become Rubbish Movement member), Fan Si (凡斯), asked Zhou Jun "do you think all badly written poems are called Rubbish?" to which Shen Wu (神武) replied, "Old Fan, you fell into his trap, this is a famous poem used by this person to make fun of us". Although the last stanza of the poem does appear to have been copied from elsewhere,[14] it is a fair

[14] Internet searching of the last few lines reveals mention of similar song lyrics and perhaps a Hungarian poem.

assumption that Zhou Jun's request for feedback from established forum members was made in earnest.

The only poet to take this request seriously was Training Piglets to Fly in the Sky, who a few days later on November 20 posted in response her own interpretation of what constitutes Rubbish Poetry, entitled "Rubbish Poetry worships the low, the three standards of worshiping the low are [...]." In it she rearticulates the basic interpretive strategies of Rubbish Poetry as defined by Lao Touzi and summarizes by adding her own interpretation. This takes the form of another set of numbered slogans, reminiscent of CCP political policy: "one opposition, three disposals, and nine departures." Yang Chunguang (杨春光), an influential member of the School of Rubbish before his death in late 2005 and advocate of "Post-Political Writing" (后政治写作), clearly approved, stating that "this theory of Little Pig's is the most clear-headed theory in the School of Rubbish, I recommend that all Rubbish poets get to grips with it." Zhou Jun responded by asking, "Little Pig, have a look at my poem, is it School of Rubbish?" Training Piglets to Fly in the Sky did not answer this question, but what does follow is a series of posts from her and other poets asking that "personal abuse" (骂人的话) be deleted, suggesting that Zhou Jun (or someone else) had originally posted a further, presumably foul-mouthed reply which has now been deleted. Pidan's only intervention in all these exchanges is brief, promising to remove the offending post immediately.

We can presume from the responses to this poem that Zhou Jun's attempt to join the School of Rubbish had failed – although the same name can be found responding to other posts around the same time, it soon stops appearing in late 2003, and he or she is not listed as a member of the school. Although Zhou attempts to express a commitment to the school ("In order to be rubbish I am rubbish") and the last two lines ("in order to be born/I die/in order to die/I am born") could be said to echo the Daoist sentiments of the Rubbish principle of "both dead and alive", judging by the responses to this poem, the general consensus was that the poet had failed to meet the criteria for membership of the interpretive community – successful application of the school's interpretive strategies.

Other School of Rubbish hopefuls are even more deliberate in their attempts to join the school. On February 25 2006 a poet named A Feisty Pig (一头血气方刚的猪) posted a series of three poems and a personal manifesto on *Beijing Review* under the heading "Going against the tide: I announce that from now on I have officially joined the School of Rubbish, don't stop me!" (A Feisty Pig 2006). I have translated the first three items in full:

1. Going against the tide (倒行逆施)

I walk upside down
in this upturned world
using my sordid arse
to catch that
rapidly falling shit
I use my arsehole
to eat it
past my anus, rectum, caecum, large intestine, small intestine
duodenum, stomachus pyloricus, stomachus cardiacus, oesophagus, pharynx and larynx

turning that discarded shit
into food
finally pulling it out
from my throat and mouth
I will go and kiss
those precious arses
use my mouth
to take aim at
their glorious arseholes
take the food and
feed myself
mouthful by mouthful
when I do odd jobs
because I stand upside down
my penis
from beginning to end
points straight up at the sky

2. My school of rubbish manifesto

> *Rubbish poets can't be bothered to hide their own opinions and intentions. They clearly state that their aims can only be achieved by using violence to overthrow the entire current poetry system. Let the world's poetry scene shake in the face of the Rubbish Revolution. What the School of Rubbish will lose in this revolution is only their shackles. What they gain will be the whole world.*
>
> *Schools of Rubbish of the world, unite!*

3. Rubbish imagery

I worry myself to death
because there really is
too little rubbish imagery
where can I find things
with an ugly feeling?
I use my fingers to count
shit, faeces,
anus, arsehole
nostrils, maggots
periods, reproductive organs
bits and pieces on the human body
really are few and far between
God is truly unfair
giving us, the School of Rubbish,
such a tiny bit of imagery

oh, I forgot
the School of Rubbish doesn't believe in god
annihilate god
fuck him up the arse
then god in his
new mirror image
will appear
but it's still not enough
what should I do
I think so much I nearly lose hope
then suddenly I broaden my mind
and think of
Rubbish teacher
Comrade Pidan
what a fantastic image
strange that no one has used it
as Rubbish poets
we will never come across
a stroke of genius
more cool or more striking than
"annihilate Pidan
fuck Pidan up the arse"

The influences in these two poems are plain to see. It is almost as though the poet (whose choice of web-name is also typical of School of Rubbish pseudonyms) has taken all the archetypal features of School of Rubbish poetry, mixed them up together in his or her own poems, and then attempted to go one step further. The first, "Going Against the Tide," opens with a reference to a poem by Xu Xiangchou entitled "I Stand Upside Down," and uses the theme of physical and temporal inversion to describe a process of digestion reversed, thus allowing him to make copious references to characteristic "low" or "rubbish" symbols, as well as a list of the scientific terms for all the other organs food passes through during ingestion, digestion and egestion. It is hard to tell whether it is intended as parody or serious imitation.

The second poem, "Rubbish Imagery," is classic meta-poetry, describing in short lines, colloquial language and stream-of-consciousness the mental processes of an aspiring Rubbish poet as he or she tries to come up with an original School of Rubbish image to use in a poem. Again, the tone is flippant and tongue-in-cheek, and the concluding choice of imagery in particular – with its desecration of School of Rubbish figurehead Pidan – represents an attempt to break new taboos and thus embody the predominant Rubbish spirit of opposition and destruction, included in some earlier versions of the "Three Principles." Mentioning School of Rubbish members by name is also, as already discussed, the ultimate demonstration of community membership, and is usually practiced only by core members of the group. It implies a familiarity or intimacy with Pidan and thus with the group as a whole. The poet's personal manifesto, too, is characteristic of School of Rubbish slogans in its satire of communist revolutionary ideology: "Schools of Rubbish of the world, unite!"

A Feisty Pig was more successful than Zhou Jun in his or her declaration of allegiance to the School of Rubbish – all eight of the individual responses to this post were positive. Amongst other replies, Blue Butterfly Lilac responded with "Ha ha! I support you;" the First Review (第一评论) commented "no one's stopping you;" Pidan, unperturbed by the violence he had been subjected to in the poem, simply posted "greetings, A Feisty Pig;" and School of Rubbish poet ufo spelt out the general consensus by announcing "I agree: you are now a member of the School of Rubbish!" The whole thread has been moved to the Information Archives section of *Beijing Review*, an honor reserved for poetry, criticism and theory deemed to be of importance to the school as a whole.

The manner in which the poet's affiliation to the School of Rubbish is confirmed by other poets indicates that for these Internet-based poetry groups, membership of the interpretive community is something much more tangible, expressible and perhaps less open to interpretation than it seems in Stanley Fish's theory. Moreover, although in this case the interpretive principles and strategies followed by the group were largely settled upon by one individual (Lao Touzi), when it comes to poetry criticism and decision-making regarding admission to the school, interpretive authority is shared by all approved members of the community.

Conclusion

Xu Xiangchou has made the following assertion regarding the nature of the School of Rubbish (Xu 2003a):

The "School of Rubbish" are several brothers and mates with basically unanimous artistic tendencies who have ended up together in order to facilitate communication and learning from each other. However, the "School of Rubbish" is an open school of poetic art, and can take in new members at any time – you only need to be willing to explore with us, and to have already written works with Rubbish tendencies.

This statement encapsulates the nature of the interpretive community as described by Stanley Fish and epitomized by the School of Rubbish, describing how individuals are drawn together by shared poetic "tendencies" or interpretive strategies, and confirming that community membership is ultimately demonstrated and validated through writing rather than just reading (Fish 1980: 13). Where the School of Rubbish differs from Fish's description of interpretive communities is the way in which these strategies are not only spelled out in manifestos, slogans and theoretical essays, but also actively demonstrated in a number of texts that include both poetry and commentary. This means that those interested in joining the school have ample opportunity to clarify their understanding of Rubbish principles, and more importantly, to put them into practice through participating in Internet forums. Community membership, in other words, often forms the motive behind the application of certain interpretive principles to poetic texts: poets write in a Rubbish style *in order to identify as* a Rubbish poet. Furthermore, mechanisms are clearly in place for the confirmation of community membership – rather than Fish's elusive "nod of recognition", would-be community members have their interpretive efforts picked to pieces by current members, and if they are successful (like A Feisty Pig) are openly declared to be so.

The importance of the immediate context of this poetic activity – poetry forums – deserves highlighting here. The sheer accessibility of information on the Internet, as well as the speed, ease, anonymity and immediacy of online communication, have significant implications for the development of Chinese poetry and the discourse that surrounds it. In this paper the focus has been on the close connections between poetic text and metatext observable in online forums, and not on any formal distinctions of poetry produced online: the texts examined here could equally easily be reproduced in print form, and do not exploit the Internet's potential for technical experimentation (for example multimedia poetry and hypertext writing, discussed in Glazier 2002). Nonetheless, whilst aided in part by a typically close relationship between poetry discourse and poetry practice in modern and contemporary China, one could easily argue that the Internet as mode of production (Barmé and Davies 2004: 76) has had and continues to have an effect on literary practice in an online environment, not least in drawing attention to increasingly strong ties between text and metatext, and the enhanced community-forming possibilities that they provide.

The focus of this paper has been less on the efforts of the School of Rubbish to be accepted within a larger poetry scene, and more on issues of community identity observable within the poetry group itself: an internalizing, rather than an externalizing perspective. This is at odds with most investigations of identity politics, which usually seek to raise the consciousness of a certain social group and position it within a larger framework by means of demarcation based on social experience, ethnicity, sexuality, gender, or other differentiating factors. A similar approach could be adopted in the study of poetry groups, especially those like the School of Rubbish which are relatively marginalized both in terms of the numbers of poets who identify with the group's poetics (28 members by the end of 2003 certainly did not reflect universal acceptance of their principles within wider poetry circles) and the frequently negative reactions their poetic views and writings attract from other, non-Rubbish poets and critics.

A study of the group's interaction with other poets and rival groups would likely be rewarding as regards their attitudes towards other schools of poetry, and how their own poetic identities might be in part shaped in relation or in opposition to this Other.[15] Indeed, the current live scene (现场) of contemporary Chinese poetry is to a large extent defined by its divisiveness, by frequent poetry polemics, and by each poet or group of poets' awareness of their own standpoint(s) (立场) within this scene (Jiang 2003: 556-558). In this paper it has been my thesis that for online poetry groups such as the School of Rubbish, association with the Self of the poetry school, and the expression of this through regular writing and interaction on designated poetry forums, is the key factor in the formation of their poetic identity. Ultimately, this points to the predicament of so many culturally minded Chinese netizens, at once liberated by the Internet's defense of creative individualism and the possibilities this allows, and yet still inextricably bound by the overriding desire to belong.

References

A Feisty Pig (一头血气方刚的猪) (2006) "Daoxing nishi: wo xuanbu cong jintian kaishi wo jiu zhengshi jiaru laji pai le, bie lan wo!" 倒行逆施: 我宣布从今天开始我就正式加入垃圾派了, 别拦我! [Going against the tide: I announce that from now on I have officially joined the school of rubbish, don't stop me!] <http://hk.netsh.com/eden/bbs/6411/html/tree_7544870.html>, accessed 3 February 2008.

[15] Members of the School of Rubbish, for example, have participated in extended online debates with poets associated with the Lower Body school, especially Shen Haobo. See, for example, Xu 2003b.

Barmé, Geremie R. and Gloria Davies (2004) "Have We Been Noticed Yet? Intellectual Contestation and the Chinese web," in Edward Gu and Merle Goldman (eds) *Chinese Intellectuals Between State and Market*, London: Routledge Curzon.

Blue Butterfly Lilac 蓝蝴蝶紫丁香 (2006) "Lao Touzi shi ge fangpi dawang," 老头子是个放屁大王 [Lao Touzi is a king of farts]. <http://my.clubhi.com/bbs/661473/19/10671.html>, accessed February 3, 2008.

Day, Michael (2006) "China's Second World of Poetry: The Sichuan Avant-garde, 1982-1992," Digital Archive for Chinese Studies (DACHS). Leiden University. <http://www.sino.uni-heidelberg.de/dachs/leiden/poetry/md.html>, accessed February 3, 2008.

Fish, Stanley (1980) Is There a Text in this Class? The Authority of Interpretive Communities, Cambridge, Mass: Harvard University Press.

Glazier, Loss Pequeño (2002) *Digital Poetics: The Making of E-Poetries*, Tuscaloosa and London: The University of Alabama Press.

Hockx, Michel: (2005) "Virtual Chinese Literature: A Comparative Case Study of Online Poetry Communities," in *The China Quarterly* 183, pp. 670-691.

Jiang Tao 姜涛 (2003) "Xianchang yu yuanjing" 现场与远景 [The current scene and future prospects] in Tan Wuchang 谭五昌 (ed.) *Zhongguo Xin shi Baipishu 1999-2002* 中国新诗白皮书 1999-2002 [Chinese new poetry white papers 1999-2002] Beijing: Kunlun Chubanshe.

Landow, George P (1997) *Hypertext 2.0: The Convergence of Contemporary Critical Theory and Technology*, Baltimore/London: The Johns Hopkins University Press.

Lao Touzi 老头子 (2003a) "Shi zha" 诗札 [Poetry epistles] <http://hk.netsh.com/eden/bbs/6411/html/tree_4095350.html>, accessed February 3, 2008.

Lao Touzi 老头子 (2003b) *Zhongguo laji pai shige daibiaozuo shi shou zuopin yu dianping* 中国垃圾派诗歌代表作十首与点评 [Ten representative works and commentary of China's school of rubbish poetry] <http://tw.netsh.com/eden/bbs/704883/html/tree_5753831.html>, accessed February 3, 2008.

Lao Touzi 老头子(2003c) *Lajipai Xuanyan* 垃圾派宣言 [School of rubbish manifesto] <www.yanruyu.com/jhy/author/34926.shtml>, accessed 3 February 3, 2008.

Lao Touzi 老头子(2003d) "Laji pai jishi (2003 nian 3-5 yue)" 垃圾派纪事 (2003 年 3—5 月) [School of rubbish chronicles (March to May 2003)] <http://www.yanruyu.com/jhy/author/34836.shtml>, accessed 3 February 2008.

Lao Xiang 老象 (2003) *Lao Touzi zenme le?* 老头子怎么了 [What's up with Lao Touzi?] <http://hk.netsh.com/eden/bbs/6411/html/tree_5357898.html>, accessed February 3, 2008.

Li Zehou 李泽厚 (2003) *Zhongguo xiandai sixiang shilun* 中国现代思想史论 [A history of Chinese modern thought] Tianjin: Tianjin shehui kexueyuan chubanshe.

Lovell, Julia (2002): "Misty in Roots: Chinese Poetry after Mao," in *Poetry Review* 92/3.

McDougall, Bonnie and Kam Louie (1997) *The Literature of China in the Twentieth Century*, London: Hurst & Company.

Ouyang Youquan 欧阳友权 (2003) Wangluo wenxue lungang 网络文学论纲 [A thesis on Internet literature] Beijing: Renmin wenxue chubanshe.

Pidan 皮旦 (2003a) *Lun zuowei yundong de lajipai* 论作为运动的垃圾派 [On the school of rubbish as a movement] <http://hk.netsh.com/eden/bbs/6411/html/tree 2496931.html>, accessed February 3, 2008.

Pidan 皮旦 (2003b) *Lajipai jiyao* 垃圾派纪要 [School of rubbish synopsis] <www.yanruyu.com/jhy/author/46807.shtml>, accessed February 3, 2008.

Pidan 皮旦 (2003c) *Lun zuowei geming de lajipai* 论作为革命的垃圾派 [On the school of rubbish as revolution] <http://www.yanruyu.com/jhy/author/detail.aspsendid=35434 &detailpage=1>, accessed February 3, 2008.

Pidan 皮旦 (2005a) *2005 nian beiwanglu* 2005 年备忘录 [2005 memorandum] <http://hk.netsh.com/eden/bbs/6411/html/tree_6656043.html>, accessed February 3, 2008.

Pidan 皮旦 and Li Xia 李霞 (2005b) *Pidan Li Xia duihualu: laji shige, zai sheng hai shi reng diao?* 皮旦李霞对话录：垃圾诗歌，再生还是扔掉？[Transcript of a conversation between Pidan and Li Xia: rubbish poetry, rebirth or disposal?] <http://tw.netsh.com/eden/bbs/704883/html/tree_4683287.html>, accessed February 3, 2008.

Qin Yuhui 秦宇慧 (2007) *Di san dai shige de meixue yuanze* 第三代诗歌的美学原则 [Aesthetic principles of third generation poetry]. <http://www.bhgx.net/html/classic/20070816/103.html>, accessed February 3, 2008.

Turkle, Sherry (1995) *Life on the Screen: Identity in the Age of the Internet*, New York: Simon and Shuster.

Van Crevel, Maghiel (2003): *The Horror of Being Ignored and the Pleasure of Being Left Alone: Notes on the Chinese Poetry Scene* in MCLC Resource Center Website <http://mclc.osu.edu/rc/pubs/vancrevel.html>, accessed February 3, 2008.

Van Crevel, Maghiel (2005a) "Not Quite Karaoke: Poetry in Contemporary China," in *The China Quarterly* 183, pp.644-669.

Van Crevel, Maghiel (2005b) "Desecrations? The Poetics of Han Dong and Yu Jian," in *Studies on Asia* (Spring & Fall 2005), <http://www.isp.msu.edu /studiesonasia/vanCrevel.3.pdf>

Xu Xiangchou 徐乡愁 (2003a) *Xu Xiangchou wenxuan* 徐乡愁文选 [Collected writings of Xu Xiangchou] <http://my.ziqu.com/bbs/665167/4/145.html>, accessed February 3, 2008.

Xu Xiangchou 徐乡愁 (2003b) *Niubi shi zhuang chulai de: da 'Shijianghu' de yi qun wei xianfeng* 牛逼是装出来的：答"诗江湖"的一群伪先锋 [Being shit hot is a pretence: a reply to the fake avant-garde of poetry vagabonds] <http://www.yanruyu.com/jhy/author/40634.shtml>, accessed February 3, 2008.

Xu Xiangchou 徐乡愁 (2006) *Xu Xiangchou jianta renmin xilie (20 shou)* 徐乡愁践踏人民系列（20首）[Xu Xiangchou's trampling on the people series] <http://www.yanruyu.com/jhy/author/63679.shtml>, accessed 3 February 2008.

Yang Chunguang (2003) *Guanyu lao touzi* 关于老头子 [About Lao Touzi] <http://hk.netsh.com/bbs/6411/html/tree_5357898.html>, accessed February e, 2008.

Yeh, Michelle (1991) *Modern Chinese Poetry: Theory and Practice since 1917*, New Haven: Yale University Press.

Zhou Jun 周军 (2003) *Wei le laji wo laji* 为了垃圾我垃圾 [In order to be rubbish I am rubbish] <http://my.clubhi.com/bbs/661473/19/10671.html>, accessed June 20, 2006.

Carsten Storm

Postmodernism, Historicity, and Historical Fiction

Writing on the topic of "postmodernism in China" calls for a preliminary consideration of the relationship between the two terms involved. Is postmodernism[1] to be understood as a globalised phenomenon, though Western in origin, which relegates China to just one of the many examples of the very globality of postmodernism? This would concomitantly promote a notion of postmodernism as the inevitable fate which befalls non-Western cultures and states and build a construct of China as a marginalized entity. The identities emerging from this marginalized status are thus forced into challenging transition by the newest encounter with a dominant Western discourse – this time the discourse on postmodernism. This is contradictory insofar as postmodernism with its critique of the processes of hegemony, alienation, and 'othering' seems to offer the perfect tool to oppose marginalization, although it does so with a specific Western notion of the methods and objectives to be used in the struggle.

Or does, on the other hand, the focus on China refer to the image of a cultural stronghold with its long history of assimilation and the sinicization of everything that becomes important in China? In this case, the underlying argument of this article – and in fact of the whole book – should aim to conclude with an understanding of 'postmodernism with Chinese characteristics.'[2] This option transfers the object of the challenging transition in China from the Chinese self to the concept of postmodernism originating in the West. Of course, the dichotomy arising here is, in the end, of little analytical use following Michel Foucault, "what is interesting is always interconnection, not the primacy of this over that" (Foucault 1999: 141).

These two options reveal the contesting versions of Chinese history: one version constructs the formative experience of Chinese history on the basis of the encounter with the dominant European and Western powers, starting from around 1850. From this standpoint, the transition of the Chinese dynastic world to modernism is a story of constant oppression beginning with colonialism and continuing with contemporary Western economic and military dominance. Chinese modern history is thus constructed as an ongoing struggle to regain the country's own traditional hegemonic status. The other version clings to the image of China as a cultural, political, and not least, military hegemon. It constructs China in the role of assimilating and sinicizing its neighbors, foreign ideas and systems of values and draws one constant line from the introduction of Buddhism, via the integration of alien dynasties (Jurchen, Mongols, Manchus) to modernism, nationalism, Marxism, and now, postmodernism.

The experience of modernism scattered the Chinese self to a larger extent than most of the Western nations. While the transition to modernity in the West offered new strongholds to

---

[1] The term "postmodernism" is defined in this article in two intertwined dimensions: firstly, in terms of its meaning as a set of ideas and practices and, secondly, in terms of time as a specific period in which this set of ideas formed a body of legitimate knowledge.

[2] Although an epithet "with Chinese characteristics" is often used since, in fact, China's encounter with the West, it is, of course, highly problematic to add an ethnic signifier like "Chinese" to a term like "postmodernism". It is, however, beyond the scope of this article to investigate further the theoretical difficulties of these politics of labelling. Rey Chow (1998) has convincingly dealt with the impacts of such ethnicising practices, especially within the academic world.

Berliner China-Hefte/Chinese History and Society 34 (2008), pp. 95-112

the majority of Westerners in terms of nationalism and economic power, it was perceived in a much more ambiguous way in China. One major reason was that modernity developed in an autonomous way in the West, while China was confronted with a more or less fully configured predominant system. The encounters with the Western powers paved the way for the decline of the former Chinese self-awareness as the imperial power dominating the region. The rise of Chinese nationalism was thus turned into debates on the contradictory issues of 'weak nation' vs. 'national pride'. After the victory of the CCP in 1949, mainland China was not only ruled by a communist regime, but for the first time in half a century, a period of stable rule was established that was ultimately modern in its ideology, its policies, and its construction of the Chinese national self.[3] Since 1949, however, China's ongoing and currently quite successful struggle to regain the status of a leading world power has been accompanied by the constant awareness of international marginalization.

The deconstruction of the communist historical master narrative on the decline of traditional China and the glorious communist war against Japanese aggression as well as the Guomindang brought the Republican Era back into focus. The May-Fourth-Movement of 1919 was marked as a starting point and as a fore-runner of the student movement of 1989.[4] The rewriting of Republican history and of the anti-Japanese war in particular opened up the possibility of reconstructing national and personal identities according to alternative readings by crossing the discursive borders set by the CCP. At the same time, in fact, after the end of the Cultural Revolution, the dominant narrative on the Chinese tradition as a feudalist gentry-system oppressing the majority of the Chinese populace came under scrutiny and this resulted in attempts to rewrite the entire history of China. Within this process, however, some highlights have been given special attention, for instance, the Qin dynasty and the First Emperor, the Kangxi- and Qianlong-reigns, and the Taiping uprising. The re-evaluation of the Chinese past allows for alternative identity constructions that may fill the gap in values caused by the shifts in contemporary Chinese policies advocating a market economy, individual enrichment, and radical competitiveness.

The impact of history on forming a new Chinese self-awareness in postmodern times is quite visible in all processes of re-narrating the Chinese past to a wide audience, not least within the genre of the historical novel. History here serves as a major device to construct – namely national – identities, not only in historiography, in political and cultural discourses, and in psychoanalysis, but also in personal writings, such as diaries and autobiographies. The genre of historical novels and films is, without doubt, one of the most successful and influential genres not only in China.

History and the historical novel

[3] There were, no doubt, important transitions towards modernism before 1949 in China, especially in the aftermath of the May-Fourth-Movement of 1919. However, in general, these earlier manifestations of partly alternative, non-communist modes of modernism were limited either regionally or in scope. Shanghai, for instance, has certainly deserved to be called a 'modern city' from the 1920s on and also had a strong influence on its hinterland. Yet, compared to the CCP after 1949 it failed to unfold a similar modernising effect on China as a whole. Groups of (leftist) intellectuals, such as Lu Xun, Qu Qiubai, Xu Zhimo, Ding Ling and others formed a social stratum advocating and, to some extent, embodying modernism, but their achievements in transmitting modernist modes of thinking and living to other layers of society were quite limited in the end.

[4] Examples of such rhetoric are, for instance: Widmer and Wang 1993, Yeh 2001, or Kong 1997.

Since its beginnings, the major focus of criticism with regard to the 'historical novel' genre has been its relation to historiography and therefore the relation between fiction and 'truth.' This dichotomy widely ruled the analysis of the Chinese and the Western variants by academics and literary critics.[5] The work of Hayden White had a strong influence on the discussion on the historical novel, first of all, in Western literature and, soon afterwards, in Chinese academic writing as well. Furthermore, psychology and the linguistic turn caused a transformation of poetic and mimetic processes in historical novels. Shifting these processes towards radical self-consciousness allows the re-evaluation of the contesting relations of history – story, past – present, factionality – fictionality, or essentialism – constructivism.

In modernity, the structure of legitimizing (fictional) historical narratives has operated quite ambivalently. The idea of progress which had paved the way for the industrial revolution also caused a shift to a notion of history that was categorically determined by a linear-teleological and processual principle. Progress, understood first of all as technological progress, became measurable when placed on a linear timescale. Exact reference to academically legitimized knowledge of material history serves as the main criterion for inscribing authenticity and legitimacy into historical novels or films. The differences between the technological capabilities, trade and craft, tools and equipment as well as civilization described in these fictional historical texts on the one hand and contemporary achievements on the other are constructed as a deficit of the past. Thus, the novel is marked as "historical." These changes in the epistemology of history which gained momentum during the 19th century (Hardtwig 1990: 30) are visible, for example, in the detailed descriptions of wine production in Mo Yan's 莫言 novel *Red Sorghum* (*Hong gaoliang jiazu* 红高粱家族) or the design of the armament in Zhang Yimou's 张艺谋 *Hero* (Yingxiong 英雄).

This technique is quite different from premodern styles, where legitimacy was gained by repeating a canonical and thus generally acknowledged plotline, but where the material aspects were shifted into the time of writing. For instance, the material world described in the *Outlaws of the Marsh* is not that of the Song dynasty in which the story is set but that of the Ming dynasty during which the existing manuscripts were published.

While, in terms of literary techniques, these material aspects create a measurable temporal distance between the world described in the text and the world of the contemporary reader, other aspects allow identification. The establishment of psychology often results in a notion of timeless validity of psychological phenomena which are uncritically employed in historical novels and inscribed into the protagonist's motivation, especially with regard to notions of love. The result is a chrono-centric 'streamlining' of the past. Ideological threads, seemingly authentic ways of life, destiny and meaning, are inscribed into history to provide the audience with an identity that legitimizes political, social, and cultural action in the present time.

Thus, the construction of time, the 'timing' of the plot is of eminent importance for the narrative and the aesthetic structure. This leads to several concluding questions: first of all, how time itself is structured and how events and processes are linked to each other in time?

---

5 A prominent example is the dispute on the *Outlaws of the Marsh* (*Shuihu zhuan* 水滸傳), which is not regarded as a historical novel by some researchers because of the level of fictionalisation of the original Song dynasty uprising (see i.e. Ma 1975: 278). The dichotomy of fiction vs. historical truth is emphasized in almost every analysis on *lishi xiaoshuo* 历史小说 in Chinese, for instance: Ouyang 2003: 15–25, Lei 2003.

This question leads far beyond labeling structures as (Western) linear or (Eastern) cyclical which is a simplifying dichotomy. Instead, the question has to be: which roles do time and chronology play in creating links between events and processes? Secondly, how is biographical time to be understood, which instantly implements a specific cultural notion of individual life-time and the meaning of life? Finally, how does time constitute the very processes of writing and reception?

The discursive pattern of postmodern history challenged the modern academic methodology of producing historical knowledge to a lesser extent than the ways in which findings are inscribed into a "master narrative." The criticism of a term such as "master narrative" focuses not so much on the "narrative" but on the "master." The strategies of valuation and of producing legitimacy for a dominant narrative within the media, the public arena and academia are central to postmodern criticism. One major aspect of the resistance to the dominant "master narrative" is the categorical individualization of history. A person's individual biography serves as the final legitimate pathway to history that can claim authenticity. History is decreasingly understood as the history of a national, social, or ideological community, but as one of smaller groups, bound together by common heritage, locality, or other aspects, that reinstall moments of destiny, as constructed, for instance, in *Red Sorghum*.

Authors have reacted differently towards postmodern epistemologies. Many recent novels aim at questioning traditional or mainstream images (often confused with each other) namely of identities, by rearranging object and subject positions; they try to show discontinuities and to break down chronological causalities. This new and, in a sense, postmodern type of historical novel was conceptualized by Hans V. Geppert, who labeled it 'the other historical novel.' It tries to evade empirical (that is pre-postmodern) history by employing a self-referential mode, thereby problematizing its own narrative structures and statements (Geppert 1976, Febel 2000: 69). A Chinese variant of postmodernism in historical novel writing emphasizes the deconstruction of the master narrative provided by the CCP as well as pre-communist narratives of Chinese history. It employs narrative strategies such as non-linear constructions of time or de-subjectivisation to regain a new identity and selfhood uncorrupted by the CCP's images and language. This variant is mostly labeled the new historical novel (*xin lishi xiaoshuo* 新历史小说) but terms, such as *xiandai lishi xiaoshuo* (现代历史小说, modern historical novel), *lishi zhuyi xiaoshuo* (历史主义小说, historicist novel), or *changpian lishi xiaoshuo* (长片历史小说, long historical novel) can also be found. The 'new historical novel' is often seen as a postmodern enhancement from the revolutionary historical novel (*geming lishi xiaoshuo* 革命历史小说). [6]

The attempts of Chinese researchers to theoretically underpin these changes are ambiguous. Wang und Chen, for instance, emphasize that the "historical viewpoint of the 'new historical novel' takes a rebellious stance against [those traditional modes, C.S.] following only historical facts and historical determinism"(Wang/Chen 2005: 44). However, they attempt to delimit the impact of postmodernism in China by interpreting it as a result of Western economic development. This argument constructs the development towards postmodernity

6 The terms do not refer to completely identical phenomena. They are, however, often inaccurately used and mixed up. This is caused by an "over-categorisation" in which formal, content related and intentional aspects are connected. See for instance Liao 2004, Zhang 2005, Zhu and Zeng 2003, Wu 2002. An important study in Western language is Lin 2005.

on a linear timescale and, additionally, within the framework of Marxist materialism. Not only is China at a different stage of economic development, but, as they go on arguing, the aspects of harmony (*hexie* 和谐) and the doctrine of the mean (*zhongyong* 中庸) were constitutive for Chinese traditional culture. Thus, China can either accept only some superfluous features of postmodernism, or a 'misreading' of postmodernism followed by (a sovereign) reproduction.[7] A similar focus on the characteristics of Chineseness is to be found in Peng Wenxiang's term 'folksiness' (*renminxing* 人民性) which for him is central to Chinese authenticity as constructed in the media (Peng 2005: 16).

In another article, Chen Lianjin emphasizes aesthetic aspects of the 'new historical novel.' He lists three important elements of postmodern influence starting with (i) the cutting down of the mode of historical depth (*lishi shendu mushi xueping* 历史深度模式削平) by dismantling history through gender and violence (*xing yu baoli zhejie lishi* 性与暴力折解历史) and by fading out of time (*shijian de danchu* 时间的淡出). Next comes (ii) dispelling the subject (*zhuti de tuiyin huo xiaojie* 主体的退隐或消解) including the absurdity of human existence (*ren shi yi ge huangmiao de cunzai* 人是一个荒谬的存在) and the status of characters being a sign (*renwu fuhaohua* 人物符号化). His last element (iii) hints at the irony of history (*lishi de ziyi xixue* 历史的恣意戏谑) which he divides into the categories of satire (*fanfeng* 反讽) and imitation (*xifang* 戏仿) (Chen 2004). Chen describes these elements as aesthetic devices which are employed by authors to give their texts a postmodern shape. Although he might be correct in claiming a consumer or even market-oriented aspect in authors' decisions to construct their historical novels in this way, he nonetheless reduces important categories of postmodernism to empty signifiers which no longer carry central aspects of the postmodern set of ideas. It is precisely this understanding which opens up postmodernism for a reconstruction 'with Chinese characteristics.'

The general differences in the Chinese approach to postmodernism within the 'new historical novel' is also emphasized by Wang and Su. Like Chen and Wang before, they stress the importance of tradition which continues to influence historical novel writing and is molded into a new form with postmodern elements.

Although nowadays the 'new historical novel' is already declining again, no matter how we see it, it has departed from tradition and has stepped onto the path of postmodernism in a sustainable way. It has substituted the traditional meaning of the historical novel and has developed new patterns for its creation. We should be well aware of this aspect. In a new evaluation of the 'new historical novel' we can take the following stance: the 'new historical novel' is traditional and postmodern; it is a particular cultural phenomenon that is moving back and forth between tradition and postmodernity (Wang/Su 2006: 129).

Wang and Su take a number of elements into consideration in order to validate their argument. Like Peng, they focus on a disposition of folk culture within history (*minjian wenhua lichang de lishi* 民间文化立场的历史) which primarily links the historical novel to tradition, while a history of defamiliarization and individualization (*moshenghua, gerenhua de lishi* 陌生化，个人化的历史) as well as a history of the individual (*gexinghua renwu de lishi* 个性化人物的历史) are seen as signifiers of adaptations of postmodern ideas. Postmodernism here is clearly understood as temporal cum theoretical. The position of

---

7 "*... Zhongguo suo jiena de zhi neng shi houxiandai zhuyi de yixie qiancengxing de tezheng, huozhe shuo shi dui houxiandai zhuyi 'wudu' er chansheng de*" 中国所接纳的只能是后现代主义的一些浅层性的特征，或者说是对后现代主义‘误读’而产生的 (Wang/Chen 2005: 44).

phenomena such as, in this case, the 'new historical novel' can be fixed on an axis in terms of progress or backwardness. This assumption sets forth a materialist linear concept of history, which itself is modern rather than postmodern. However, Wang and Su's procedure is, in a certain sense, typical in that it denucleates and resignifies Western postmodern theory in order to adapt it to a Chinese framework.

Authors often associated with the 'new historical novel' are, for example, Yu Hua 余华, Mo Yan 莫言, Su Tong 苏童, Ye Zhaoyan 叶兆言, Ge Fei 格非, Liu Zhenyun 刘震云, Chen Zhongshi 陈忠实, or Bei Cun 北村 among many others.[8] Directors who are constructing their films in a similar way are, for example, Zhang Yimou 张艺谋, Chen Kaige 陈凯歌 , or Jiang Wen 姜文.[9] In the following, two techniques of rewriting the historical master narrative by constructing alternative meanings and by renegotiating time structures will be analyzed in more detail. In order to encompass different modes of cultural production, the focus will be on one novel and one film, namely, Mo Yan's *Red Sorghum* (1986) and Zhang Yimou's *Hero* (2002).

Narrative causality and time in Mo Yan's *Red Sorghum*

Mo Yan's novel, first published 1986 in a serialized form in five different magazines, is set in a rural area of north China, Gaomi, Shandong province, mainly between 1923 and the early 1940s. The story focuses on several struggles that the protagonists (the first person narrator's grandfather, Yu Zhan'ao, grandmother, Dai Fenglian, father, Yu Douguan, second grandmother, Liu Lian'er, and uncle, Liu Luohan) have to endure in order to live a self-determined local life. Mo Yan unfolds a kaleidoscopic panorama of modern ideological and military forces that threaten local practices. The protagonists thus fight against the Japanese army, troops of the Guomindang and the CCP, local bandits, and a highly symbolic band of dogs. *Red Sorghum* is a postmodern novel in terms of its narrative construction, its game of timing the plot, and in its self-reflective mode of praising the pre-modern archaic hero who symbolises a non-alienated life.

Mo Yan employs a complex system of references in timing the plot, which at first, refers to the arrangement of 'event-time' and, secondly, deals with specific modes of history's processes. Many of the often presented dates refer to the Western Christian calendar, yet the months and days are presented according to the Chinese lunar calendar. Mo Yan the-

---

8 Novels at least partly informed by postmodern styles are Yu Hua's *1986* (*Yi jiu ba liu nian* 一九八六年), *An Landowner's Death* (*Yi ge dizhu de si* 一个地主的死), Mo Yan's *Big Breasts and Broad Hips* (*Fengru feitun* 丰乳肥臀) or *Red Sorghum*, Su Tong's *Rice* (*Mi* 米) or *My Life as an Emperor* (*Wo de diwang shengya* 我的帝王生涯), Ye Zhaoyan's *Story of the Date Tree* (*Zaoshu de gushi* 枣树), Ge Fei's *The Enemy* (*Diren* 敌人) or *Margins* (*Bianyuan* 边缘), Liu Zhenyun's *Hometown* series (*World and Yellow Flowers*, *Contact and Circulation*, *Flour and Flowers*, *Guxiang, Tianxia huang hua*, *Xiangchu liuchuan, Mian he huaduo*, 故乡：天下黄花，相处流传，面和花朵) Chen Zhongshi's *The Field of the White Dear* (*Bailu yuan* 白鹿原), or Bei Cun's *The Baptizing River* (*Shi xi de he* 施洗的河). A more comprehensive collection can be found in Lin 2005.

9 Films informed by postmodern styles are for instance: *Red Sorghum* by Zhang Yimou, *Life on a String* (*Bianzou bianchang* 边走边唱) by Chen Kaige or *Devils on the Doorstep* (*Guizi laile* 鬼子来了) by Jiang Wen. Outside of the PRC, Taiwanese director Hou Hsiao-hsien (侯孝賢) has to be mentioned, especially his films *City of Sadness* (*Beiqing chengshi* 悲情城市) or *Millennium Mambo* (*Qianxi manpo* 千禧曼波). However, the question whether or not this would hint to a notion of a 'Chinese postmodernism' that refers to Greater China is beyond the scope of this article.

reby blurs traditional and modern elements. Hinting at common practices during the warlord era in rural China, this system of time references might be accurate in the sense that mixing different calendar styles was common in daily life. As such, it is a narrative act of historicizing the plot. Nonetheless, used as narrative tool by a fictional first person narrator who records family history in the 1980s, the plot is consciously placed in a space between modernity and tradition.

The extensive use of dates seems to offer the audience the possibility of associating knowledge of world history and placing the plot into a Chinese or even global framework. Yet, the novel almost completely lacks any reference to history outside Gaomi. The events and processes, including the invading Japanese army, are constructed as an autochthonous history unconnected to the outside. Historical identity results exclusively from the 'local' and opposes any notion of globality.

The plot's time line is highly fragmented by numerous flashbacks which establish a non-linear approach to time. This critical understanding of the modern linear uniqueness of time seems to reveal a postmodern stance. However, the ambivalence of the simultaneous fragmentation and the fixation of time install a potential for different readings of the text depending on the mode of reception. Readers believing in traditional modes of constructing historical meaning – which includes aspects of 'historical truth' – may understand the author's play with several levels of time merely as an aesthetic device. Similar to reading a crime story, these readers' attention may focus on the correct rearrangement of – in this case: temporal – hints in order to reconstruct a 'correct' time line of the overall plot. The fragmentation of time would be little more than an intellectually challenging time-puzzle. On the other hand, for readers sensitive to a postmodern construction of historical meaning, the potentially reconstructable linearity may serve as a signifier for a lost tradition which the 'other' historical novel (in the sense of Geppert) rejects but still needs as a background reference.

References to the ages of the protagonists are more significant in terms of postmodern strategies to deconstruct a linear time structure, for example for Yu Zhan'ao, Dai Fenglian, Douguan, and the first person narrator. History is thus shifted from a grand narrative of important events and persons to a biographical time, which comes close to the notion of "inner time" as proposed by Henri Bergson. This shift also scrutinizes the rules of selection inherent in the ascription of 'importance.'

Another narrative technique employed to determine time is the linking between events within the plot. Here a time line is not set up by placing events on an extrinsic calendar scale but by their mutual internal relations which are not necessarily linear. Historical meaning is thus constructed in an open system of mutual references. Historicity is embedded in a space of individual and local memory and reconstruction. Traditionally, history is defined by regional, national, and/or global processes or events of which the individual is merely a minor part. Contrastingly, in *Red Sorghum*, history only exists within the individual and the local. In the process of reconstructing history, knowledge gained through individual investigation, imagination, and a mythical connection to one's own past and origin form the decisive matrix in which history is meaningfully organized. Identity is not rooted in ideology or any other commonly shared categories of order, neither for the acting protagonists (Yu, Dai) nor for the first person narrator. Instead, identity is shifted to a psychologized individual. Consequently, identity and meaning only gain significance in comparison to other individuals. The status of being extraordinary serves as a border vis-à-vis other biographies and reveals the concept of the extraordinary person: the hero.[10]

In order to reconstruct processes, a wide and somewhat contradictory range of different modes is created to construct temporal meaning. The first person narrator, for instance, thinks that his father's notion of causality is not primarily determined by rationality (as the modern reader would assume). During a ceremonial burial, a cracking ceramic bowl ritually thrown against the coffin reminds Douguan of his relative's splintered forehead. "He had a vague inkling that the two events were somehow linked. The collision of one event with another always produces a third inevitability" (Mo 1993: 61, see also 1994: 56). The specific mode of connectivity is not rationally explained but attached to a mythical awareness that the non-alienated characters of the past obtained.

Later in the text, the first person narrator comments on his father's understanding of overall historical and social coherences:

He never did figure out the relationship between men and politics or society or war, even though he had been spun so violently on the wheel of battle. He was forever trying to squeeze the light of his nature through the chinks in his body armor (Mo 1993: 185, see also 1994: 173).

Arbitrary association is the new significant mode of linking historical events and a means to construct alternative meanings in *Red Sorghum*. For example, the description of a sword Yu used to murder Dai's first husband, Shan Bianlang is followed by a scene in which the adolescent Yu plays with another sword and uses it to murder a monk who is in adulterous love with Yu's mother (Mo 1994: 103, 1993: 112). The exhumation of Dai to prepare for her late funeral procession leads to the description of another procession in which Yu took part when he was working as a pallbearer (Mo 1994: 269, 1993: 277–278).[11] The notion of a rationally recognizable causality between events is shifted into mystified references that place events in chains of pictorial associations. The first person narrator, according to his own words well trained in Marxism,[12] acknowledges the lack of objective categories of historical processes and laws, and at the same time, avoids inscribing precisely this type of external meaning into his own narrative. Thus, officially sanctioned approaches to history are marked as contradictory to an individual, non-rational, yet original approach.

These chains of sometimes arbitrary or trivial associations transform history into an open space of memory that is not structured chronologically or cyclically. On the contrary, it allows the free movement of constant re-interpretation which creates new linkages between any chosen events in the sense of the "lines-of-flight" concept introduced by Gilles Deleuze and Félix Guattari. This concept relies on arguments on resistance developed by Foucault

---

[10] It has to be noted, however, that in this argument the meaning of the term 'extraordinary' changes. With reference to biography it hints at experiences, at things that happened to the individual and which are labelled as being 'extraordinary'. It therefore encompasses a passive mode. Linked to the concept of the hero, on the other hand, it hints to action and capabilities. It is the hero him/herself, who creates the 'extraordinary' through his/her actions.

[11] Further associative links are: the shift from Dai's death in the sorghum field to Douguan's face and on to the introduction to the begetting of Douguan (Mo 1994: 65-66, 1993: 71); links set within the introduction to the 'weasel story' (Mo 1994: 336, 1993: 334); the shift from Shan's death to that of Dai (Mo 1994: 69, 1993: 75); the links between the open mouths of two children's corpses (Mo 1994: 356, 1993: 354), etc.

[12] This sentence is omitted in Goldblatt's translation (Mo 1994: 2).

and serves as a metaphor for an every-day resistance against dominant systems of representation. Normally, a fixed set of connections between single significations within those systems provides us with a hyper-organized framework. Transforming these connections does not simply reconnect the entities but is thought as flinging spontaneously and thus as an opportunity for a constantly emerging transversal trajectory which is characterized as non-dialectical and non-linear.[13]

Mo Yan employs the memory of the first person narrator to construct a radical individualization of history, which contrasts the official CCP historical narrative precisely because its focus on subjectivity gives it authenticity and legitimacy. The recovery of subjective history and the making of historical meaning critically challenges any historical epistemologies based on collective (political, social, or else) or seemingly objective formations.

These aspects become quite visible in a range of songs, of which the earliest in plot-time follows the Japanese attack against the village of second grandmother Lian'er, during which she is raped and her daughter killed.

大刀向鬼子们的头上砍去! — *Swing your sabers at the heads of Japs!*
高粱红了，东洋鬼子来了. — *The sorghum is red, the Japs come from the east.*
蹂躏我国土，玷污我二奶奶. — *Trampling our soil and disgracing my second grandma.*

全国爱国的同胞们， — *Patriotic brethren everywhere*
抗战的一天来到了！ — *The day of resistance is now!*
拿起刀，拿起枪，拿起掏灰耙，拿起擀饼杖， — *Raise your swords, raise your guns, raise your dust harrows, raise your rolling pins,*
打鬼子，保家乡，报仇雪恨！ — *Beat the devils, protect the families and villages, take revenge!*[14]

Before the battle at Blackwater River, the Adjutant of Yu Zhan'ao, Ren, taught the soldiers a revolutionary song that takes up some motives and phrases of the first song and that therefore can be regarded as a variant developed from an original:

高粱红了，高粱红了, — *The sorghum is red, the sorghum is red,*
东洋鬼子来了，东洋鬼子来了. — *The Japs are coming, the Japs are coming.*
国破了，家亡了, — *The nation is lost, our families scattered.*
同胞们快起来，拿起刀，拿起枪 — *Rise up, countrymen, take up arms*
打鬼子保家乡... — *To drive out the Japs and protect your homes ...*

---

13 On "lines-of-flight" see, for example, Fleming 2002 and Roach 1997. In general, the "lines-of-flight" concept offers possibilities for alternative and heretical signification. Applications of such alternatives, documented for instance by Liebes and Katz (1990), concerning the reception of the US series *Dallas* among non-US audiences and their resistance to dominant signification have informed the theory of audiences and relevant processes of reception. The idea of an ideologically and culturally passive audience, which also is important in Edward Said's study on orientalism, was shifted towards an understanding of an "active audience" and polysemy.

14 Goldblatt omits the last two lines in his translation (Mo 1994: 343–344, 1993: 342).

(Mo 1994: 52, 1993: 57).

Again some time later, we see a child goatherd, possibly the first person-narrator himself, urinating on the grave of Grandmother Dai while singing a third variant of the song:

高粱红了,	*The sorghum is red,*
日本来了.	*The Japanese are coming.*
同胞们准备好,	*Compatriots, get ready,*
开枪开炮.	*Fire your rifles and cannons (Mo 1994: 2, 1993: 4).*

The repeated phrases allow the three songs to be interpreted as variations on the topic of nationalism and resistance. The changes elucidate developments in national rhetoric and national consciousness. In a very emotional and direct manner, the first song offers the reason for resistance, the motifs of protecting the homeland, and of immediate revenge. The national element is conceptualized as a society of victims, directly and immediately defending themselves. Calling the Japanese aggressors "devils" highlights horror and contempt and is quite common in Chinese texts describing the time of the anti-Japanese war, yet it also. In an interview, Mo Yan emphasized his mistrust of the idealization of the resistance by the CCP propaganda and stated that "most peasants did not have the awareness to resist the Japanese. [...] They only wanted to have a peaceful life. So to depict a peasant standing up to fight the Japanese, the rape scene was an artistic necessity" (Leung 1994: 150).

In the middle version, the detailed description of Japanese atrocities is omitted as well as the motif of revenge. Instead, the composition is more even in its poetic form. The song is now turned into a revolutionary tool that does not express the same level of horror and indignation. It contains an ideological component, and therefore an intellectual transition as well as a form of alienation.

The last version substitutes "devil" with the term "Japanese" (in fact, only *Riben* 日本 which is, literally, Japan). The analogy of "Fire your rifles and cannons" with the urinating boy turns the song of resistance into an empty signifier showing a folksy and propagandistic historical narrative initiated and employed by the CCP. Mo Yan rejects the notion of the Chinese populace as a unity in resistance – the protagonists fight against the Japanese as well as against Chinese nationalist and communist troops – and reveals it as a propagandistic (mis-) use of the national memory. Since he constructs resistance in the exceptional heroism of the archaic individual, memory in his view is distorted by the official discourse instead of being properly celebrated.

In the novel, this development from spontaneous and immediate resistance to the ideologically motivated attempt to monopolize resistance and finally to reconstruct resistance as an empty signifier of history is presented in reverse temporal order. The way forward in the text is transferred into a way back into history plus a way into identity. The growing layers of alienation covering the spontaneous and direct resistance are removed one by one. The audience is thus guided to a vision of the original archaic human being: victimized, yet legitimized in his spontaneous, immediate actions, unfiltered by processes of civic sublimation. This archaic mode exclusively symbolises the existence and behavior of heroes. The layers of civilization are deconstructed. The earliest version transports an outcry following the Japanese slaughter in a very unsublime manner. It is characterized by mourning, sorrow, rage, and an unfiltered desire for revenge. It emphasizes an image of uncontrolled, yet authentic drives and motivations. Neither the second nor the third versions are attached to the hero, Yu, himself. The second revolutionary version is taught to his men. For them, resistance is not caused by authentic sorrow but by an indirect approach based on national and patriotic duties. The last version represents a complete loss of the heroic and of any authentic way of life.

The heroism transported by the characters of Yu Zhan'ao, Dai Fenglian, and – to a lesser extent – their son Douguan is part of a lost world. The first person narrator belongs to a hybrid, postmodern world and finds a way back into the non-alienated archaic cum heroic existence of his ancestors only through the typical postmodern form of action: the collection, interpretation and reconstruction of information. There is, however, no way back into this way of life for him other than through processes of construction. The ideal world of unalienated existence he reconstructs is thus instantly lost again by the very means of its achievement. Presenting parallel versions of a story in order to deconstruct a normative reading of history is an aesthetic tool that is also used in film.

Fragmentation and authenticity in Zhang Yimou's *Hero*

Hero, released in 2002, can be regarded as a postmodern movie especially because of its modes of constructing the plot. Zhang Yimou plays with narrative elements to fragmentize historical truth. The plot is told in three different versions, thus seemingly rejecting the notion of a legitimate "master narrative." During an audience with King Zheng of Qin, later known as Qin Shi Huangdi, the martial arts master Nameless (*Wuming* 无名), whose initial aim is to assassinate the king, tells him the story of how he succeeded in killing three other famous assassins. He brought their weapons as evidence and was thus granted the privilege of approaching the king up to a distance of ten paces, which he regards as near enough to carry out his attempt on the king's life. He is so impressed by the king's moral and intellectual qualities during their dialog that he abandons his plan and thus follows the example of Broken Sword (*Canjian* 残剑) who had been one of the three other assassins and who came close to killing the king three years before. The movie emphasizes the subordination of formerly independent and free characters under the regime of the idea of *tianxia* 天下 (all under heaven) which represents a higher value than individual deeds or single lives (Häse 2006: 223–228).

Guo Yuelian suggests that "as a metaphor of real existence for the contemporary world, the historical movie *Hero* contains Zhang Yimou's wish to provide the world after the 9/11-incident with a highly ambitious narrative" (Guo 2003: 8). The king's notion of *tianxia* in the film is thus set out as a promising ambition of authority and authenticity unlimited in space and time. *Tianxia* becomes a modernized signifier for regaining political order in a world that noticeably falls apart; in fact, in a similar way as the central power of the Zhou reign had fallen apart into the Warring States. The combination of *tianxia* and peace (*heping* 和平) as aims of the strong ruler reflects the awareness of a defective present time.

In setting up three plot versions, Zhang also re-evaluates the traditional verdicts on Qin Shi Huangdi. The first version refers to the "master narrative" of Chinese historiography condemning the first emperor as a tyrant and destroyer of culture. He is contrasted by Nameless who refers to the meaning of music. He plays the fife-string-zither (*qin* 琴)[15] and marks himself as a man of culture (*wen* 文) and martial arts (*wu* 武) thus combining the two

[15] In the film, a seven-string zither was used (maybe erroneously), while in Qin-times usually a fife-string zither was used.

elements of Chinese statehood. The Qin-army attacks the calligraphy school and the school's head urges his frightened pupils to keep practicing their characters despite the hundreds of arrows launched by the Qin artillery. The practice of culture thus symbolises the last shelter the military cannot destroy. Rejecting this version incidentally means rejecting this projection of Qin Shi Huangdi.[16]

The second version, told by the king, makes extensive use of images of water. This seems to follow a re-adaptation of the theory of five elements, which Qin Shi Huangdi took up in a form attributed to Zou Yan (鄒衍, ca. 305–240 BC). Here, water corresponds with the Qin dynasty, with the color black (which is used as the color of the Qin-army's uniforms), and with harshness (Fung 1973: I, 169). It must be pointed out, however, that the doctrine of the five elements in the exact form of the early Qin times is not adopted here in an overall correct way. Zhang rather plays with a hybrid image of color correlations thus referring to authentic Chinese knowledge *and* to contemporary images of water (softness). It must also not be underestimated that the abundant images of water employed in this version serve aesthetic aims and address different audiences' expectations of beautiful pictures. In this version, the king imagines Nameless destroying the complete library (into which the calligraphy school of version one has been transformed) in order to demonstrate his fighting skills. This scene obviously refers to the normative historical image of Qin Shi Huangdi's burning of books, yet this connotation is contrasted by Nameless' using a teapot in the fighting scene thus setting another sign of refined culture.

The third version, again told by Nameless, takes up some motifs of the king's version. The location of the meeting of Nameless, Broken Sword, and Flying Snow (*Feixue* 飞雪) is the library again, but this time it is only partly damaged. In this sequence, Nameless again sets an emblematic sign of Chinese culture (that of calligraphy again) encoded in the brushes he throws up. This mingled third version is also the one in which Broken Sword initiates Nameless' devotion to a larger notion of *tianxia* followed by the latter's abandoning the assassination plot.

These three versions of history told one after another all encompass the same basic features: the chronological order in which Nameless gathers the weapons from the three other martial arts masters, the close relationship between Flying Snow and Broken Sword, the considerations of Nameless, Broken Sword, and Flying Snow in the latters' refuge, the ambivalent mixture of jealousy and devotion shown by Broken Sword's female student Moon (*Ruyue* 汝月), and the fight between Nameless and Flying Snow in front of the king's army. Zhang Yimou thereby elucidates that mere 'facts' alone do not form a consistent story. Instead, it is – to use a phrase by Hayden White – the 'emplotment,' here to be understood as the combination of these events with the protagonists' motifs, values, convictions, and emotions, which provides meaning to a story. Consequently, the main questions are not who and what but how and why. It is about the linkage of events in a discursive matrix and about the processes of which they are part. The outcome of the three versions –

16 The historiographical mainstream of condemning Qin Shi Huangdi as a tyrant for not meeting the Confucian standards of benevolent reign does not mean that there had been no alternative evaluations. The Ming scholar, Li Zhi 李贄 (1527-1602), for instance, criticised official historiography and presented a radical reevaluation of the biographical chapters by praising Lü Buwei 呂不韋 († 235 BC) for his moral standards and by arguing that Qin Shi Huangdi was, in fact, the only emperor who had really earned this title (Spaar 1984: 54).

Nameless delivers the three weapons to the king – is the same, but the historical narrative differs. Nameless' first version is doubted by the king precisely because he does not believe in the motifs made up by Nameless. Nameless claims that his plan to overcome Flying Snow and Broken Sword was successful because he succeeded to cause an outrage of jealousy between these two. He rejects Nameless' version because such a lack of emotional control seems unbelievable to the king, since it does not suit his experience of them both. He remembers them as martial arts masters with exceptional strength of mind and morality. Zhang Yimou installs the category of psychological plausibility as a main signifier of historical meaning. In the second version, the king constructs his own reading of the events in which devotion, mental strength, and sublimation all play an important part. In the third version, Nameless adopts another element suggested by the king: the superior morality of Flying Snow and Broken Sword. For the king (and in fact at this stage of the narrative: for the audience as well) this version ends after the death of Flying Snow and Moon's delivering her master's sword to Nameless. Only after Nameless has abandoned his assassination attempt and been executed, we do learn that Flying Snow has survived the fight in front of the army due to Nameless' unique fighting skill. This allows him to wound enemies with his sword without hitting vital organs. Until the last sequence, neither the king nor the audience know that she is still alive. When she and Broken Sword finally commit suicide,[17] history follows its own projections. Here Zhang reverses the generic order which traditionally develops from event to narrative.[18] In a postmodern framework, this hints at the emblematic and formative power that a narrative can unfold when placed at a discourse's centre of validation and legitimacy.

Both ways of fragmentation, de-spacing and de-authenticating, are employed ambiguously manner in the film. The three versions elucidate how differently a story and history can be constructed along different narrative aims. Yet, the film also refuses postmodern hybridity and delivers what can be regarded as the 'real' story from which the three versions are drawn. The third version is, in fact, mingled with a fourth which is the director's own version. The suicides of Flying Snow and Broken Sword follow Nameless' execution in terms of the chronological and the narrative order of events. Placing this final event after the execution of Nameless, and thus outside the dialogue between Nameless and the king, authenticates this version as the "real" one. Zhang's play of colors closely links the third and fourth versions and thus authenticates – of the three versions told by the protagonists – the third as nearest to "reality" and only purposely inaccurate concerning single aspects. Zhang uses color as a main aesthetic tool in his movies. Possibly most striking in this respect is his use of colored cloth (*Judou*, *The Red Lantern*, *Hero*) and the coloring of landscape (*Red Sorghum*, *Hero*). Here, both elements are employed to separate the different versions notably in the central "Flying Snow and Broken Sword" sequences. Nameless'

[17] In fact, Flying Snow urges Broken Sword into a fight after she discovered that he initiated Nameless to rethink his plan. She feels betrayed by him. In the middle of the fight Broken Sword suddenly stops defending himself, hoping that by sacrificing his life to her he might convince her of his honesty and love for her.

[18] The notion of events following their own narration resembles a "self-fulfilling prophecy." It is, however, only a modern framework in which the generic order of act and word violates fundamental discursive rules. In a premodern understanding, divination and fortune-telling are based on the assumption that a narration can precede its realisation.

first version is marked in the color red, the king's second version in blue, and Nameless' third version in white. White is also the color of the final director's version which marks it as a continuation of the third story.

The director's version serves as a master narrative and the other versions are as much alternative narratives in the postmodern sense as scheming plots employed by the protagonists to manipulate each other and the audiences. It depends on the audience's sensibility towards postmodern narrative techniques as whether they interpret the multi-version story as a signifier of a fragmented history and a self-reflective mode in the sense of Geppert or very traditionally as a stratagem in the mental combat between Nameless and the king, much in the sense of the classical text on the art of war *Sunzi bingfa* 孫子兵法 (or both).

Differently to a Western postmodern stance, these various versions of history do not represent equally valid viewpoints of history and thus do not hint at a concept of a multitude of relative and parallel "truths" in the sense that they are believed to be adequate and meaningful by different agents. In contrast, in a shift addressing a specific contemporary Chinese framework, the versions elucidate the arbitrary use of information and narratives in order to legitimize power. While Mo Yan in *Red Sorghum* has shown that the deconstruction of history as a narrative which serves the ideological aims obviously opposes the CCP's hegemonic claim to normatively interpret and narrate the world, Zhang Yimou provides his own master version and thus reduces his deconstruction to a strategy to uncover a reality that was 'only' arbitrarily distorted by individual interest and power. Thus it offers the notion of a 'true history' that can, finally, be decoded. Even more ambiguous is Zhang's notion of a strong authority possessing the legitimacy to employ violence and oppression in order to reinstall harmony and peace in the world, a role that the CCP still claims and enforces in China. The wish for strong leadership in the sense of a modernized *tianxia* can easily be attached to certain forms of neo-authoritarianism and its intellectual backing provided by modern Neo-Confucians (*dangdai xin rujia* 当代新儒家) like Du Weiming 杜維明, Yu Yingshi 余英時, or Liu Shuxian 劉述先.

The aspect of de-spacing the story is likewise ambiguous. The de-spacing of the area historically attached to the Qin dynasty is encoded in the emblematic use of places that were far beyond the grasp of Qin Shi Huangdi in Qin-times, but which today are easily recognizable signifiers of Chinese ethnic borderlands, namely the Gobi desert around Dunhuang in Xinjiang, the poplar forests (*huyang* 胡杨) in Inner Mongolia, and the lakes and forests in Jiuzhaigou on the border between Sichuan and the Tibet provinces (Xu 2007: 38–40). The movie constructs these areas as part of the world that the king will later unify, which bear a striking resemblance to the size of the area covered by the Chinese communist state today. The king's unclear answer to Nameless' question as to whether unifying the six feudal states of the Warring States would not be a sufficient aim reveals that the claim to power is unlimited. The modern notion of *tianxia* is global.

Postmodernism – sinicised cum global

Postmodernism reacts to a set of social and philosophical formations mainly established by modernity. It is closely connected to a range of other formations either emphasizing resistance or criticizing modern epistemologies of stability or dichotomies (postcolonialism, post/structuralism, gender theory, new historicism etc.). It is further enhanced by a range of processes adding to a general awareness of crisis in the West, namely globalization, limits of growth, destruction of environment, etc. Postmodernism focuses on marginalized communities and their relation to the 'mainstream' and aims at strengthening the periphery against the center. Its epistemology is primarily set up to deconstruct modern forms of essentialism and to transform them into a world of fragmentariness and hybridity.

For a Western audience sensitive towards the crisis of modernity, postmodernism offers at least theoretically the utopia of a diverse and highly self-aware society; a society in which mutual processes of constructing and oppressing the other are presumably not eliminated per se but in which everyone is offered the opportunity and the methods to successfully address and overcome these injustices caused by these very processes. In Western societies, especially those whose population is highly diverse, postmodern theory has to offer something positive: an exodus from a modernity in crisis and the establishment of a community of individuals who are free to construct and maintain their own identities and to participate in and equally contribute to a diverse society.

In many non-Western societies, the case is different, first of all, due to other histories and the often violent encounter with modernity. In the case of China, the major crisis evolving from reform policy since the 1980s challenges identities that were enforced by the CCP's propaganda machinery since the founding of the PRC. The challenges to the contemporary Chinese self are caused by planned political acts aiming not at deconstructing but at rebuilding a Chinese nation state that successfully symbolises and enacts national pride, political strength, moral firmness, social stability, and economic capability.[19]

Recalling the aims of the reform and given the CCP's level of power to implement policies and to model society, it could be concluded that the crisis in Chinese self-awareness is caused by changes which are less postmodern than modern in character. The failure of the modern socialist experiment has resulted in an attempt to implement another modernity that is already the third if the May-Fourth-Movement of 1919 is counted as the first to gain momentum in China. The attempt to simultaneously remodel state, society, ideology, and identity is further weakened by the same aspects that contribute to the Western feeling of crisis as well, namely globalization and environmental issues. Since the CCP was and is the responsible agent leading China into modernity, whatever form this may take, it is precisely the continuity of the CCP's rule that is now diminishing the ability to systematically and compulsorily enforce changes in values, policies, and identities upon the populace.

The subject of crisis is, however, categorically different from the West: in China, the mainstream society has itself lost its values and identities. It is thus the center and not the periphery that is radically devaluated. Only to a lesser extent is an awareness of fragmentation and hybridization caused by forms of resistances rooted in postmodern attitudes. This awareness is primarily caused by processes of re-implementing modernity and its forms of stability. Western postmodern theory has therefore to be de-nucleated and reshaped in order to serve the needs of the Chinese mainstream. Postmodernism thus turns into a cultural practice which seems to be – at least, when seen from a Western point of view – formulaic in many ways, but which is nonetheless not merely an empty signifier, devoid of any meaning.[20] The mode of being ripped off from essentialized notions of identity for the third time

[19] Sheldon Lu argues that "the discourse of Chinese postmodernism at the end of the twentieth century was a response to both the legacy of Western modernity and China's own modernization project" (Lu 2001: 70). A third factor has to be added: that is its also a response to Western postmodernity.

[20] It must, however, not be neglected that in many cases Western voices on postmodernism are as formulaic as Chinese ones. The reason differs from the Chinese case though. At least in academic discourses postmodern

has caused an intertwining of the categories of self-alienation and fragmentation and therefore of modern and postmodern forms of identity crisis. In China, the vision of a lost mainstream free from the notion of crisis is at stake and shall be (re-) gained through an apparatus offered by postmodernism. Thus, postmodernism promises an exodus from alienation, fragmentation and hybridity; an exodus that leads into a shared but mandatory identity placed in a fairy-like locus of an original past that never existed. This past is created as a matrix of original heritage which is practically unachievable. It is, however, different from the past related in the dominant CCP discourse, a history that is worth being lost in (post-) modernity. It determines a valuable point of departure from pre-modern, dynastic China, and thereby offers a heritage of positive identity.

Therefore, the question is not: global postmodernism in a Western sense or postmodernism 'with Chinese characteristics.' Constructing this question as a dichotomy offering only mutually exclusive options proves to be inadequate. Instead, both options are meaningful. This is precisely not to be understood as a 'middle way', since hybridity does not refer to a middle position. It hints at a necessary process of constant renegotiation and contestation. As such, it offers – though not in the liberal understanding of individual freedom – choice and constructability. Postmodernism represents a set of ideas that reacts to a growing awareness of modernity in crisis. However, the meaning and the emanations of modernity differ between cultures and nations and thus the appearance of postmodernism as a reaction differs as well. While in the West, the aim of criticizing and deconstructing typical modern hierarchies and marginalization processes might be to overcome modernity, this is not necessarily the case in China. Here, it sometimes seems as if postmodern theory is rather employed in a formulaic way to *repair* modernity. In this sense, it might be precisely the possibility to meaningfully adopt postmodernism to specific cultural and/or national modes that reveals its very globality.

References

Chen Lianjin 陈连锦 (2004) "Xin lishi xiaoshuo de houxiandai shenmei quxiang 新历史小说的后现代审美取向 [The postmodern aesthetic orientation in the new historical novel]," in *Guizhou shifan daxue xuebao (shehui kexue ban)* 贵州师范大学学报〔社会科学版〕3, pp. 90-94.

Chow, Rey (1998) "On Chineseness as a Theoretical Problem," in *boundary 2*, pp. 1-24.

Febel, Gisela (2000) "Michel Foucaults Begriffs des Archivs und das Modell des historischen Romans," in *Internationale Zeitschrift für Philosophie* 1, pp. 63-81.

Fleming, Peter (2002) "'Lines of Flight': A History of Resistance and the Thematic of Ethics, Feath and Animality," in *ephemera* 2/3, pp. 193-208.

Foucault, Michel (1999) "Space, Power and Knowledge. Interview with Paul Rabinow," in Simon During (ed.) *The Cultural Studies Reader*, 2nd edition, London: Routledge, pp. 131-141.

Fung, Yu-lan (1973) *A History of Chinese Philosophy. Vol. 1: The Period of the Philosophers (From the Beginnings to Circa 100 B.C.), Vol. 2: The Period of Classical Learning (From Second Century B.C. to the Twentieth Century A.D.)*, transl. by Derk Bodde. 2nd edition, Princeton: Princeton University Press.

Geppert, Hans Vilmar (1976) *Der ‚andere' historische Roman: Theorie und Strukturen einer diskontinuierlichen Gattung*, Tübingen: Niemeyer.

---

theory is part of the mainstream while it keeps instrumentalising the attitude of resisting the mainstream.

Guo Yuelian 郭月莲 (2003) "Lun 'Yingxiong' yu xin lishi zhuyi" 论《英雄》与新历史主义 [On 'Hero' and new historicism] in *Dianying wenxue* 电影文学 4, pp. 7-9.

Häse, Birgit (2006) "Tianxia – ‚alle unter dem Himmel'. Zur Konstruktion kultureller Identität in ausgewählten chinesischen Filmen," in Raimund T. Kolb und Martina Siebert (eds) *Über Himmel und Erde. Festschrift für Erling von Mende (Abhandlungen für die Kunde des Morgenlandes 57/3)*, Wiesbaden: Harrassowitz, pp. 209-228.

Hardtwig, Wolfgang (1990) *Geschichtskultur und Wissenschaft*, München: dtv.

Hero aka *Yingxiong* 英雄 (2002) Zhang Yimou 张艺谋 (dir), Elite Group Enterprise, Miramax Films, Edko Films, Zhang Yimou Studio Production, China Film Co-Production Corporation, SIL-Metroploe Organsiation, Beijing New Picture Film. China.

Kong, Haili (1997) "The Spirit of ‚Native Soil' in the Fictional World of Duanmu Honglian and Mo Yan," in *China Information* 11/4, pp. 58-67.

Lei Da 雷达 (2003) "Guanyu lishi xiaoshuo zhong de lishi guan" 关于历史小说中的历史观 [On the historical view in historical novels] in *Fuyin baokan ziliao, J3: Zhongguo xiandai, dangdai wenxue yanjiu* 复印报刊资料：J3，中国现代，当代文学研究 11, pp. 40-41.

Leung, Laifong (1994) *Morning Sun. Interviews with Chinese Writers of the Lost Generation*, Armonk: M.E.Sharpe.

Liao Feng 廖锋 (2004) "20 shiji lishi xiaoshuo chuangzuo guannian de yanbian" 20 世纪历史小说创作观念的演变 [Changes of the concepts of historical novel writings in the 20th century] in *Yunnan dianda xuebao* 云南电大学报 6/2, pp. 48-51.

Liebes, Tamar and Elihu Katz (1990) *The Export of Meaning. Cross Cultural Readings of Dallas*, Oxford: Oxford University Press.

Lin, Qingxin (2005) *Brushing History Against the Grain. Reading the Chinese New Historical Fiction (1986-1999)*, Hong Kong: Hong Kong University Press.

Lu, Sheldon H. (2001) *China, Transnational Visuality, Global Postmodernity*, Stanford: Stanford University Press.

Ma, Yao-woon (1975) "The Chinese Historical Novel: An Outline of Themes and Contexts," in *The Journal of Asian Studies* 34/2, pp. 277-294.

Mo Yan 莫言 (1994) *Mo Yan wenji. Juan 1: Hong gaoliang* 莫言文集。卷 1：红高粱 [The works of Mo Yan. Vol 1: Red Sorghum], Beijing: Zuojia chubanshe.

Mo, Yan (1993) *Red Sorghum*, transl. from the Chinese by Howard Goldblatt, London: Heinemann.

Peng Wenxiang 彭文祥 (2005) "Yishi xingtai lilun yu meijie chuanbo de 'zhenshixing' yanjiu 意识形态理论与媒介传播的"真实性"研究 [On authenticity in ideology and media]," in *Jiaxing xueyuan xuebao* 嘉兴学院学报 17/5, pp. 11-16.

Roach, Colleen (1997) "Cultural Imperialism and Resistance in Media Theory and Literary Theory," in *Media Culture & Society* 19/1, pp. 47-66.

Ouyang Jian 欧阳健 (2003) *Lishi xiaoshuo shi* 历史小说史 [History of the historical novel], 中国小说史丛书 Zhongguo xiaoshuo shi congshu, Hangzhou: Zhejiang guji chubanshe.

Spaar, Wilfried (1984) *Die kritische Philosophie des Li Zhi (1527–1602) und ihre politische Rezeption in der Volksrepublik China*, (Veröffentlichungen des Ostasien-Instituts der Ruhr-Universität Bochum 30), Wiesbaden: Harrassowitz.

Wang Junzhong 王俊忠 and Chen Lianjin 陈连锦 (2005) "Xin lishi xiaoshuo de houxiandai lishi guan 新历史小说的后现代历史观 [The new historical novel and postmodern historical consciousness]." in *Qinzhou shifan gaodeng zhuanke xuejiao* xuebao 钦州师范高等专科学校学报 20/2, pp. 42-44.

Wang Qifan 王启凡 and Su Feng 宿丰 (2006) "Zai chuantong yu houxiandai wenhua jian shengteng yu zhuiluo de 'xin lishi xiaoshuo' 在传统与后现代文化间升腾与坠落的"新历史小说" [Rise and fall of the 'new historical novel' between tradition and postmodern culture]," in *Neimenggu shehui kexue (hanwen ban)* 内蒙古社会科学〔汉文版〕27/1, pp. 127-129.

Widmer, Ellen and David Wang (eds) *From May Fourth to June Fourth. Fiction and Film in Twentieth-Century China*, (Harvard Contemporary China Series 9), Cambridge, Mass: Harvard University Press.

Wu Xiuming 吴秀明 (2002) "Wenhua zhuanxing yujing zhong de lishi xushi yu benti yanbian" 文化转型语境中的历史叙事与本体演变 [Shifting the narrative in historical fiction and cultural transformation] in *Zhejiang daxue xuebao (Renwen shehui kexue ban)* 浙江大学学报〔人文社会科学版〕32/1, pp. 62-68.

Xu, Gary G. (2007) *Sinascape. Contemporary Chinese Film*, Lanham: Rowman & Littlefield.

Yeh, Catherine Vance (2001) "Root Literature of the 1980s: May Fourth as a Double Burden," in Milena Dolezelova-Velingerova and Oldrich Král (eds.) *The Appropriation of Cultural Capital. China's May Fourth Project*, Cambridge, Mass.: Harvard University Asia Center, pp. 229-256.

Yeh, Ching-ying (1990) "The Reassessment of Confucianism in Contemporary Mainland Chinese Fiction," in *Issues & Studies* 26/2, pp. 103-114.

Zhang Weizhong 张卫中 (2005) "Lishi xiaoshuo de jiexian yu xin lishi xiaoshuo de guishu. Jian lun xin lishi xiaoshuo mingming de luoji yiju" 历史小说的界限与新历史小说的归属。兼论新历史小说命名的逻辑依据 [Seperating the historical novel from the new historical novel. A double discussion on logical categories in labelling the new historical novel] in *Lilun yu chuangzuo* 理论与创作 3, pp. 24-28.

Zhu Wenbin 朱文斌 and Zeng Yiguo 曾一果 (2003) "Xin lishi xiaoshuo 'xin' lun" 新历史小说"新"论 [The 'new' of the new historical novel] in *Shantou daxue xuebao* (renwen shehui kexue ban) 汕头大学学报〔人文社会科学版〕 19.4, pp. 14-20.

Martin Gieselmann

Humor, History, and Postmodernity: Exploring Contemporary Chinese Cinema

The relation between the Chinese cinema and postmodernism points back to the more general issue of China's quest for modernity. From this historical perspective, the impact of postmodernism on Chinese culture in general and on cinema in particular could be perceived as short-lived and therefore of secondary importance, but despite the brevity of the time span during which postmodernism was a significant and influential factor for Chinese film production, it has to be considered an important agent of change. This article aims to examine the historical development and relations of postmodernism and the Chinese cinema, and to discuss their relevance for contemporary Chinese film production. By doing this, the article also aims to counterbalance the commonly-held opinion that cinema is a rather underprivileged arena for the development or application of postmodernism (Welsch 2004).

Today, postmodernism is acknowledged to be a "lebensweltliches Phänomen" (Riese/ Magister 2002), that is, a phenomenon that has entered into many aspects of cultural life. Using this notion as a frame of reference, this article concentrates on aspects of postmodern aesthetic articulation in the Chinese cinema within the oeuvres of several well-known directors. Here, China is understood in the context of what has been conceptualized as "Transnational China," in our case, the three film markets of the People's Republic of China (PRC), Hong Kong and Taiwan. By selecting and examining examples from these three politically and historically specific and diverse Chinese film cultures, the understanding of postmodernism in China can be tackled more systematically and more broadly. Last but not least, tracing postmodernism in the contemporary Chinese transnational cinema might offer answers to the question as to whether there is a particular "Chinese" postmodern aesthetic at work in the cinema.

Humor as Analytical Category of Postmodernism in Chinese Cinema

Among the changes in film aesthetics most often cited by postmodernism are the mimicking and/or reinventing of existing genres; the granting of privileged treatment to nostalgia; the blurring of the boundary between high and low art; the rejecting of easy readings; and the deep distrust of any supporting ideology or belief such as that which any socially committed or political film would require. To varying degrees, all these attributes of postmodernism can be found in the Chinese cinema. However, in the course of this article, preference is given to one further characteristic of the postmodern, namely the use of humor. Humor, as such, is a surprisingly under-researched element of cinema. Although humor can be found in almost all movies, very few theoretical approaches are available for the study of these. Many of the better approaches rely on genre studies, but humor is a constituent factor of film production and reception that is not restricted to a particular genre. Rather, humor constitutes a major cultural technique, which defines the borders of a particular culture. Generally, humor is a precious source and has a widely unexplored potential to serve as a productive category for many forms of inter-cultural and trans-cultural analysis.

In postmodern cinema, humor is mainly applied in two forms: as irony and/or parody. Both forms offer the potential to blur the notions of dualistic concepts such as good/bad or

Berliner China-Hefte/Chinese History and Society 34 (2008), pp. 113-129

right/wrong. In Chinese cinema, these have been applied for a long period of time. Indeed, both the socialist film industry in the PRC and its ideological archrival – the nationalist movie production industry in Taiwan – share a preference for these dualisms. As a result, both have offered rather limited doses of humor to their audiences for a substantial period of (film) history. When, in the context of postmodernism, irony and parody were revived in the Chinese cinema, this push for differentiation was of the highest importance: filmmakers were given a powerful tool with which to challenge the dominant political beliefs and systems. In contrast to the situation in other parts of the world, postmodernism and postmodern humor meant an opportunity for Chinese intellectuals. As political control was strictly exerted in the PRC and Taiwan, and also under the only marginally more liberal political system in Hong Kong, the dominance of the "beliefs" and "truths" given out by the local authorities was able to be significantly undermined. It is for this reason that the post-socialist Chinese cinema in the PRC and the post-nationalist cinema in Taiwan can be defined precisely through their quality of poking fun at the dominant ideology.[1]

In her definition of postmodern cinema, Susan Hayward differentiated between two sets of postmodern culture, namely mainstream and oppositional (Hayward 1996: 259-272). According to Hayward, these two are characterized by different aesthetic concepts. While in mainstream cinema, postmodern culture appears as a pastiche, the oppositional cinema relies on parody. The difference between parody and pastiche is that parody innovatively subverts existing codes, while pastiche merely uses formulae without striving for innovation or change. Pastiche in principle might be humorous, for example, when offering a recombination of already existing elements – but it does not necessarily rely on humor. Elements recombined in pastiche might be recognized, but recognition is not a precondition for reception. Pastiche might therefore be understood as a technique of production rather than a means of perception. In contrast, parody works solely if the intended target – the parodied – is identified. Parody is a humorous redefinition of a given situation. In the process of reception, the audience has to be aware of the "original" that is parodied. Moreover, to fully grasp the mode of parody the recipient has to share, to some extent, the idea that this original is worth being parodied. In the context of postmodernism, parody as the subversion of existing codes might in principle be directed towards any "stable" system which is challenged, questioned or demystified – more often than not by use of humor.[2] In the Chinese cinema, the dualism of mainstream and oppositional cinema has become an issue in recent years. In the PRC, the emergence of filmmakers with a dissident image in the 1980s and the advent of the so-called underground as well as of independent filmmaking in the 1990s have counterbalanced official mainstream filmmaking for more than twenty years. In many cases, however, single films or individual filmmakers shift back and forth between support for official notions and utterances of criticism. Any final categorization therefore seems difficult to achieve, especially when looking at the overall careers of filmmakers: debates in

---

1 For definitions of postsocialism in the PRC cinema, see the studies carried out by Chris Berry (Berry 1999) and Paul Pickowicz (Pickowicz 1994). For the post-nationalist cinema in Taiwan, see the section on Taiwan cinema.

2 In a more general sense, parody did exist in the Chinese cinema before the advent of postmodernism. Depictions of foreigners or class enemies in movies of the 1950s and 1960s are but pure parody. Although this cannot be discussed at length here, the author sees a difference between the applications of parody in the earlier periods and since the 1980s. Rather than subverting existing codes, the use of parody in earlier periods established codes of reception for socialist cinema.

China and beyond show that deciding the position of a single film within a category is not an easy task. In a similar way, numerous filmmakers in Hong Kong shift from a market orientation to independent filmmaking and back, while in Taiwan serious artistic approaches that do not cater to mainstream needs meet with wide-spread disapproval. In this complex context, humor becomes another suitable category for defining the position of particular film/filmmaker between the opposing poles of mainstream and opposition.

History, Chinese Cinema and Postmodernism

Frames of reference that have been crucial for postmodernism in Western countries are not so readily applicable in China. Different economic systems and multiple layers of time and space have existed contemporaneously here. Furthermore, postmodernism has not been the only shaping factor. Looking at the construction of national identity in the PRC, for example, it is obvious that postmodernism cannot solely be defined by its opposition to modernity: it has also had to deal with the concurrent paradigms of post-revolution and post-socialism.[3] In Hong Kong, postcolonialism served as a major frame of reference for the discussion of postmodernity, and in Taiwan, the advent of postmodernism coincided with the fundamental questioning of a coherent national ideology. The conditions for post-modernism in China differed in general from those in the West, but there were also differences in the conditions in Taiwan, Hong Kong and the PRC.

This had implications in many fields including history and, more specifically, the treatment of history in the Chinese cinema. As a main agent for the construction of a national identity, history is a major asset for establishing a common ideological basis and the Chinese cinema has played a crucial role in this context. This holds true for the PRC as well as for a pre-1997 Hong Kong identity or the "Republic of China on Taiwan" ideology. In all these cases, the depiction of central historical events as a basis for common national identity contributed to a specifically Chinese form of identity. Any derivation of this identity was for a long time considered to threaten the logic of a dominant historical truth. Even when a shift towards differentiation and a more "objective" depiction of history became visible (as, for example, in the case of a comparison of different cinematic versions of the Opium War) a serious, that is, non-humorous approach was adopted for the treatment of historical events (Gieselmann 2007). Insisting on the serious treatment of history seems to imply that the moment humor takes over, the tight overall approach of a common ideology based on a rigidly defined interpretation of history is in danger. Thus a close look at the interconnection of humor, history and cinema reveals to what extent a given ideology is able to deal with this challenge. Looking at humor, the depiction of history and the cinema might therefore well describe a field within which the rise and impact of postmodernism in the Chinese cinema can be categorized.

Struggling with Nostalgia in Taiwan: Lai Shengchuan and Edward Yang

Taiwan cinema and postmodernism have been explored by Frederic Jameson who brought *Terrorizers/Kongbu fenzi* (Edward Yang, 1986) into the canon of postmodern Chinese cinema. Jameson was interested in the film because it was a perfect example of the spatial dislocation that postmodernism stood for at that time – although, as he carefully pointed

[3] Other dimensions have also been mentioned. See, for example, Sheldon Lu: Lu adds (amongst others) liberalism, the humanist spirit and the New Left as major trends in intellectual topics of debate (Lu 2001: 84).

out, one with Taiwanese characteristics (Jameson 1994). In recent years, many authors have criticised this article, including Sheldon Lu, Emilie Yeh, David Desser and Yvonne Chang (Lu 1997: 14; Yeh/Desser 2005: 127-131, and Chang 2005). While the dispute about Jameson probably reveals many of the problems related to the difficult and different applications of postmodernism in East and West, the details of this dispute will not be dealt with here. Within the analytical framework of this article, *Terrorizers* is of secondary importance: although the historical reading follows along postmodern critical lines, the film lacks the second category of humor, which was clearly not a basic ingredient in the conception of *Terrorizers*. It was only in Yang's later films in the mid-1990s that humor became more significant. It came in the form of an ironical comment regarding Western influence in Taiwan, as in *Mahjong/Majiang* (1996), or in the form of irony that sometimes turned into mild sarcasm, as in Yang's exploration of the state of the art of Taiwan society and its well-educated middle-class in *Confucian Confusion/Duli shidai* (1994). The ironic tones prevailing in these two films were well suited to the condition of postmodernism. At the same time, the exposure of "modern" life styles through ironic commentaries revealed that the director was aware of the fact that Taiwan had not travelled far on the road to modernity. Beneath the surface of economic success, Yang found a lot of problems in Taiwan. His films diffuse the existing beliefs (in the view of history, in the market economy, in the modern lifestyle etc.). This critical attitude was not compatible with the taste of the masses and it could, to some extent, be associated with postmodernism. At the same time, Edward Yang aimed at change and innovation in terms of content as well as aesthetics. His films carried a message and as a director, he achieved a great deal for the reputation of the Taiwan cinema.

By the time the tide of postmodernism was generally considered to have turned, Yang was employing humor much more decisively. In his last work, *A One and a Two/Yiyi* (2000), Yang depicted the midlife crisis of a Taiwanese, middle class father of a family and entrepreneur. The film reworks the agenda of a single human being into a greater spatial context. Very much like Taiwan as such the protagonist is lost between East-East (Taiwan, Japan) as well as East-West relations. The absence of nationalist rhetoric is an indication of the irrelevance of these questions concerning the existential quest to live a decent life in the 21st century. The entire film, which dwells on the situation of a small man for whom the world is too big a place to be tackled, shows a subtle use of irony. The protagonist, NJ, (played by Wu Nianzhen) is, in similar ways to Taiwan as a "nation", just too small to have a voice in the concerto of international business. Edward Yang shows a protagonist who has lost the ability to find any fun in joining in the moneymaking game and who asks, instead, what life is all about. The film reveals that Edward Yang has long left behind any "great ideas" for the future of Taiwan. He is interested in the very personal situations that tell stories of the everyday lives of everyday people. Differently to Ang Lee, whose movies dealing with Taiwan presented characters that were optimistic and going all out for success in international business, Yang remains cautious about "worldly success" within the biographies of his protagonists.

The relation between humor and history in *A One and A Two* clearly shows that parody, one of the characteristic features of postmodernist cinema, is not used in the work of Edward Yang; instead, a constant flow of irony is used to build up empathy with the main character. The anti-hero, NJ, is the cinematic proof of a line of heritage and also the overcoming of postmodernism in the oeuvre of Edward Yang. By focusing on the human side of the small-scale tragedy in modern day Taiwan, Yang moved beyond the restrictions that postmodernism would have imposed. At the same time, the film owes a debt to postmodernism because Yang uses irony to dissolve any feelings of superiority in the political, economic and moral status of Taiwan people.

Compared with Edward Yang, the Berkeley-trained film and theatre director, Lai Shengchuan, had a different approach to postmodernism. Lai built up one of the most influential theatre companies, the Performance Workshop (*biaoyan gongzuo fang*), after his return to Taiwan. In one of his earlier successful plays, Lai made extensive use of comic elements. *Peach Blossom Land/Anlian taohua yuan* from 1985 was turned into a film seven years later. It is a cleverly combined and neatly interwoven play-within-a-play in which two theatre groups struggle for one rehearsal stage. The overall title of the play consists of the two titles of the single dramas, namely, *Secret Love/Anlian* and *Peach Blossom Spring/Taohua yuan*. This collage of titles and plays offers several characteristics of postmodernism: spatial dislocation is applied in a broadly developed form because the play presents three locations at the same time which belong to different historical times: present-day Taiwan, pre-1945 Shanghai (*Secret Love*), and the mythic Peach Blossom Spring. Thus the Chinese past with a strong reference to paradise is juxtaposed with the historical and the contemporary situation of a non-unified China. Present-day Taiwan is a point of reference as it appears at two levels: at the level of the play, *Secret Love,* it represents a nostalgic glance back into the lost past (lost Mainland). By depicting this glance as nostalgic, the play makes a strong stand for a reshuffle of official GMD-ideology. The return to the Mainland is depicted as a fantasy, a dream kept up by old, tired, and homesick men (represented by Jiang Bingliu, the male leading role in *Secret Love*). At both levels of the play, the Taiwan of today is depicted as inhabited by young and energetic youth: in *Secret Love,* in the person of the nurse, and even more directly at the meta level of art-in-practice (rehearsal) with its young artists. The corresponding alter ego of Jiang Bingliu, at this level, is the director of *Secret Love.* Although the actors (and the audience) understand the sad situation of their director/Jiang Bingliu, there is a clear difference in opinion about the practical consequences in the historical situation of present-day Taiwan. All the actors – including those in the second play – differ from the director in one respect, namely, that their emotional experiences are solely linked to Taiwan. The spatial dislocation supports this stance. Although it places a Taiwan in the foreground where different locations are at work, it is pointing at the level of present-day Taiwan and thus privileges the now and then.

In *Peach Blossom Land,* the relation between humor and history is a suitable tool for analysis. As previously mentioned, the two plays are different from each other in every respect, but most importantly, in content and mode. One is tragedy, the other a comedy; one features a nostalgic Mainlander who has lost his first love; the other, a betrayed husband who flees from home only to be confronted with the very result of his escape. Interestingly, in the dramatic peak they are combined into one (comic) play. While they refer to each other, the two plays also begin to interact and establish a meta-play-level above the three levels already at work. What seems to be utter chaos finally turns into "something". In this process, "the nostalgic" (play 1) and "the traditional" (play 2) approaches for salvation in today's world both prove to be ineffective. With a clear stance in the here-and-now, Lai Shengchuan proves that looking back to indulge in private fantasies of a better world in the past as well as building up a modern state based on the concept of a "traditional China" are useless. The whole play thus counterbalances and parodies the hegemonic GMD idea of a reunited China grounded in the self-acclamation of being the true and only heir of Chinese tradition. As Jon Kowallis has pointed out, Lai Shengchuan views the question of (Taiwan) identity "from a postmodern perspective of personal past/present and self/society interplay" thus rereading history within many different layers (Kowallis 1997: 183).

These two examples show how postmodernism in the Taiwan cinema can be perceived. Humor and the reshuffling of the official view of history have joined forces to diffuse the formerly dominant historiographical and political dogmas. Both examples show that belief in modernity has been shaken or is in doubt. Edward Yang and Lai Shengchuan started their respective explorations of modern life in Taiwan with sensitivity, seriousness and the utmost caution. Both offer accounts in the present tense and they are concerned with solutions for the questions of the present. In this sense, both Yang and Lai bear the two souls of a Taiwan intellectual in their hearts: They are postmodern in the sense that it enables them to challenge and, to some extent, overcome modernity, yet at the same time they remain committed to social and political concerns and as such stay certainly un-postmodern.

Lost in the Present Tense in Hong Kong: Wong Kar-wai und Stephen Chiau

In the closing chapter of his groundbreaking study, Stephen Teo argues that the Hong Kong cinema came to an end with the rise of the postmodern cinema (Teo 1999: 243-255). Taking into account the vitality of the Hong Kong cinema the prediction of its end would seem premature. Certainly, there was a crisis in the years that Teo was referring to and this crisis brought with it profound changes in the Hong Kong film market. And Teo is right in stating that the postmodern cinema played a significant role during this period, first and foremost because it was an appropriate means of reflecting anxiety about the uncertain political future after 1997. But what did this crisis actually look like? And was it solely (or to a great extent) occupied with postmodernism?

Janice Tong conceptualized this period of Hong Kong cinema as characterized by a double haunting which was nurtured by an anxiety about the future and an obsession with the past (Tong 2003). Tong elaborates her argument by looking at the films of Wong Kar-wai which, although obviously set in present-day Hong Kong, reveal a high degree of ambivalence about the present. Several authors, such as Chris Berry, Mary Farquhar and Cui Shuqing, have argued along the same lines. They stress the fact that the Hong Kong cinema at that time expressed feelings of lost centers (Cui 2000: 61), highlighting the fact that the protagonists in many films were stuck between future and past (Berry/Farquhar 2006). Caught between the modes of time (past/future), Hong Kong cinema seemed to be especially prepared for the influence of postmodernism. But was postmodernism a dominant driving force or rather a specific characteristic of the time? Chuck Kleinhans argued that postmodernism in Hong Kong was not so much influential in the sense that it was displacing existing forms, but rather that it was transforming them. According to Kleinhans, it was one of those floating concepts that met in the mainstream Hong Kong cinema. Kleinhans concludes that "commercial culture today is not simply "postmodern" and different, but also "modern", and "realist", and especially "romantic (Kleinhans 2003: 168). Looking at the diversity of forms and formulae in Hong Kong cinema, the solution offered by Kleinhans seems to describe the relation between postmodernism and the cinema in Hong Kong very accurately, namely, as a melange of different concepts and forms of expressions. But what about other driving forces? Concerning the situation in those years, Helen Leung argued that there was a feeling of "slipping away": "*The feeling that nothing could be "held tight" characterized the political as well as the cultural imaginary of this period of transition. Yet Hong Kong cinema responded to this pervasive milieu of change and uncertainty in a uniquely indirect manner. In the most innovative films of this period, the postcolonial predicament appears at most as an undercurrent, a not-quite visible force that nonetheless animates what is amply visible on-screen: sex, romance, family conflicts, underworld heroism, teenage gangsters, period drama, martial arts legends, and absurdist humor.*" (Leung 2001: 424) Following Leung, it seems that next to postmodernism, post-colonialism matters, too. And keeping the above-cited arguments in mind, we should come to the conclusion that postmodernism was not an almighty factor in film production in Hong Kong. It corresponded with the feelings and anxieties in a particular historical situation. It seemed that filmmakers were looking for ways to escape the danger looming ahead and, at the same time, for ways to attract their audiences. They achieved these goals by referring to and reshuffling the standard modes of cinema, among them, comedy and romance. Both modes can be considered crucial for gaining an understanding the work of the Hong Kong directors presented in this article.

When it comes to comedy in the Hong Kong cinema, probably no other actor-director has made better use of absurdist humor than Stephen Chiau. "Stephen Chiau Sing-chi is the ubiquitous star of a new genre of 'nonsense comedies', one manifestation in the multi-faceted grid of the postmodern edifice" (Teo 1999: 246). According to Teo, his protagonists are heroes of irrationality and, as such, perfect expressions of postmodernism. Chiau's career took off when he tried his hand at parody: his first box office success was *All for the Winner/Du sheng* (Corey Yuen, Jeff Lau, 1990) which was a spoof of the most successful movie of the previous season, namely *God of Gamblers/Du shen* (Wong Jing, 1989). *All for the Winner* was the first of its kind as a comedy and broke box-office records. In the years after 1990, Chiau made several films per year, and most of them were extremely popular. With breathless speed, Chiau pushed film after film onto the market and film critics started to write about the Stephen Chiau phenomenon. The majority of his films have been exceptional box office successes in Hong Kong. Chiau made spoofs of every possible film format and genre, deliberately exploiting Eastern and Western sources alike. His movies have exploited James Bond movies, police films, court drama, historical tales, adventure movies and many more.

While at the visual level, spoofs are rather easy to read and decipher, the script level was a different case. To a high degree, the films were related to local language (Cantonese) as well as to the time and place of production. Cantonese plus the knowledge of everyday gossip and news from Hong Kong were essential to fully appreciate and understand the allusions and jokes. Even Hong Kongers who were temporarily on leave from the city had difficulty in catching the points that Chiau's humor referred to and similar difficulties were also encountered by audiences when Chiau's films were exported to Taiwan and the PRC. Translations into Mandarin were in many cases inadequate. The same holds true for when Chiau later tried to market his films in the West. Almost a decade after his start in Hong Kong, Chiau was directing and starring in movies, such as *Shaolin Soccer/Shaolin zuqiu* (2001) and *Kungfu Hustle/Gongfu* (2004), which he brought to North American and European audiences. By this time, he had already significantly reduced the pace of film production and the degree of local integration. Similarly to the ways in which Jackie Chan invented strategies to become global, Stephen Chiau has managed to adapt his style: although many of the jokes were not transferable, the comic substance of the later Stephen Chiau movies proved to be sound enough to appeal to audiences far away from Hong Kong.

For an analysis in the context of postmodernism and the Hong Kong cinema, it is necessary to go back to the works of Chiau from an earlier period. *God of Cookery/Shi shen* (Stephen Chiau; Lee Lik-chi, 1996) is a good case in point. Here, Chiau uses a number of established cinematic devices for parody, for example, the Eastern hero topic as it is known from martial arts films. In the dramatic climax of *God of Cookery*, there is a cookery showdown between the protagonist, the God of Cookery (Stephen Chiau) and his rival, Bull Tong (Vincent Kok). This sequence exploits the visual attraction of the Eastern hero and showdown fighting in martial arts films – but at the same time parodies it. This is achieved with the binary presentation of cinematic codes: on the one hand, both fighters present themselves in serious fighting poses, while on the other, their weapons (kitchen tools, chairs), and facial expressions (poking out their tongues at each other) counterbalance or even break the code of serious fighting. The heroic ethos is broken by the presentation of simple and childish behavior. A second set of oppositions used and parodied in the film is that of metaphysical or religious elements (a visit to a monastery; meditation practice) and the outright vulgarities used in speech. Juxtaposing the sacred and the (more than) profane is a standard practice used by Chiau, not only in this movie.

In both examples, it is the evocation of the vulgar yet all too familiar/human side of reality which challenges the artistic and fictional character of the movie. While the audience witnesses the standard procedures of film codes, there are constant reminders of ordinary life which are usually kept out of movies. Vulgarities, curses and childish behavior do not apply to the set of standard behavior of stars within a given film. It is the extended and exaggerated use of these misfits that produce the fun and define the style of Chiau. Relying on pure nonsense, these films cater to the notion of postmodernism as they create the impression that they do not take anything seriously – neither stars, nor filmmakers nor even filmmaking itself. By the time Chiau had become prominent, this approach had changed because audiences had started to take the *star*, Stephen Chiau seriously. But the initial impulse that propelled Chiau to fame was a serious non-seriousness.

The notion of non-seriousness can be traced in yet another storyline of *God of Cookery* that is not concerned with hero rivalry. The second story line is a romantic one. Throughout the major part of the film, the God of Cookery is haunted by a terribly ugly woman named Turkey (Karen Mok). He does everything he can to escape from her. Turkey is presented as having a heart of gold which makes the strong disapproval and open disgust that Chiau shows towards her seem unfair. The longer the film lasts the more empathy is directed towards Turkey. By changing a beautiful actress – as Mok is known in the public perception as a movie star outside the film – into an ugly woman uttering primitive curses, the film plays with the expectations and pre-knowledge of its audience. Mok displays her talent for comedy here, which includes terrible singing and clumsy movements. This interplay with the expectations of the audience is resolved in the last sequences of the film: Turkey is finally presented as the beautiful Karen Mok, as she is in "real life". The romantic storyline thus leads the film into a standard happy ending. The way this ending is presented shows, again, the playfulness of the film. The final part plays with, yet, at the same time, fulfils the expectation of such a happy ending. This double strategy hints at the "obvious" fact that the end (like the movie) is constructed and perfectly unreal. And there is more ambiguity about fiction/reality and film/audience at work here. "You like it? (*ni xihuan ma*)" is the last phrase of the film. These few words have a double address, as the "you" in the phrase can be understood as the protagonist as well as the single spectator. And depending on who "you" is, the object of appreciation might change: it can be the reinstalled beauty of Karen Mok or the movie as such. As the end does not make a clear decision for any one option, the reception of this last phrase sums up the overall pattern of reading the film. Non-seriousness down to the level of film genres and the conscious blurring of the final "message" is tantamount to playing seriously with codes of filmmaking. The Chiau-films work perfectly in this regard as they reshuffle existing forms and formulas – including comedy and romance – and create a unique fabric with numerous postmodern strings.

Romance of a truly different kind is at work when we turn to the movies of Wong Kar-wai. Wong was dubbed a postmodern romanticist by Stephen Teo and his romanticism can already be observed in earlier films such as *Days of Being Wild/Afei zhengzhuan* (1991). It was especially true of his movies in the 1990s and culminated in recent works, such as *In the Mood for Love/Huayang nianhua* (2000). As a prime example of postmodern romanticism, we should turn to *Chungking Express/Chongqing senlin* (1994). For Teo, this particular film was "an expression of the convergence of postmodern aesthetics and a curiously old-fashioned but not outmoded, romanticism" (Teo 1999: 196). What Teo describes here hints at the different ways in which Stephen Chiau and Wong Kar-wai treat romance. While Chiau deliberately uses romance as a given standard ingredient of filmmaking which he parodies, redefines and integrates into his non-serious cinematic universe, Wong takes romanticism much more seriously. In his cinematic approach, there is almost no protagonist who is not utterly romantic – which creates his charm for the audience and is, dramatically, often his major problem. Men as well as women are utterly romantic in Wong's films and their romanticism is obsessed with the past – in Teo's terms "curiously old-fashioned". They run after each other, or better, after the emotions they project upon each other, but their present feelings are nurtured by their past experiences. No single Chinese filmmaker has managed to bring out so well this kind of hopeless romanticism obsessed with an obscure dominance of the past. However, one element in this picture has often been overlooked. It is mostly a silent, gentle humor that constitutes the empathy directed towards the protagonists in Wong's films. By referring to the intended laughter at the absurdities of life or by creating funny solutions to deal with their romances, Wong produces a very personal form of humor.

In *Chungking Express,* humor is often developed out of one of the key dramatic ingredients, namely food. Food plays a central role in *Chungking Express* in several respects: firstly, the title points to a location that is associated with the simple meals eaten by Indian immigrants in Hong Kong. Secondly, the meeting and communication points for the male and female protagonists are located at food stalls. Wong used these locations before and he continues to demonstrate his belief in the importance of food venues in later films – the central killer scenes in *Fallen Angels/Duoluo tianshi* (1995) and the major kitchen dance in *Happy Together/Chunguang zaxie* (1997), to name just two examples. But what is unique in *Chungking Express* is the combination of food and obscure fun: several of the most poetic, most beautiful and obviously disturbing scenes are related to food. The often quoted pineapple cans with expiring dates is one of them, the ride in an ice cream van with a kidnapped family through night-time Hong Kong, another; or the massage of the dead corpse of a pig. Skillfully, the usual frames of reference are displaced and put out of order in all these sequences: food is not simply for consumption or to define the family bonds as in many other films from China. It becomes a symbol for longing (pineapple), there is a high degree of force involved (kidnapping), it is without limitation (ice cream), and, last but not least, it is charged erotically (massage). All these symbols are absurd and taken separately do not make any sense, but they reveal not so much a frightening, but rather a charming degree of obsession. Seen within the larger picture of the whole movie, they define the quality of humor that Wong Kar-wai has to offer.

While Stephen Chiau presented skillfully carved vulgarities, Wong Kar-wai's created poetic pictures. These work with banalities but hint at important layers in the characters of his protagonists. Both Wong and Chiau were successful in inventing an individual style of filmmaking that addressed a particular audience. While Chiau went for local, big audiences of mostly young recipients, Wong addresses the somewhat older art house viewers – both in China and the West. By skillfully playing with the possibilities that the medium of film has to offer, their oeuvres clearly reveal traces of postmodernism. Yet neither of the two film makers finds a way out of the postmodern stance.

Whither Postmodernism: The PRC-directors Jiang Wen and Zhang Yimou

In PRC film history, the use of humor signaled profound changes. From the 1950s until about the time when postmodernism made its entrance into China, traces of irony and/or parody were extremely rare in Chinese cinema. PRC-Cinema tended to be deadly serious and humor was – if at all – applied in simple black and white forms. More technically speaking, the cinematic code of the early PRC-cinema was based on simplicity and trying to avoid double standards. The heroes of socialist realism were those who might insert a joke in order to show their superior moral status, but they were not funny per se. Rather, humor was an additional sign of their "goodness", thus directing empathy towards them. Humor was the dividing line between good and bad in comedies such as *Li Shuangshuang* (dir.: Lu Ren, 1962) or even *Big Li, Little Li, and Old Li/Da Li, xiao Li he Lao Li* (dir.: Xie Jin, 1962) where all the central characters had the fun on their side. By directing humor towards what were, at the time, considered to be non-sensitive (*bu mingan*) topics, the overall belief system of a "good" socialism (Zhou Xing 1999: 502-506) was not challenged. In general, socialist humor in the early days of the PRC cinema has to be understood as a means of illustrating the victory over the (class) enemy. The in-between modes, such as irony or parody, were not standard tools for filmmakers in the PRC. If applied at all, they were directed towards the "outside," that is, to ridicule class enemies. The "messages" in the films had the advantage of being easy to understand and the national organs for film production and control made sure that misunderstandings and ambiguities were excluded.

By the 1980s and early 1990s, this picture had changed fundamentally. Humor was on the rise and this reflected the overall changes in society and the film industry as well. There were many prominent remakes of classical comedies from the 1930s, such as *Orphan Joins the Army/Sanmao congjun ji* (Zhang Jianya, 1993), but humor also took ambiguities into consideration and started to use its critical potential. One early result was *Black Cannon Incident/Heipao shijian* (Huang Jianxin, 1985) which included major portions of unhidden black humor. Seen from today's perspective, the film is a perfect example of the 1980s, since it questions hitherto basic beliefs in radical forms that were characteristic for the second half of the decade. That a career like Huang's was possible after 1978 shows that humor had regained considerable space for development although it lost, all too soon, its more critical potential. Other prominent directors of Huang's generation, among them Zhang Yimou, did not make use of humor in the early stages of their careers.

Zhang started his career as an underdog, and challenged the hierarchies of the post-Cultural Revolution film industry in the early 1980s in unprecedented ways. Although he was successful throughout his professional life as a trained cinematographer, actor and director, it seems that his career as a filmmaker was on the verge of extinction between 1989 and 1992. The release of his latest films was stopped or reportedly postponed and on more than one occasion, Zhang was prevented from leaving the country to promote his work. For a filmmaker who was reliant on foreign reception as Zhang was at that time, this was a dramatic situation. In the perception of the West, Zhang was a unique figure in aesthetic and political terms. Aesthetically, he was dubbed an outstanding filmmaker, who, next to Chen Kaige heralded the new Chinese cinema, often associated with the catchword, 5th Generation. Politically, he was at the same time in the West considered to be something of a dissident. It was taken for granted here that Zhang would be permanently in opposition and this perception established his reputation and support. The impression of Zhang as an oppositional filmmaker was further nurtured by the fact that, in China, his films did not have mass appeal. Known and sometimes hotly debated among Chinese intellectuals – themselves a group with a partly dissident flavor – Zhang Yimou was at this time not widely popular at home. This picture has changed significantly in recent years, as Zhang's ambition to cater to mainstream Chinese tastes cannot be overlooked. Since the second half of the 1990s, his films have become tremendous box-office successes in China and he himself is one of the few international celebrities of Mainland China. It did not come as a surprise, then, when Zhang took over the preparations for the official bid for the Olympic Games – and he has also become centrally involved in the promotion of the 2008 event. Zhang has now become a representative of official PRC culture and towards the outside world, one of the most important agents of official culture. But to criticize him for changing sides is an all too simple accusation that overlooks one principal characteristic of his outstanding career: Zhang always considered himself to be part of the cultural elite of the PRC and was consequently eager to stay within this group. He was certainly always perfectly aware of this positioning, its implications, limitations, risks and opportunities.

There were and, to some extent, still are heated debates held in China about the relevance of Zhang Yimou and his films. Especially in his earlier works, Zhang offered interpretations of Chinese history that were not in line with the mainstream agenda of historiography. He turned towards contemporary China with *The Story of Qiu Ju/Qiu Ju da guansi* (1992). This film set an example for the realistic approach that the 6th generation would explore some years later, but, more importantly, it was a critical account of the legal system and its limitations particularly in the countryside. The image of pre-Cultural Revolution China was cleverly played upon with some touches of nostalgia in *The Road Home/Wode fuqin muqin* (1999); a rather monumental depiction of 20th century China, culminating in the catastrophe of the Cultural Revolution, was offered with *To Live/Huozhe* (1994); a crucial point in Chinese history, namely the founding of the Chinese Empire under the first emperor, was restaged (and of course reinterpreted) in *Hero/Yingxiong* (2002). To sum up, Zhang Yimou used history in order to reflect critically upon the current socio-political situation of China.[4]

4 For a comparision of how different PRC-directors, including Zhang Yimou, dealt with contemporary history during the 1990s, see: "Ein Medium und die Wunden der Nation. Zur inneren Befindlichkeit des

Supporting this stance the serious tone made a lot of sense as it contributed to the attitude of an artist who was critically concerned.

In all these films mentioned above, Zhang Yimou was not, therefore, known for making use of humor. Tragedy was the basic dramatic mode that he employed during the early part of his career, worked out in the depictions of the tragic lives of women, who were strongly resisting the much too powerful male world. In 1997 and 2000, however, Zhang presented two films that had the potential to perplex his audiences and these films showed that Zhang Yimou's talent for using comedy should not be underestimated. Interestingly, these two comedies were largely overlooked in the West: in Europe, for example, where almost all Zhang Yimou's other works were in circulation, these two films only sold in Italy and Spain. *Keep Cool/You hua haohao shuo* (1997) and *Happy Times/Xingfu shiguang* (2000) were two standard comedies with ethical undertones. Zhang, with a light touch, manages to comment on contemporary China. He does not parody people or situations but rather uses humor to point out actual problems between individuals as well as within Chinese society. In its overall structure, *Happy Times* has a playful element: it is one of the few films, in the history of the cinema, which offers two endings. The purpose of these endings could roughly be described as being directed towards foreign and domestic audiences.[5] Although this was nothing new in the context of commercial filmmaking (in the Hong Kong cinema, for example, Jackie Chan has explored the production of different versions very successfully), the adaptation of the narrative ending of a film to a particular cultural environment by a filmmaker like Zhang Yimou was something special. Although this is not only a postmodern characteristic, it is a playful technique for responding to Chinese and Western audiences alike. And this element of playfulness owes a debt to postmodernity.

Zhang did not employ this technique of playing with endings to this extent in his other films, but the second comedy being considered here has something else to contribute to our discussion of postmodernism and Chinese cinema. *Keep Cool/You hua haohao shuo* (1997) is a comedy about contemporary China, which focuses on the ups and downs in life and love in the city as exemplified by two protagonists. Both protagonists are parodies of particular types of males, a petty bourgeois intellectual and a young redneck, who meet by sheer coincidence. For different reasons, they find themselves in a similar situation. They both want to find the same person in order to obtain compensation from him. Although their attempts do not meet with success, these two unequal brothers-in-arms consider and implement partly naïve, partly sophisticated strategies which trigger off numerous funny scenes. *Keep Cool* thus plays with male role types that are both unable to find solutions for their particular problem. Neither the clever, intellectual type nor the more robust and physical, rascally type has a chance against an opponent who is always invisible. Although their demands are rational, the means they employ are not. This basic dramatic construction pokes fun at the lack of ability of the male protagonists. They reshuffle the male gender roles and stake a claim for a new ethical code that is not derived from socialism.

In his earlier movies, Zhang Yimou had already made it clear that he did not go along with official policies and readings of history – but the two comedies even go one step beyond a critical re-examination. By implication, they declare that revolutionary or socialist histories are not relevant issues. Instead, Zhang goes back to a more fundamental moralistic attitude

chinesischen Kinos der 90er Jahre" (Gieselmann 2006).

5 For a detailed account and discussion of the two versions, see David Li's analysis (Li 2007).

and shows protagonists with high standards of ethics. Rather than relying on any kind of ideology, it seems necessary to remember ethical standards in order to cope with the problems of China today. Although in *Keep Cool*, the protagonist does not actually have a chance to apply ethical standards, the moral orientation is given. In neither of the films is there a collective identity, let alone an ideological message. Rather, individuals are shown struggling for their rights in what could be termed a humanist way of life.

Much has been written about the directorial debut of Jiang Wen, one of the best-known actors of his generation in China. When Jiang tried his hand at directing films, he was taking the risk of damaging his first rate reputation as an actor by achieving only second rate success as a film director. The results, however, showed that Jiang was endowed with a second above-average talent. The first two films under his direction must be considered major contributions to filmmaking in China. Both of them dealt extensively with history: *In the Heat of the Sun/Yangguang canlan de rizi* (1995) was one of the most powerful redefinitions of the cinematic memory of the Cultural Revolution and *Devils on the Doorstep/Guizi laile* (1999) tackled an even more sensitive topic, that of the Sino-Japanese war. In both cases, Jiang was trying to push beyond the limits set for the cinema by the discourse on history at the point of filming. While both films make serious comments on history, they also both rely on humor to a great extent.

In the Heat of the Sun rewrites several key issues that belong in the standard memory of the Cultural Revolution. The storyline is related from the perspective of a teenager entering adolescence. In his account of 1960s Peking, there are no mass rallies, no campaigns, no self-criticism, and no mental or physical destruction by mass interrogation. The film thus carefully avoids evoking the images which are usually presented to describe the political catastrophe that the Cultural Revolution came to mean. Instead of being described as an exceptional event, the Cultural Revolution period is presented and told as a "normal" coming of age story. From the perspective of the protagonist, this "normality" is first of all perceived as a period that is free from the presence of authorities. All the young people in the movie are completely independent, and when they fight it is not for political but for very personal reasons. *In the Heat of the Sun* thus situates the private lives of its protagonists in the calm eye of a political storm that is not visible.

Jiang thus found a means to present a very effective counter-history of those years. But he did not postulate this depiction of history as the only truth. Rather, the director skillfully played with versions of the story and competing strings of memory. In this regard, *In the Heat of the Sun* is perfectly in line with postmodernity as it does not only doubt ideology but also plays with private memories. Moreover, the playfulness of memory is paralleled with the playfulness of the protagonist. Although his memory is imperfect, contradictory and not reliable, at least when judged by the standards of objective historiography, his memories are perceived as authentic. This is mainly due to the fact that empathy is with the protagonist and one major strategy for the construction of this empathy is humor. In this respect, his name is telling: Ma Xiaojun – little soldier Ma, which is but pure irony as there is nothing at all military about him. Had his parents known what he was doing, they would have been disappointed because Ma seems to be the exact opposite of what his name seems to promise. This constructed frustration of parental expectations is in itself an ironic comment. Moreover, on many occasions, he serves to remind us of the famous monkey king, Sun Wukong, a cheeky yet intelligent and therefore widely respected figure in the canon of mythological animals. Ma Xiaojun is addressed as "monkey" by his friends and there are sequences that directly evoke parallels of him as monkey king – for example, when he climbs down the chimney and jumps out at the bottom, with his shirt and face all covered in black. His appearance and performance, at this point, use the Chinese stage convention of the monkey while the very dangerous act he has just performed points at the courageous Sun Wukong. This multilayered character construction points at the ironic potential. This, again, serves to direct empathy towards Ma Xiaojun, building up his reputation as a clever rascal in whose story we want to believe.

Devils on the Doorstep focuses on the history of the Japanese occupation, and it works very differently from Jiang's previous movie. The dramatic setting is thrilling and dangerous but, at the same time, absurd: one night, in a small village near the coast, the Chinese resistance dumps two Japanese prisoners of war on one household. The unknown guerrilla fighters say they will come to pick them up soon, but they never show up again. The villagers are afraid that they will be punished if the hostages are found and they try to find a way to get rid of them. Their attempts all fail, however, and the more desperate they become to solve the problem, the funnier the story becomes. With *Devils on the Doorstep,* Jiang Wen tapped into the terrain of official historiography again, but in this case, he chose a theme that in the PRC and Japan was loaded with prejudices that catered to the desires of the Cold War period. In films, even today, Japanese people, – and particularly Japanese soldiers – are seldom cast as anything but stereotypes of vicious and evil characters. This holds true even for more sophisticated, longer treatment of Japanese protagonists. Readjustment seems difficult for both sides and Jiang managed to go beyond stereotype depictions. *Devils on the Doorstep* achieves a more balanced view by confronting the "vicious" Japanese with the "good" Chinese: both of these are funny when they try to stick to their beliefs. In this setting, Jiang Wen – who himself plays the male lead Ma Dasan – appears like a modern Ah Q. This famous literary figure created by Lu Xun in the early 1920s, presented a stubborn peasant through whose fate the author wanted to awaken and enlighten his readership. Being a bitter satire, the story of Lu Xun ends with the death of Ah Q for reasons he does not wholly understand. The parallel to *The True Story of Ah Q* (*a q zhengzhuan*) goes so far that in *Devils on the Doorstep*, the protagonist, Ma Dasan is finally executed, too. The irony goes full circle when we consider what the meaning of the evocation of Ah Q is, namely the appeal to wake up and face reality. The film implies that this is not achieved, or not yet achieved, one must think. Watching the film, one cannot but come to the conclusion that the *spirit of Ah Q* (*a q jingsheng*) – an euphemism for ignorance in the face of reality – is exactly what Jiang Wen had in mind when he made this film about the Sino-Japanese war. Although Jiang Wen owes a debt to postmodernism here, *Devils on the Doorstep* is a clever and powerful adaptation of one of the key figures of Chinese national identity.

Conclusion

The analysis of the relation of humor, postmodernism and Chinese cinema has been conducted by looking at the œuvres of a number of individual filmmakers stemming from Taiwan (Lai Shengchuan and Edward Yang), Hong Kong (Wong Kar-wai and Stephen Chiau) and the PRC (Jiang Wen and Zhang Yimou). While other choices would have been plausible, limiting the number to six directors had several advantages: firstly, the major regions of Chinese film production were covered and thus representative insights were gained into the relation between postmodernism and (transnational) Chinese cinema. Secondly, the choice of two directors per region paved the way to an understanding of the range of options which can be used to deal with postmodernism and cinema in a particular part of China. Thirdly, the article went for a more balanced view that included mainstream popular filmmakers (Stephen Chiau and, more recently, Zhang Yimou). It continued the work of authors, such as Stephen Teo (Teo 1997) and Leo Ou-fan Lee (Lee 1993), who have already discussed popular actor-directors and postmodernism. The more up-to-date and comprehensive view of postmodernism and Chinese cinema that has been undertaken here, however, reveals that postmodernism and its heritage can be traced in many recent films, going well beyond the core period during which postmodernism was introduced to China. Humor proved to be an important analytical category that made the comparison more concise and fleshed out the differences of the application of the postmodern in the PRC, Hong Kong and Taiwan. Furthermore, a high degree of diversity has been revealed yet, at the same time, parallel developments in the application of postmodernism to Chinese cinema within transnational Chinese cinema. Thus it is possible to tackle the question of whether or not postmodernism has accomplished a "monolithic panoramic view" that has denied the diversity of cultural reality – as a critical voice once stated with regard to Peking (Dai Jinhua 2003: 159). As the article has shown, this is rather not the case at the transnational level. The given examples indicate that postmodernism can be traced in many works since the mid-1990s – even in the oeuvres of filmmakers who are, at first glance, not associated with postmodernism. Postmodernism in the examples presented here also reflects cultural diversity not only in the PRC (or Peking) but also in Hong Kong and Taiwan. On the other hand, postmodernism in contemporary Chinese cinema is but one ingredient of filmmaking. At the same time, postmodernism is preparing the ground for an evaluation of commonly held beliefs, opinions and ideologies. In this sense, the examples cited above point to the functional aspects of postmodernism that is aligned with the potential to reshuffle the given. Systematically, the combination and application of a thematic (history) and a modal (humor) thread proved to be effective to trace otherwise not such obvious notions related to the postmodern in the transnational cinematic spheres of China.

Literature

Berry, Chris (1999) *Towards a postsocialist cinema: The representation of the Cultural Revolution in films from the People's Republic of China, 1976-1981* [Ph.D. dissertation] Los Angeles: University of California.

Berry, Chris and Mary Ann Farquhar (eds) (2006) *China on Screen. Cinema and Nation*, New York: Columbia University Press.

Browne, Nick; Paul G. Pickowicz, and Esther Yau (eds) *New Chinese Cinemas: Forms, Identities, Politics*, Cambridge: Cambridge University Press 1994.

Chang, Yvonne Sung-sheng (2005) "The Terrorizers and the Great Divide in Contemporary Taiwan's Cultural Development" in Chris Berry and Lu Feiyi (eds) *Island on the Edge. Taiwan New Cinema and After*, Hong Kong: Hong Kong University Press, pp.13-26.

Chen, Xiaoming (1997) "The Mysterious Other: Postpolitics in the Narrative of Chinese Film," in Dirlik/Zhang 1997, pp. 222-238.

Cui, Shuqin (2000) "Stanley Kwan's Centre Stage: The (Im)possible Engagement between Feminism and Postmodernism" in *Cinema Journal* 39/4 (Summer 2000), pp. 60-80.

Dai Jinhua (2003) "Immediacy, Parody, and Image in the Mirror: Is There a Postmodern Scene in Beijing" in Jenny Kwok Wah Lau (ed.) *Multiple Modernities: Cinemas and Popular Media in Transcultural Asia*, Philadelphia: Temple University Press, pp.151-166.

Dirlik, Arif and Zhang Xudong (eds) (1997) *Postmodernism and China*, Durham: Duke University Press.

Gieselmann, Martin (2006) "Ein Medium und die Wunden der Nation. Zur inneren Befindlichkeit des chinesischen Kinos der 90er Jahre" in Martin Schulz and Birgit Mersmann (eds) *Kulturen des Bildes*, München: Wilhelm Fink, pp. 403-417.

Gieselmann, Martin (2007) "History Film and National Myth: The Opium War Revisited," in Andy Jackson, Michael Gibb, and Dave White (eds) *How East Asian Films Are Reshaping National Identities: Essays on the Cinema of China, Japan, South Korea, and Hong Kong*, London: Edwin Mellen Press, pp. 29-46.

Hayward, Susan (1996) *Key Concepts in Cinema Studies*, London and New York: Routledge.

Jameson, Frederic (1994) "Remapping Taipei" in Browne et al. (1994), pp. 117-150.

Kleinhans, Chuck (2003) "Terms of Transition: The Action Film, Postmodernism, and Issues of an East-West Perspective" in Jenny Kwok Wah Lau (ed.) *Multiple Modernities: Cinemas and Popular Media in Transcultural Asia*, Philadelphia: Temple University Press, pp.167-178.

Kowallis, Jon (1997) "The Diaspora in Postmodern Taiwan and Hong Kong Film: Framing Stan Lai's The Peach Blossom Land with Allen Fong's Ah Ying" in Lu (1997), pp. 169-186.

Lau, Jenny Kwok Wah (ed.) (2003) *Multiple Modernities: Cinemas and Popular Media in Transcultural Asia*, Philadelphia: Temple University Press.

Lee, Leo Ou-Fan (1994) "Two Films from Hong Kong: Parody and Allegory" in Browne (1994), pp. 202-215.

Leung, Helen Hok-sze (2001) "Queerscape in Contempory Hong Kong Cinema" in *positions* 9/2 (Fall 2001), pp. 423-447.

Li, David Leiwei (2007) "Capturing China in Globalization: The Dialectic of Autonomy and Dependency in Zhang Yimou's Cinema" in *Texas Studies in Literature and Language* 49/3 (Fall 2007), pp. 293-317.

Lu, Sheldon Hsiao-peng (ed.) (1997) *Transnational Chinese Cinemas,* Honolulu: University of Hawaii Press.

Lu, Sheldon Hsiao-peng (2001) *China, Transnational Visuality, Global Postmodernity,* Stanford: Stanford University Press.

Pickowicz, Paul (1994) "Huang Jianxin and the Notion of Postsocialism" in Browne (1994), pp.57-87.

Riese, Utz and Karl Heinz Magister (2003) "Postmoderne" in Karlheinz Barck, Martin Fontius, Dieter Schlenstedt, Burkhart Steinwachs, and Friedrich Wolfzettel (eds) *Ästhetische Grundbegriffe*, Vol. 5, Stuttgart: Metzler, pp.1-39.

Teo, Stephen (1999) *Hong Kong Cinema. The Extra Dimensions*, London: British Film Institute.

Tong, Janice (2003) "Chungking Express: Time and its Dislocation" in Chris Berry (ed.) *Chinese Films in Focus. 25 New Takes*, London: British Film Institute Publishing, pp. 47-55.

Welsch, Wolfgang (2004) "What was Post-Modernism – and what might it become?" in Ingeborg Flagge and Romana Schneider (eds) *Die Revision der Postmoderne*, Hamburg: Junius, pp.32-39.

Yeh, Emilie Yueh-yu and Darrell William Davis (eds) (2005) *Taiwan Film Directors. A Treasure Island*, New York: Columbia University Press.

Zhou Xing 周星 (2002) "Lun xin zhongguo xiju dianying de yishu bianqian" 论新中国喜剧电影的艺术变迁 [Über den künstlerischen Wandel in den Komödien des neuen

China] in: Ding Yaping 丁亚平 (ed) Bai nian zhongguo dianying lilun wenxuan 百年中国电影理论文选 [Ausgewählte Texte aus 100 Jahren chinesischer Filmtheorie], Beijing: Wenhua yishu chubanshe, pp. 499-514.

Filmtitles

A Brighter Summer's Day Gulingjie shaonian sharen shijian 牯嶺街少年殺人事件 (Edward Yang, 1991).
A One and A Two Yiyi 一一 (Edward Yang, 2000).
All For The Winner Du sheng 赌圣 (Corey Yuen /Jeff Lau, 1990).
Big Li, Little Li, and Old Li Da Li, xiao Li he Lao Li 大李小李和老李, (Xie Jin, 1962).
Back to Back, Face to Face Bei kao bei, lian dui lian 背靠背, 臉對臉 (Huang Jianxin, 1994).
Black Cannon Incident Heipao shijian 黑炮事件 (Huang Jianxin, 1985).
Chungking Express Chongqing senlin 重慶森林 (Wong Kar-wai, 1994).
Confucian Confusion Duli shidai 獨立時代 (Edward Yang, 1994).
Days of Being Wild A fei zhengzhuan 阿飛正傳 (Wong Kar-wai, 1991).
Devils on the Doorstep Guizi laile 鬼子来了 (Jiang Wen, 1999).
Eat Drink Man Woman Yinshi nannü 飲食男女 (Ang Lee, 1994).
Fallen Angels Duoluo tianshi 墮落天使 (Wong Kar-wai, 1995).
Get Up, Don't Bend Over Zhanzhilou, bie paxia 站直嘍，別趴下 (Huang Jianxin, 1992).
God of Cookery Shishen 食神 (Stephen Chiau/Lee Lik-chi, 1996).
God of Gamblers Dushen 賭神 (Wong Jing, 1989).
Happy Times Xingfu shiguang 幸福時光 (Zhang Yimou, 2000).
Happy Together Chunguang zaxie 春光乍洩 (Wong Kar-wai, 1997).
Hero Yingxiong 英雄 (Zhang Yimou, 2002).
In the Heat of the Sun Yangguang canlan de rizi 陽光燦爛的日子 (Jiang Wen, 1995).
In the Mood for Love Huayang nianhua 花樣年華 (Wong Kar-wai, 2000).
Keep Cool You hua haohao shuo 有話好好說 (Zhang Yimou, 1997).
Kungfu Hustle Gongfu 功夫 (Stephen Chiau, 2004).
Li Shuangshuang 李双双 (Lu Ren, 1962).
Mahjong Majiang 麻將 (Edward Yang, 1996).
Orphan Joins the Army Sanmao congjun ji 三毛从军记 (Zhang Jianya, 1993).
Shaolin Soccer Shaolin zuqiu 少林足球 (Lee Lik-chi/Stephen Chiau, 2001).
Surveillance Maifu 埋伏 (Huang Jianxin, 1996).
Terrorizers Kongbu fenzi 恐怖分子 (Edward Yang, 1986).
The Peach Blossom Land Anlian taohuayuan 暗恋桃花源 (Lai Shengchuan, 1992).
The Road Home Wode fuqin muqin 我的父亲母亲 (Zhang Yimou, 1999).
The Story of Qiu Ju Qiuju da guansi 秋菊打官司 (Zhang Yimou, 1992).
To Live Huozhe 活著 (Zhang Yimou, 1994).

Jens Damm

The Chinese Diasporic Cyberspace: Cultural Essentialism, Nationalism and Hybrid Identities

It is beyond dispute that, from a historical perspective, the mass media, including Chinese language newspapers, have played an important role in linking up the Chinese diaspora to the "homeland(s)," and also in fostering various identities ranging from strong Chinese nationalist sentiments to the assimilation and acculturation of Chinese migrants in various host societies (Zheng 1953, Huang 1955, Suryadinata 1971, Ng 1999, Chen 2002, Chan 2006). More recently, the new information and communication technologies, such as the Internet with its various, often interactive features, have become widely employed within the diaspora and the Chinese homelands and have changed the relations between the diaspora and the homelands and within the diaspora itself to a hitherto unknown degree. In particular, the Internet thus functions as an extension of a global network within the Chinese diaspora, offering an accelerated rate of communication and reinforcing the linkages to the homeland which have existed for centuries; it also provides unique features, which foster new diversity and hybridity within the diaspora, thus creating new structures in the globalized world of this new millennium. In analyzing these relations, a very broad definition of the Chinese diaspora and of the Chinese "homelands" should be employed, resembling, to some extent, what has been called "Greater China," "Cultural China," the "Chinese World" and the "Sinosphere" (Tu 1994, Harding 1995m Tu 1996, Meyer-Clement/Schubert 2004). Thus, Chinese "homelands" is taken to refer to the People's Republic of China (PRC) proper, Hong Kong and Macao as part of the PRC's "one country, two systems formula," and Taiwan/ROC, which until the 1990s regarded itself, from the KMT perspective, as the homeland for "all Chinese," but has, since then, started to focus more attention on the newly established Taiwanese diaspora (Meyer-Clement/Schubert 2004: 6; Damm 2007). The Chinese diaspora, then, would include various places all over the world where ethnic Chinese reside – according to any definition, be it self-perception as "Chinese from China" (*Zhongguoren* 中國人), as "ethnic Chinese residing outside China" (*huaren* 華人), as being "of Chinese descent" (*huayi* 華裔), as "nationalist Chinese outside China" (*huaqiao* 華僑), as someone with a "hyphenated" identity, such as Thai-Chinese or Asian-American with Chinese background,[1] or be it the perception of others, for example, the surrounding society, country of residence or the view of the "homelands."[2] These overseas Chinese communities / the Chinese diaspora can thus be divided into several different areas: Singapore, the only country in Southeast Asia with an ethnic Chinese majority (approximately 77 per cent ethnic Chinese); countries such as Malaysia, which have very distinctive groups of ethnic Chinese (24 per cent) and a high degree of Chinese language ability within these groups; other Southeast Asian countries, such as Thailand (14 per cent), Indonesia and the Philippines, with strong minority groups of ethnic Chinese who are almost completely assimilated and have only limited knowledge of (written) Chinese; over-

1 For problems related to the terminology, see (Ge 2001; Damm 2007: FN 1).

2 The World Huaren Federation (http://www.huaren.org) even talks about "Huaren-Governments" (PRC, ROC, Hong Kong Government, Macau Government) which is rather strange, considering that the term "*huaren*" is most frequently used to refer specifically to people who accept a third homeland as their mother country (Wang 1993).

Berliner China-Hefte/Chinese History and Society 34 (2008), pp. 130-148

seas communities found outside Southeast Asia (Pan 1999); the newly-emerged communities where the so-called new migrants (Wang 2002, Charney et al. 2003,Chan 2005) form a majority and where these migrants are supposed to show a great interest in their countries/regions of origin, particularly with regard to the PRC (Barabantseva 2004).

When referring to an increasingly fragmented globalized and transnational world, then the term "diaspora" is certainly the most helpful in describing the newly developed postmodern and hybrid Chinese cyberspace.

According to the definitions employed by the most important theorists, Stuart Hall and Paul Gilroy, "'diaspora' references a connection between groups across different nation states whose commonality derives from an original but maybe removed homeland; a new identity becomes constructed on a world scale which crosses national borders and boundaries" (Anthias 1998: 559-60), which obviously could be transferred to the world of cyberspace. Thus, unlike nationalist approaches, this concept of diaspora transcends the view of homogeneity and sameness, by stressing difference, diversity and heterogeneity: "The diaspora experience as I intend it here is defined, not by essence or purity, but by the recognition of a necessary heterogeneity and diversity; by a conception of 'identity' which lives with and through, not despite, difference; by hybridity. Diaspora identities are those which are constantly producing and reproducing themselves anew, through transformation and difference" (Hall 1993: 401-02).[3] Hu-DeHart – with reference to the Chinese diaspora in particular – even lists the characteristics of a diaspora "Tradition and modernity, localization and globalization, territorialization and deterritorialization, belonging and leaving, integration and exclusion, exile and return, sojourner and citizen, national and transnational, nation-bound and border-crossing, purity and hybridity, ethnicization and assimilation, localism and nationalism, parochialism and cosmopolitanism, displacement and integration, cooperation and competition, rigidity and flexibility" (Hu-DeHart 2005: 435). By explicitly rejecting the definition of a diaspora as dispersed worldwide communities maintaining a collective memory of the homeland (Hu-DeHart 2005: 428), she prefers a wider definition of diasporas and it could be argued that her definition of "luo di sheng gen"[4] ("growing roots where they land") (Wang 2003a: vii and 2003b, Huang 1999, Hu-DeHart 2005: 432-33) avoids any trace of essentialism and might be especially useful in the case of the Chinese diaspora which does not comprise any explicit "trauma" or a collective memory based on a collective trauma as the characteristics of any diaspora (Cohen 1997: 22). Interesting enough, the current trend in the Anglo-Saxon world of employing the concept of a transnational and non-essentialist diaspora in the popular media and particularly in the new curricula for cultural and literary studies, means that it has begun to spread from a purely academic discourse to a wider audience, has not yet gained an equivalent foothold in the Chinese language. In the Chinese world, the term "*huaqiao huaren*" meaning "nationalist Chi-

---

3 It remains unclear, however, whether a diasporic situation is always connected to global capitalism as Hu-DeHart states "modern diasporas seem to emerge, unfold, move, change, and fade within the successive modes of capitalist political economies, be they colonialism, slavery, new world plantation, free market capitalism and imperialism, state or monopoly capitalism, and currently, late capitalist or neoliberal globalization" (Hu-DeHart 2005: 435).

4 落地生根, Hu-DeHart calls it "*luo-di-sen-gen.*"

nese and ethnic Chinese" is still employed in a collective and rather essentialized sense[5]. Occasionally, however, *lisan* 離散 (be away from home + scattered) is used (Liao 2003), that is, "Chinese diaspora" is equated to "group of ethnic Chinese being away from home and scattered" 華人離散社群 (Cai 2006)[6]. In this context, Cai Sulong relates the term *lisan* to new forms of globalization and the increasingly important "net society" (*wangluo shehui* 網絡社會) which has come into existence during recent decades. Unlike Hu-DeHart, however, Cai links the new term *lisan* and its postmodern interpretation to the emergence of a new group of migrants who are usually well-educated and members of the middle class, but who - unlike the classic Jewish Diaspora - still have strong connections with the (existing and prospering) homeland (that is the PRC) in terms of private connections, business links and academic links (Cai 2006).

In my analysis, a differentiation is also made between the so-called "old diaspora," that is, the diaspora formed between 1850 and 1930, when (under the colonial system which existed at that time) the largest number of Chinese left China and moved mostly to Southeast Asia (McKeown 2004; Damm/Gransow 2007). The "new diaspora" was born when the PRC opened its doors after 1978 and an increasing number of new migrants, often better-educated, began to move to Anglo-Saxon countries (United States, Canada, Australia), Europe, and even to Singapore, where a small number of highly educated Chinese was once more allowed to settle; this new "PRC diaspora" was accompanied by economic globalization which led to another boom in re-migration, with ethnic Chinese also moving from Taiwan and Southeast Asia to North America and Australia, so that the large Chinese diaspora today is not composed of members deriving from only one place of origin – remigration has become very common in recent decades and people who might identify themselves or might be perceived by others as members of the Chinese diaspora could have originated from many other places, such as Taiwan, Hong Kong Singapore, Indonesia and Thailand, or Cuba, Peru, Jamaica or Guyana (Hu-DeHart 2005: 434). This new diaspora is shaped by fluidity and steady changes, particularly with regard to the new "elite migration," which has been described by Aihwa Ong and Donald Nonini as being composed of "astronaut migrants," who are never really "at home" anywhere but are able to switch easily from China, Hong Kong and Bangkok to New York and London, while their families are also often dispersed, for example, when the children are sent to North America to take advantage of the superior education system there (Ong/Nonini 1997). That is to say, the Chinese diaspora itself experienced drastic changes after the 1980s, within the new era of globalization, even before the arrival of the new information and communication technologies.

Regarding the Chinese cyberspaces in the homelands, Taiwan, Hong Kong and Macao are – to varying degrees – forerunners in the new information and communication technologies. But also in the PRC, the places of origin of the "old migrations" (the old *qiaoxiang* 僑

5 A Google search with only simplified Chinese provides 2,400,000 hits, and a CAJ search, 2648 hits, for *huaqiao huaren*, but only 234 hits in Google, and 3 in CAJ for 華人離散 (other terms occasionally found are 海外散居 meaning "scattered residences of overseas").

6 Hu-DeHart, for example, states that "It is astounding to me that the word and concept of 'diaspora,' which until a few years ago was unknown even to many academics and which was certainly unheard of among the general reading public, has taken hold in the popular imagination. Not only in business and the arts, but on the food and culture pages, as well as plastered frequently across the national and international sections of major purveyors of news and opinions … the word or idea of 'diaspora' has become almost commonplace." (Hu-DeHart 2005: 429)

鄉 in Guangdong, Fujian and Wenzhou) today belong to the better developed coastal regions. New migrants, often highly educated people from Beijing, Shanghai, Tianjin and Canton have grown up using the new information and communication technologies and their "computer literacy" functions as a plus for the green-card screening processes in the new host countries. While some of the "old diaspora" still reside in places where the new information and communication technologies are not easily accessible, the new migrants have moved to the "most wired places on earth," so that continuous connections with the "homelands" are guaranteed. The average user rate varies from almost 70 per cent in Hong Kong, 60 per cent in Taiwan, and 40 per cent in Macao down to only 10 per cent in the PRC[7]. In addition, millions of Chinese-speaking users access the Net outside the areas mentioned. Nevertheless, a huge digital gap still exists between, for example, Asian Americans who are the most wired people in the United States[8] and the ethnic Chinese in Singapore and urban Malaysia; a similar divide can be observed between the ethnic Chinese in Vietnam, where the number of users has increased exponentially [9] in recent years, and the ethnic Chinese living in Burma, Laos and Cambodia, which are among the few remaining countries in Southeast Asia with limited and restricted access to the Internet and with an Internet penetration rate of approximately one per cent.[10] Thus, the many features of the Internet are employed in various ways by the diaspora: websites are offered by diasporic institutions, overseas Chinese organizations, and academia; various news/press organs have developed into online news portals; the Web 2.0 provides specific Internet forums, Bulletin Board Systems (BBSs), online chats and self-produced videos and clips from TV shows and films.

In the following paper, the various developments within the Chinese diasporic cyberspace will be analyzed, first of all, by taking a close look at the academic research and research institutions which are dealing with these issues, particularly when they are available online and thus themselves form part of the Chinese diasporic cyberspace; secondly, by presenting a brief overview of the state of the field with regard to research on the specific topics; thirdly, by examining the nationalist Chinese diasporic cyberspace, which, in some ways, interrelates with a more essentialist version of Chinese culture; fourthly, by studying the diaspora and hybridity through postmodern approaches which build on current examples derived from the Web 2.0. In the conclusion, it will be shown that the seemingly contradictory developments can be described as signifiers of an increasingly fragmented globalized world, in which a global, postmodern, and hybrid diasporic Chinese identity has emerged, but that due to "offline" developments and the improved information and communication technologies, the new and the old Chinese diasporas are now building links with China which can trigger new nationalistic sentiments, even within this fragmented and hybrid discourse.

---

7 Http://www.internetworldstats.com/asia.htm.

8 According to a survey by the Pew Internet and American Life Project (quoted in Saunders/Ding 2006: 269-70).

9 The situation in Vietnam has changed since these observations were made by Ann Shu-ju Chiu (2005: 352); the Internet penetration rate today stands rather higher, at about 20 per cent, and is thus even higher than in China and Thailand, see http://www.vnnic.vn.

10 If not mentioned otherwise, all websites quoted were accessed on May 7, 2008.

Research on the Internet and the Chinese Diaspora: State of the Field

The relations between the Chinese diaspora and the use of the Internet have been the focus of some preliminary studies, which, however, rarely take into account the differences between the old and the new migrants and the contradiction between a global, postmodern and hybrid Chinese diaspora and a new sense of nationalism related to the "rise of the PRC" within the diaspora. Ann Shu-ju Chiu, for example, analyzes the use of the Internet by Chinese overseas organizations, pointing out that the Internet does not only accelerate "the communications between people of similar interest, [but…] also rapidly conveys the diverse ideologies of Chinese overseas establishments worldwide. This socio-technical media fosters a new communicative practice and an emerging terrain of online communities" (Chiu 2005: 344). Chiu thus employs an anthropologically inspired approach to investigate the virtual ethnography of Chinese overseas organizations. She also has a rather optimistic view of the Internet as allowing "the unprecedented flow of current information and speedy de-territorialized interactions between writers and viewers" (ibid.: 345). While her research is given substance by the great variety of examples offered, problems arise with regard to the question of how to define Chinese overseas organizations. She groups various organizations under this term; for example, when dealing with the Hakka community, she mentions the privately owned Hakka Global Network, the Huaren E-Magazine[11] published by the World Huaren Federation, a variety of academic institutions with an online presence worldwide which are carrying out research on the Hakka (to name but a few: the Hakka Research Institute of Jiaying University PRC; the Shijie Kejia Zixunwang in Meizhou, PRC; the College of Hakka Studies of National Central University, Taiwan; the International Center for Hakka Studies of National Chiao Tung University, Taiwan and the Hakka World, Taiwan) and older, more established Singapore institutions, such as the Foong Shoon Fui Kuan and the Ying Fo Fui Kun (ibid.: 346).[12] This leads to the blurring of some important differential aspects, such as, the relation between online and offline (Damm 2001); that is to say, although the above-mentioned Singaporean organizations are able to present their activities online, the question still remains as to whether they are able to reach out to a wider audience beyond their local place of operation. The Ying Fo Fui Kun (http://www.yingfofuikun.org.sg) in Singapore, for example, offers very localized services on its website, ranging from timetables, photos of recent events, a brief history of the organization, an introduction to the board members, an application form and a special log-in area reserved for members, while the US-based World Huaren Federation obviously employs ethnic, nationalist and essentialist approaches to unite "ethnic Chinese" all over the world and is particularly interested not in local, but in international politics or in politics in

11 Hakka Global Network: http://www.asiawind.com/pub/forum/fhakka/mhonarc/msg02144.html; Huaren E-Magazine: http://www.huaren.org/Text/1124691451962-7684/E-Magazine.

12 World Huaren Federation http://www.huaren.org; Hakka Global Network http://www.asiawind.com/pub/forum/fhakka/mhonarc/msg02144.html; The Hakka Research Institute of Jiaying University 嘉應大學客家研究所 http://www.jyu.edu.cn/kejia/index1/index1.htm; Shijie Kejia Zixunwang 世界客家資訊網 in Meizhou 梅州 http://www.worldhakka.org; The College of Hakka Studies of National Central University 國立中央大學客家學院 http://hakka.ncu.edu.tw/Hakka; The International Center for Hakka Studies of National Chiao Tung University 國立交通大學國際客家研究中心 http://hakka.nctu.edu.tw/Hakka-A-webpage/hakkacenter_A_001.php; The Hakka World 客家世界網 http://www.hakkaworld.com.tw; Foong Shoon Fui Kuan 豐順會館 http://www.sfcca.org.sg/foongshoonclan; Ying Fo Fui Kun 應和會館 http://www.yingfofuikun.org.sg.

various regions outside its location (Ong 2003, 2005). It is clearly essential to take into account the different organizational structures which are behind the researched websites, for example, academic organizations, traditional *huiguan* 會館 (native place organizations, especially in Southeast Asia), online newspapers, and privately owned websites.[13]

An extensive database presenting examples of websites related to the Chinese diaspora and some preliminary research results has been compiled by Vincent D. Pollard (Pollard 2007; Pollard 2008) as part of the Chinese WWW Virtual Library and arranged in geographical regions, such as Southeast Asia, Japan, Asia-Pacific, S. Pacific Islands, Hawai'i, Canada, United States, Latin America, Europe, and Africa; there is also a specially designated "transregional" section. According to this author, the database "consists of detailed entries and links to an experts' sample of 124 websites" which "share and discuss the experience and influence of immigrant and post-immigrant Chinese diaspora and transnational communities" (Pollard 2008). The websites in the database use various languages in addition to Chinese, such as, English, Bahasa, Japanese, Filipino/Tagalog, French, Spanish, German, Dutch, Polish and Hungarian and cover the following subjects: "overseas Chinese social services; newspapers, TV stations; youth, women, clan, family; preserving community traditions, history; business networks, professional associations; political advocacy, anti-discrimination struggles; and philosophy, religion, health, self-cultivation, education and fine arts" (Pollard 2008). Pollard's project thus refers to the "online presence of Chinese diaspora," but fails to provide a satisfactory explanation for his choice of certain Chinese diaspora websites, stating only "details aside, maintaining or claiming Chinese identity of some sort is a common underlying theme" (Pollard 2007: 142).

Guobin Yang (Yang 2003), despite the title of his article, "The Internet and the Rise of a Transnational Cultural Sphere," is more interested in the question of a Habermas-inspired public sphere within the PRC which is linked and related, via various networks, to a transnational operating Chinese cyberspace. His definition of a cultural sphere is influenced by Tu Weiming's concept of a "Cultural China" (Tu 1994).[14] Yang focuses on BBSs, including their usage in China (PRC) and in North America. In fact, his "transnational public sphere" resembles a broad definition of an "open space for communication" (Yang 2003: 470). As many researchers have found when carrying out research into the Internet and interconnected networks, solid empirical data is hard to come by and for this reason, Yang employs "participative observation in an ethnographic inspired field work" (Yang

[13] Online newspapers also play also an important role, since regional Chinese language newspapers are now usually accessible in China, while at the same time, Chinese newspapers are available in the diaspora (leaving aside the often discussed question of censorship: in general, explicitly anti-PRC newspapers and websites, such as the Epoch Times http://www.epochtimes.de/ and Tang Dynasty TV http://www.ntdtv.com/ are not accessible in China and nor are most of the Taiwanese news websites). In addition, there are the websites of localized political Chinese organizations, such as the Malaysian Chinese Organization, a political party in Malaysia (http://www.mca.org.my), which provides a very interesting example of a multiethnic policy, unique in the case of Malaysia. Another interesting area of research could include the various web-sites of the Chinese Chambers of Commerce, such as the Singapore Chinese Chamber of Commerce, http://english.sccci.org.sg/ and the Thai-Chinese Chamber of Commerce, www.thaiccc.or.th.

[14] Tu Wei-ming has described "Cultural China," as an emergent cultural space produced through the interaction of three symbolic universes: societies with ethnic Chinese majorities (China, Taiwan, Hong Kong, and Singapore), diasporic Chinese communities, as well as non-Chinese individuals who interact with the idea of "China" (Tu 1994).

2003: 471). Regarding language, he restricts his research to the Chinese language sites often provided by the big commercial portals (such as SINA, Sohu, Netease, Yahoo) which offer different portals for various Chinese regions including North America; thus Guobin Yang completely omits the large non-Chinese diasporic cyberspace.

Other researchers deal with local studies on the use of the Internet by the Chinese diaspora: Chen Wenhong (Chen 2005/2006), for example, analyzes Chinese language websites in Canada with the aim of tracing transnational entrepreneurship within the Chinese diaspora and between the Chinese diaspora and China, Taiwan and Hong Kong. "The Internet is critical to entrepreneurship. However, [...] the Internet is not a silver bullet that can solve all problems... [...] While it creates new social practices, the online and the offline are intertwined with each other. Cyberspace is not an isolated space separated from real life" (Chen 2005/2006: 13). Eugenia Siapera (Siapera 2006) in "Multiculturalism Online: The Internet and the Dilemmas of Multicultural Politics" focuses on minority communities in the UK and their Internet presence, including the Chinese diaspora. This research draws on more normative positions vis-à-vis multiculturalism in the works of Charles Taylor, Jürgen Habermas, Jeremy Waldron and Nancy Fraser. In her research, she deals with the question of whether their websites are directed towards a general audience or to a specific community, and also with the question of whether news from the homeland is included. She concludes: "It seems that in their quest to preserve and highlight their cultural uniqueness, these websites have fallen prey to essentialistic identity formation processes" (Siapera 2006: 17).

In a research project which includes an extensive content analysis on British Chinese websites, David Parker and Miri Song argue that "these new communicative practices are best understood through a reworking of the social capital problematic" (Parker and Song 2006: 178). They first of all see networking and bonding taking place which leads to the establishment of social capital within the groups involved, but "judgment on the social capital consequences of Internet interactions must await a longer-term assessment of whether British Chinese institutions emerge to engage with the wider polity" (Parker/Song 2006: 178).[15]

From Essentialist to Nationalist Approaches

A closer look at overseas Chinese websites – taking Pollard's database as a main source – reveals that many of the diasporic websites belong to the categories of "essentialist websites" which stress the essential/eternal/unchanging nature of Chinese culture. This view is often related to the large number of academic websites and specific museums dealing with overseas Chinese and the Chinese diaspora – these websites are mostly related to "offline" research institutes and situated in China, Hong Kong, Taiwan, Southeast Asia, Australia, North America and Europe. There is a digital gap, that is, many of the PRC research insti-

---

[15] The number of specific articles dealing the specific use of the Internet and the Taiwanese diaspora and a Taiwanese identity are very limited, On the other hand, there are quite a number of online articles which deal with questions related to Taiwanese identity and consciousness; Yu Jung-hui (2007), for example, mentions the importance of the Internet and blogs for raising awareness of this identity. For related articles dealing in general with Taiwanese nationalism and which also use the Internet to spread their argumentation, see Shi 1999, Chiu 2007, Su 2007. Cai Mingzhe (2004) examines the characteristics of cyberspace in the light of post-structuralism, contemplating the effect of new information technology in the "Electronic Era" with specific regard to curricula and learning.

tutes do not have their own web presence, while especially North America, Singapore and most of the time, Taiwan, offer fairly comprehensive websites.[16]

Chinese research institute websites focus in general heavily on the relation between overseas Chinese and China; for example, the Center for Overseas Chinese at the Jinan University (http://hqhr.jnu.edu.cn) is particularly interested in the successes of overseas Chinese worldwide and in the links with overseas Chinese and China besides in providing information on academic activities. The positive image of overseas Chinese is shown by sections with headings offering, for example, an "overview of overseas Chinese in China," an "overview of overseas Chinese in the world besides China," "the success story of overseas Chinese," "the overseas Chinese elite achievement" the "overseas Chinese and science and technology," and a "list of Chinese businessmen." A positive image of the "overseas Chinese hometowns" is created by sections on topics such as the "charisma of overseas Chinese hometowns," an "introduction to overseas Chinese hometowns," the "culture of overseas Chinese hometowns," and the "overseas Chinese donation." There are also links to other researchers, but the links refer to other institutes and scholars within the PRC only: "overseas Chinese studies," "academic activities," "academic services," "research institutions," and "scholars' directory." Others, such as the Center for the Research on Overseas Chinese at Zhejiang Normal University (浙江師大華僑華人研究中心), are interested in the "the characteristics of overseas Chinese originally coming from Zhejiang" and the "the overseas Chinese policy of the province of Zhejiang" (http://rw.zjnu.net.cn/kxyj/yjjog12.htm).

The increasing number of museums world-wide which are specifically involved with Chinese diasporic themes should also be considered; some of these offer comprehensive websites with world wide access. The approaches they employ, however, differ widely and the under-representation of most PR Chinese overseas museums on the Net is striking: the Huaqiao Xiamen Museum is only briefly mentioned on the local website of the Siming district of Xiamen and the Overseas Chinese Historical Museum of China in Beijing does not possess any website at all.[17] These museums, such as the one in Xiamen, accept Chineseness as being an essential value." In this way, they differ from Southeast Asian, websites such as the one of the Chinese Heritage Centre in Singapore which emphasizes identity and Chineseness: "About the New Exhibition on 'Chinese More Or Less' […] An exhibition on Overseas Chinese Identity will be a central attraction in the Chinese Heritage Centre's newly renovated galleries… the theme of 'Chineseness' and Chinese Identity is explored and translated into visually interesting exhibits," but also deals with questions of "Self, Other Self and Other Than Chinese."[18]

---

16 A comprehensive list of academic institutions is provided at http://www.overseaschineseconfederation.org/directories/inst.php by the Dr. Shao You-Bao Overseas Chinese Documentation and Research Center at Ohio University, Athens. Just to give a brief indication of how many of these academic institutes, including local societies and journals, have an online presence: according to the regions, all 8 listed institutes in Canada are online, 5 of the 42 in the United States are not online, none of the 9 listed in Cuba are online, in Taiwan 10 out of 11 are online and in China, 29 institutions are listed, but only 8 are online.

17 Huaqiao Xiamen Museum 廈門 華僑博物館 http://www.siming.gov.cn/lyjd/lyjd/t20040911_0904.htm; China's Overseas Chinese Historical Museum 中國華僑歷史博物館.

18 Http://www.chineseheritagecentre.org/exhibit.htm. An article on museums was published by Xinhua in 2006 (n.a. 2006) which focuses on the "struggle and success" of the overseas Chinese, thus omitting questions of identity and/or the contributions to host societies.

Besides these websites of overseas Chinese organizations, especially in the PRC and research institutes, many websites found outside the PRC are unique in their efforts to combine essentialist concepts of Chinese culture with hybrid and localized forms of society, culture and politics, and thus do not refer to the PRC as the sole bearer of Chinese cultural nationalism.

"Tsinoys on the Web" (http://www.tsinoy.com/), a Philippine website, is a rather interesting example because this website aims, on the one hand, to bring together "the global village of Chinese and Filipinos," but on the other, many of its so-called "main channels", such as "Roots, Chopsuey, Poetry, and Feng Shui," refer to traditional values and roots. Nevertheless, this website offers a wide range of hybrid forms, that is to say, it describes the influence of "mixed people": one article, for example, (http://www.tsinoy.com/article_item.php?articleid=749) relates the story of a man named Ye, who grew up in the Philippines but then moved to the PRC and was only able to return to the Philippines in the late 1980s, after the end of the Cold War. In another article, the "Confessions of a Muslim Tsinoy,"[19] religious expectations are challenged: in the Philippines, the Chinese are assumed to be either Buddhists or Catholics and when the woman who is the main focus of the story is asked if her Tsinoy identity had any contradictions to her new faith," she describes her living in between the Muslim and Chinese world, that is, although she practices the Chinese geomancy science of feng-shui, she still has to contend with certain Chinese "superstitions." Tradition-wise, she still participates in certain Tsinoy customs, such as the celebration of the Lunar New Year but totally desists from taking part in specific Chinese rites, such as ancestor worship. A more academic analysis of the Chinese in the Philippines is also provided by Allen Chua on this website: "The Filipino-Chinese have managed to survive and adjust through the times, but to generalize the Filipino-Chinese as just one community is a horrible mistake. […]Some […] have embraced Filipino values while others are still holding on to the old tradition."[20]

To return to the question of how the relation between the "homelands" and the diaspora is described, one important feature here is "Chinese cyber nationalism," which is based on essentialist concepts of Chineseness, where Chineseness is equated with the Chinese nation. Until the 1980s, a fierce struggle raged between Beijing and Taipei (that is between the PRC and the ROC) for the loyalty of the overseas Chinese, and the mass media played an essential role in fostering a very nationalist attitude. While Taiwan, after the 1990s, showed much less interest in the overseas Chinese (focusing instead on overseas Taiwanese, see (Damm 2008 (forthcoming)), the rapid spread of "traditional" news media online changed the spatial relations between newspapers and their audience: local newspapers became available globally, and media deriving from the "homelands" (PRC, Taiwan and Hong Kong) were able to transmit to a global audience without interference from local governments who, in the past, had frequently enough blocked both PRC and Taiwan traditional news media in response to their specific political stances.[21]

---

19 Jul 13, 2007 –Ivan ManDy, http://www.tsinoy.com/article_item.php?articleid=376.

20 Http://www.tsinoy.com/article_item.php?articleid=642.

21 Just to name a few of the newspapers which are now easily available worldwide (and portals such as Yahoo, Sina, Google News, Sohu, also offer either their own news in Chinese or provide an overview of already existing news): PRC: Chinese newspapers from the PRC available online, include the People's Daily (人民日報) (http:// www.people.com.cn), the PLA Daily 解放軍報(http://www.chinamil.com.cn), the news offered by the Xinhua News Agency (新華社) (http:// www.xinhuanet.com), the Guangming Daily (光明日

The inherent features of the Internet as a borderless media, of course, also mean that "Chinese Cyber Nationalism" – the term used by Xu Wu – (Wu 2007) spreads easily from China to the diaspora. Xu Wu's ideological definition of Chinese cyber nationalism thus includes the diaspora

It [Chinese cyber nationalism] is a non-government sponsored ideology and movement that has originated, existed and developed in China's online sphere over the last decade (1994- present). It is a natural extension from China's century-long nationalism movement, but it is different from both the Chinese Communist party's (CCP) official version of patriotism and the traditional Chinese nationalism movement. Taking advantages of the online communication technology (Internet, media, online chat rooms, online forums, bulletin board systems, personal blogs, etc.), Chinese cyber nationalists have utilized the Internet as a communication center, organizational platform and execution channel to promote the nationalistic causes among Chinese people around the world (Wu 2007: 2-3).[22]

Thus, one of the most fascinating features of the Internet and its relation to the diaspora is that the Internet is a very modern – or let us say – postmodern media which offers everybody the opportunity to take part, to express opinions without regard to the physical space where people are located, and to form new identities; at the same time, however, with regard to race and ethnicity, an essentializing discourse can be observed (Kalathil 2002).[23] Not only is the news available online no longer confined within national borders and thus able to bring China closer again to the diaspora; newsgroups and chatrooms, even when

---

報) (http:// www.gmw.cn), the news from local newspapers, such as the Nanfang Daily 南方報 (http://www.nanfangdaily.com.cn), and also news offered by TV stations, including video/TV clips, such as CCTV (www.cctv.com). Taiwan: All major newspapers are freely available, including the Liberty Times (http://www.libertytimes.com), the China Times (http://chinatimes.com/), the Apple Daily (http://1-apple.com.tw) und the United Daily (http://www.udn.com). Hong Kong offers the Sing Tao Daily (http://www.singtao.com), Ming Pao Daily (http://www.mingpaonews.com) and Ta Kung Pao (only partly available as free access) (http://www.takungpao.com). Others Chinese newspapers, produced outside the "homelands," include: the Epoch Times (http:// www.epochtimes.com), the US-based World Journal (http:// www.worldjournal.com), the Singaporean Lianhe Zaobao (http://www.zaobao.com), and the specific online news dwnews (http://www.dwnews.com) and boxun (http://www.boxun.com).

22 An overseas Taiwanese nationalism can also of course be found, that is websites, where the differences between Taiwanese and Chinese are stressed, as well as the idea of uniting the Taiwanese in their fight for independence, e.g. the group http://groups.yahoo.com/group/TaiwanFocus/join. A list is provided at http://www.geocities.com/CollegePark/Union/6245/taiwan_independence_movement.html#organizations. See, also, the article on the great importance of the Internet and, in particular, blogs for the course of the WUFI World United Formosans for Independence. WUFI http://www.wufi.org.tw/net.htm also provides a list of links to other Taiwan-related sources on the Net, such as political parties, Taiwanese independence organizations, (and interestingly enough, other independence organizations related to China, such as those in Mongolia, Hong Kong and Tibet) other media, online and offline, such as newspapers, TV stations, journals and radio stations, publishing houses, and also many websites in the Taiwanese language, and a list of Taiwanese student organizations worldwide (http://www.wufi.org.tw/net.htm). Yu Jung-hui (2007) describes the importance of the Internet forum TOCL.net (TOCL, Tai Oan Chheng Lian (Taiwan Young Gun) for the Taiwanese independence movement, and stresses the easy accessibility, the low cost, and also the more recent developments which make it possible to add pictures and small movie clips to this site, as the most important features.

23 For another context, see Franklin 2003.

established within a specific region are accessible from everywhere, as Brenda Chan (Chan 2005) demonstrated in her case studies of Singaporean chatrooms and forums which had been established by new students from the PRC who had moved to Singapore. Although these chatrooms have a specific Singaporean anchor, they are visited and used by people from all over the world, including many from the PRC and the topics dealt with often include Chinese nationalism, and criticism of the loss of Chineseness within ethnic Chinese society in Singapore. Specific newsgroups also focus on Taiwanese identity and nationalism, such as iDaiwan 愛台灣論壇 http://www.idaiwan.com/ and TOCL.net 台灣青年論壇 http://tocl.hopto.org/modules/newbb/. The Taiwanese Global Alliance for Democracy and Peace (http://www.gadp.org.tw/) organizes various activities and reports online in order to raise the issue of Taiwanese consciousness and identity, for example, see the report on a festival at El Pueblo in front of LA Union Station (http://www.angelenic.com/inaugural-taiwan-festival-at-el-pueblo-this-weekend/)

One of the best known instances of Chinese online nationalism was the reaction to the anti-Chinese riots in Indonesia in 1998 (Ong 2003; Ong 2005). These events led to the worldwide mobilization of the Chinese who used the Internet to protest the riots and the following murders and rapes. Popular websites, such as the newly established World Huaren Federation (http://www.huaren.org), employed essentialist approaches, not taking into account the various identities of Indonesians of Chinese descent which were not reflected in the simplified discussions found on the Internet and which could be (Aguilar 2001: 505-12; Allen 2005; Suryadinata 2007) counter-productive for the rights of the Indonesians of Chinese descent.[24]

With regard to the topic of national identity in online discussions after the attacks of September 11th, Peter Yuen – comparing the PR Chinese and the Hong Kong discourse on this issue – concludes that the "online discourse of the Chinese nation are a modern, grassroots, transborder inflection of the traditional Chinese worldview and differ from both the state-endorsed nation of the mainland Chinese press and from the nation constructed by westernized elites privileged in the Hong Kong press" (Yuen 2003: abstract). Robert A. Saunders and Sheng Ding, in a comparative research on Chinese and Russian cyber nationalism, state: "As members of the broadly defined overseas Chinese community, these Chinese Netizens share the common characteristics of this Chinese diaspora – contributing strongly to the overseas Chinese nationalist discourse" (Saunders/Ding 2006: 270). Another discussion often found on the Internet involves the so-called support of overseas Chinese for the "unification" of Taiwan; despite the fact that many of these websites are quite obviously hosted by Chinese media and the embassies (see, for example, the "'Johannesburg Declaration' Calls on Overseas Chinese Worldwide to Promote Peaceful Reunification http://www.china-embassy.ch/eng/xwss/t138039.htm); this topic is also widely found on non-government Internet sites (Wu 2007: 130-33).[25] The Internet, however, also offers opportunities for counter-reaction by the Taiwanese, be it the various sites calling/propagating for Taiwanese independence, or be it world-wide online protests against

[24] See, also, the case of the NATO bombing of the Chinese Embassy in Belgrade which led to emotional outbursts on the WorldWideWeb (Saunders/Ding 2006: 273).

[25] See, also, Chin-fu Hung (2004) who dealt with the role of the Internet in the relations between Taipei and Beijing and arrived at the conclusion that the Internet has, to some extent, played a mediating role in improving the cross-straits-relation, mostly however, with regard to economic integration while state-to-state relations have still remained weak and the Internet has reinforced mutual distrust.

the description of Taiwan as being part of China on Google Map (see Su Bing 2007) (see also http://blog.roodo.com/lifeshot/archives/530747.html). One interesting example of the struggle between Taiwanese and Chinese nationalism fought on YouTube and other Web 2.0 applications is the case of the song "Chinese language" (*Zhongguo hua* 中國話) by the Taiwanese girls' group S.H.E.[26] which first of all triggered a long list of YouTube comments from various perspectives. The content of the song describes the growing importance of the Chinese language, claiming that it has begun to rival the use of English globally, and also emphasizes the greatness of the Chinese language. As a reaction to this song, humorous Taiwanese parodies of the song were produced, for example, the song "Taiwan language" (*Taiwan hua*), which accused S.H.E of deliberately using flattery to try to increase the sales of their songs in the PRC.[27]

Internet and Postmodern Diaspora

While topics related to essentialist concepts and even increased levels of nationalism seem likely to be found on the Chinese diasporic Internet, counter-discourses could in theory be found when taking into account the more recent "diasporic approaches," which are shifting the focus more towards globalization processes and the generally ubiquitous access to the new information and communication technologies. Thus, arguments for the emergence of a Chinese postmodern and hybrid diaspora seem plausible: "Fredric Jameson - the godfather of postmodernism (1991) - might be happy to learn that ethnography has entered cyberspace, the ultimate terrain of collapsed time and space" (Watson 2004). That is to say, both, the Internet and the diaspora are shaped by transnational, global and international social processes which are not identical but are intertwined and interrelated (Lee/Shibusawa 2005: viii). With regard to identities, it could be argued that cultural identities emerge which are fluid and without fixed boundaries and which do not represent either the total negation of the past or total assimilation within the host society; cultural identities, are thus seen as "emerging 'in transition,' drawing on different traditions and harmonizing old and new without assimilation or total loss of the past" (ibid). This can, for example be observed, in many Anglo Saxon, in particular, American-based academic websites on the Chinese/Asian diaspora. The Asian American Studies at Berkeley thus focus more on hybridity, postmodernity and new forms of Chineseness and Asianness: "Asian American Studies is dedicated to the interdisciplinary study of historical and contemporary experiences of Asian Americans in local, national, and global contexts. Students will be introduced to a broad range of theories, methods, and practical tools for critical analysis and community engagement, in order to interrogate the relationships between larger social forces and lived experiences. Courses are informed by concern for social justice and organized around such concepts as panethnicity; racialization; activism and leadership; identity and community; nationality" (http://ethnicstudies.berkeley.edu/as). When the UCLA Asian American Studies Center was founded in 1969, it even emphasized the embeddedness of the Chinese diaspora within the localized society: "The Center [...] will hopefully enrich the experience of the entire university by contributing to an understanding of the long neglected history,

26 Http://de.youtube.com/watch?v=Id8i2K_2ibU.

27 Http://de.youtube.com/watch?v=HH1ZrIrpAxI, http://de.youtube.com/watch?v=H3v6xBGo9cs, http://de.youtube.com/watch?v=fM11M4FdLcw also provide a political commentary from both sides, obviously involving not only comments from Taiwan and the PRC, but also from Chinese, either in Chinese or in English, residing in the Chinese diaspora.

rich cultural heritage, and present position of Asian Americans in our society" (http://www.aasc.ucla.edu/aboutus.htm). A similar emphasis on transnationalism and interaction – probably due to different reasons – can be found at the Center for Asia-Pacific Area Studies at the Academia Sinica in Taiwan, which does not refer specifically to the overseas Chinese, but to the "interaction of the ethnic Chinese and the local societies" (http://www.sinica.edu.tw/%7Ecapas/doc/intro-english.htm). This center is particularly well-known for supporting Taiwanese independence and for promoting the idea that Taiwan belongs more to the "Southeast Asian" sphere of *huaren*-societies than to "China."[28] Much of the research available online thus describes Taiwanese interaction with Southeast Asia ranging from a historical perspective, via the Japanese time to the more recent interaction of the so-called *Taishang* 台商, Taiwanese business people in Southeast Asia.[29]

Museums situated in the diaspora itself, however, such as, the Kobe Overseas Chinese History Museum and, in particular, many museums in the US, Australia and Canada, such as the Chinese Historical Museum in San Francisco, the Chinese-American Museum in Chicago, the San Diego Chinese Historical Museum, the Chinese American Museum in Los Angeles, the Museum of Chinese in the Americas, the Kam Wah Chung & Co. Museum, the Locke Dai Loy Museum and the Chinese Canadian Military Museum and respective museums in other places all over the world from London to the Philippines, stress the local embeddedness of the Chinese and the history of migration.[30] The Chinese Canadian Military Museum, for example, states on its website "The Chinese Canadian participation in the World Wars is largely unknown within and outside the Chinese communities yet their contribution changed the social landscape of Canada forever. […] Thus the intention is to show the participation of migrants for the host society and the shaping of a multicultural society, while usually museums in China such as the one in Xiamen accept Chineseness as being an essential value."

The case of the Hakkas provides more specific examples of these new forms of hybridity.[31] One possible representation, as mentioned before, is an essentialist representation of Hakka

---

[28] See also the website of the "Transnational Chinese, Cultural Migrations" (去國汶化華文祭) conference where many of the online articles available deal with multiculturalism and the hybrid identities of various Chinese migrants (National Chiao Tung University, 2005 http://hermes.hrc.ntu.edu.tw/csa/CSA_2005/page/agenda_list.html).

[29] Http://www.sinica.edu.tw/%7Ecapas/doc/otherprog.html.

[30] Kobe Overseas Chinese History Museum http://www16.ocn.ne.jp/~ochm1979/index1.html; Chinese Historical Museum (San Francisco) http://www.sfmuseum.org/hist1/1874.html; Chinese-American Museum of Chicago (CAMOC) http://www.ccamuseum.org/; the San Diego Chinese Historical Museum http://www.sdchm.org; the Chinese American Museum, Los Angeles, http://www.camla.org; the Museum of Chinese in the Americas http://www.mocanyc.org; the Kam Wah Chung & Co. Museum http://oregonstateparkstrust.org/OurWork/EasternOR/kamwahchung; the Locke Dai Loy Museum http://www.locketown.com/museum.htm and the Chinese Canadian Military Museum http://www.ccmms.ca.

[31] Reference in this paragraph are related to: The World Hakka General Association http://www.worldhakka.com; The Taiwanese Hakka Association of the World 客家世界網 / 世界台灣客家聯合會 http://www.hakkaworld.com.tw/THAW; The Council for Hakka Affairs, Executive Yuan 行政院客家委員會全球資訊網 http://www.hakka.gov.tw/mp.asp?mp=1; The Taipei Hakka Affairs Commission 臺北市政府客家事務委員會 http://www.hakka.taipei.gov.tw; The Kaohsiung Hakka Affairs Committee 高雄市政府客家事務委員會 http://w4.kcg.gov.tw/~chakcg; the Video clip Xue Kejia

culture and the preservation of a traditionally defined culture which is found, for example, on the websites of Hakka research institutes, on various websites on Hakka culture (see Chiu 2005), on the websites of specific Hakka organizations, such as The World Hakka General Association (Hong Kong), the Taiwanese Hakka Association of the World, and also on the governmental websites of the Council for Hakka Affairs, Executive Yuan (Taiwan) and the Hakka commissions in Taipei and Kaohsiung. The Web 2.0 (Blogs, YouTube, Forums, and BBSs) with its interactive features and the opportunities it offers for collaboration between various users,[32] however, provides new forms of representation, which show a high degree of hybridity and are implicitly directed against any essentialist understanding of Hakka culture.[33] Here Hakka ethnic identity is continuously rearticulated and the Hakka cultural, linguistic and historic heritage is experienced via new technologies. In particular, YouTube and the corresponding Chinese websites with their inbuilt inter-mediality and inter-connectivity among users are changing the articulation of identity formulation, and thus the very nature of Hakka heritage on the global stage.[34] On the Web 2.0, we found various examples, such as the "Hakka Rap" by Hsieh Hsuan-chi, which play creatively with the tradition of the Hakka, the education of the Hakka and the meaning of being a Hakka today;[35] the form of music employed, American Rap, and the spread of the song via YouTube, however, highlight the fact that the transmitted version does not equate to a repetition, or re-invention of tradition, but that a new hybrid form of celebrating cultural diversity is taking place.[36] In addition, many forums, such as the PRC based "Hakka online," the

http://www.youtube.com/watch?v=NUkasnjKaxA. Hakka online http://www.hakkaonline.com/forum/forum.php?fid=2 (CHINA); Hakka board http://60.248.11.35:8105/hakkaboard.asp (TAIWAN); Hakka Chinese Forum/Asiawind http://www.asiawind.com/forums/list.php?f=1; My Space; Hakka http://groups.myspace.com/kejiaren; Taiwan Hakka, Google groups http://groups.google.com.tw/group/Taiwan-Hakka/topics; Hakka World; Forum http://www.hakkaworld.com.tw/cuteforum/index.asp; Taiwanese Hakka http://home.i1.net/~alchu/hakka/toihakka.htm; Hakka board http://220.133.97.86:8015/hakkaboard.asp.

32 There is not yet any fixed definition of Web.20, see, for example, the long discussion on O'Reilly, What Is Web 2.0 (http://www.oreillynet.com/pub/a/oreilly/tim/news/2005/09/30/what-is-web-20.html?page=1), 2005; Wikipedia defines it as follows: "Web 2.0 is a term describing the trend in the use of World Wide Web technology and web design that aims to enhance creativity, information sharing, and, most notably, collaboration among users. These concepts have led to the development and evolution of web-based communities and hosted services, such as social-networking sites, wikis, blogs, and folksonomies. The term became notable after the first O'Reilly Media Web 2.0 conference in 2004" http://en.wikipedia.org/wiki/Web_2, accessed 9 May 2008.

33 Other approaches, which try to avoid an essentialist approach built on race and ethnicity, involve ideas of collective memory which itself is also re-articulated and shaped by various kinds of experiences. For the case of the Hakka and their use of a BBS Hakka-Dream http://www.ptt.cc/bbs/Hakka-Dream/index1.html (Liao 2007).

34 Chinese versions of YouTube are, for example, video.baidu.com, v.sohu.com 搜狐, tudou.com 土豆, video.sina.com.cn, www.56.com, v.youku.com 優酷, v.zol.com.cn ZOL, 6.cn 六間房, www.movivi.com 微視網, video.pomoho.com 爆米花.

35 For the text of the song, see http://www.hakkaonline.com/forum/viewthread.php?tid=55348 ("Grateful 谢宣圻). See also a report in the Taiwan Review, on how the singer, Hsieh Hsuan-chi, began to develop an interest in Hakka Music and the problems involved with the reception of these hybrid forms within the elder Hakka community (Cheng 2007).

36 Hsieh Hsuan-chi 谢宣圻 (Xie Xuanqi), http://www.youtube.com/watch?v=NUkasnjKaxA.

Hakka Board and the Hakka Chinese Forum at Asiawind, offer a variety of Chinese and Hakka diasporic perspectives and identities which transcend "the territorial boundedness and internally homogenizing perspective of the nation-state" (Ang 2003: 3).[37] Other examples are the Hakka groups' pages found on "MySpace," where a variety of people including those who do not claim to be Hakka, but are interested in the topic of Hakka because of their business, academic or private interests, meet regularly and exchange information.[38]

Conclusion

The period after the 1980s saw dramatic changes in the political relations between China, Taiwan and the diaspora, the acceleration of (economic) globalization processes, and the emergence of a new media, in particular, the Internet, which changed the relations between the diaspora and the homeland(s) to a hitherto unknown degree. New migration waves have been accompanied by opportunities to stay in regular contact with the homeland by email; Internet phones, news and media, wherever produced, have become globally available. A fully adequate solution could not be found to reconcile the apparently contradictory claims that while a "postnational citizenship" is said to be emerging in a globalized world (Bosniak 2000: 485), the Internet is, at the same time, fostering identities which, in the case of the Chinese, resemble the earlier *huaqiao* discourses. I would doubt, however, that the Chinese diasporic cyberspace in general is shaped as much by homogenization and a nationalistic discourse as Saunders and Ding contend "Whereas the Russians are fractured by the Web, the Chinese are growing more unified. The Internet seems to act as an agent for increasing national identity among Web-enabled Chinese in diaspora" (Saunders/Ding 2006)"

In addition, the relation between offline and online developments is still very strong as was revealed in the comparison of PRC Chinese, Taiwanese and Singaporean websites. As the case of the Hakkas has shown, the PRC diasporic cyberspace is much more a pure "online" space, while the Singaporean and Taiwanese cyberspaces often represent an extension of already existing "offline" institutions and organizations – as Saskia Sassen writes, "Digital space, whether public or private, is partly embedded in actual societal structures and power dynamics: its topography weaves in and out of non-electronic space" (Sassen 2000: 198).

Of greater importance, however, are the new and hybrid forms of identity which have come into existence through the extension of the diaspora into cyberspace: the borderless Internet helps to maintain the role of the diaspora as an ideal representation of postmodernity, as Homi Bhabha claimed. For him, the hybrid and mobile subjects of diaspora, "the transnational" (Bhabha 1994: 173) [...] are themselves the marks of a shifting boundary that alienates the frontiers of the modern nation" (Bhabha 1990: 315). In the Chinese context, Ien Ang's focus on hybridity (which she contrasts with an essentialist view of diaspora),

---

37 Hakka Chinese Forum at Asiawind http://www.asiawind.com/forums/list.php?f=1.

38 See, also, the example of the song, Negarakuku, by NameWee, a Malaysian student of Chinese origin who satirized the Malaysian National Anthem employing both Chinese (Mandarin and Taiwanese) and Malay in a famous rap found in YouTube which became famous when he was threatened by Malaysian officials because of "sedition." It is still not clear whether he will face charges when going back to Malaysia (see also http://en.wikipedia.org/wiki/Wee_Meng_Chee). Huang (Huang 2000: 4) talks about biculturality and multiculturality, for example, in the case of the Hakka, where we find Chinese, simplified and with traditional characters, in the written form, English and some Hakka. – Hakka, as a as a spoken language, is most often used in the Web 2 applications, where audio and video material is accessible.

"Hybridity is a necessary concept to hold onto in this situation because [...] it emphasizes the reality of complicated entanglement, rather than the pronouncement of absolute identity" (Ang 2003: 1),[39] also lends support to my claim that hybrid identities counteract the nationalism which can be observed on the Net.

References

Aguilar, Filomeno V. (2001) "Citizenship, Inheritance, and the Indigenizing of 'Orang Chinese' in Indonesia," in *positions* 9/3 (2001), pp. 501-533.

Allen, Pamela M. (2005) ""Deconstructing the Diaspora: The Construction of Chinese-Indonesian Identity in Post-Suharto Indonesia," *UTas ePrints.* <http://eprints.utas.edu.au/1026/1/Deconstructing_the_diaspora.pdf>, accessed 5 May 2008 (2005).

Ang, Ien (2001) *On Not Speaking Chinese: Living between Asia and the West*, London: Routledge.

Ang, Ien (2003) "Representing Social Life in a Conflictive Global World: From Diaspora to Hybridity" in *Hong Kong Journal of Sociology* 4 (2003), pp. 1-12.

Anthias, Floya (1998) "Evaluating 'Diaspora': Beyond Ethnicity?" in *Sociology* 32/3 (1998), pp. 557-580.

Barabantseva, Elena (2004) "Chinese Nation-Negotiation in the Period of Modernisation," *SEAS Electronic Working Papers.* <http://www.shef.ac.uk/content/1/c6/05/02/57/Barabantseva.pdf>, accessed 5 May 2007 2/5 (2004), pp. 1-20.

Bhabha, Homi K. (1990) "DissemiNation: Time, Narrative, and the Margins of the Modern Nation" in Homi K. Bhabha (ed.) (1990) *Nation and Narration*, London: Routledge, pp. 291-322.

Bhabha, Homi K. (1994) *The Location of Culture*, London: Routledge.

Bosniak, Linda (2000) "The State of Citizenship: Citizenship Denationalized" in *Indiana Journal of Legal Studies* 7/2 (2000), pp. 447-510.

Cai, Mingzhi 蔡明哲 (2004) "虛擬、解構與拼貼： 後結構主義的網際空間課程觀" [Virtuality, deconstrction and collage – a post-structural curriculum perspective of cyberspace], in *Zixun seehui yanjiu – Journal of Cyber Culture and Information Society* 7 (2004), pp. 147-171.

Cai, Sulong 蔡蘇龍 (2006) "全球化進程中的華人離散社群問題探討" [Chinese Diasporas in the Context of Globalization] in *Dongnanya yanjiu - Journal of Southeast Asian Researches* 5 (2006), pp. 83-87.

Chan, Brenda (2005) *The Internet and the Construction of Chinese Cultural identity: a Case Study of New Chinese Migrants in Singapore* Singapore: Nanyang Technological University.

Chan, Sucheng (2006) *Chinese American Transnationalism: The Flow of People, Resources, and Ideas Between China and America During the Exclusion Era*, Philadelphia: Temple University Press.

Charney, Michael W., Tong Chee Kiong, and Brenda S.A. Yeoh (eds) (2003) *Chinese Migrants Abroad: Cultural, Educational, and Social Dimensions of the Chinese Diaspora*, Singapore, Singapore University Press.

Chen, Shehong (2002) *Being Chinese, Becoming Chinese American*, Urbana, Chicago: University of Chicago Press.

Chen, Wenhong (2005) "The Impact of Internet Use on Transnational Entrepreneurship - The Case of Chinese Immigrants to Canada", paper presented at the annual meeting of the American Sociological Association, Philadelphia, PA, Aug 12, 2005. <http://www.allacademic.com/meta/p20011_index.html>.

Chiu, Ann Shu-ju (2005) "The Chinese Overseas Organizations on the Internet, with a Note on the Socio-Cultural Phenomena beyond the Webscape" in *Zixun seehui yanjiu – Journal of Cyber Culture and Information Society* 9 (2005), pp. 343-380.

[39] See also Ien Ang's probably best-known book dealing with hybridity *On Not Speaking Chinese: Living between Asia and the West* (Ang 2001)

Chiu, Wei-Hsin 邱偉欣 (2007) "Tan WUFI buluoge de lixiang yu shixian"談 WUFI 部落格的理想與實踐 [The theory and practice of the WUFI blogs] in *Gongheguo zazhi -The Republic 55*. <http://www.wufi.org.tw/dbsql/showrwork.php?sid=284>, accessed 18 May 2008 (2007).

Cohen, Robin (1997) *Global Diasporas: an Introduction*, Seattle: University of Washington Press.

Damm, Jens (2001) "The WorldWideWeb in China and Taiwan: The Effects of Heterogenization and Homogenization in a Glocal Discourse" in *Berliner China-Hefte / Chinese History and Society* 20 (2001), pp. 66-78.

Damm, Jens (2007) "'Overseas Chinese' and Taiwan: Unresolved Questions of Identity and Belonging" in Jens Damm (ed.) (2007) *Taiwanese Identity from Domestic, Regional and Global Perspectives (*Series: *Chinese History and Society / Berliner China-Hefte 32/2007)*, pp. 79-100.

Damm, Jens (2008 (forthcoming)) "From 'Overseas Chinese' to 'Overseas Taiwanese'" in Damm, Jens (ed.) (2008 (forthcoming)) *Taiwanese Identities*, London, New York: Routledge.

Damm, Jens and Bettina Gransow (2007) "Zwischen Kuli-Export und Business-Netzwerken. Muster interner, inter- und transnationaler chinesischer Migration seit dem 19. Jahrhundert" in Jens Damm and Bettina Gransow (eds) (2007) *Migrationen. Globale Entwicklungen seit 1850*, Wien: Mandelbaum, pp. 222-244.

Franklin, Marianne I. (2003) "I Define My Own Identity: Pacific Articulations of 'Race' and 'Culture' on the Internet" in *Ethnicities* 3/4 (2003), pp. 465-490.

Ge, Weixin 葛維新 (2001) "Huaqiao shehui de yanbian yu wenti" 華僑社會的演變與問題 [Changes and issues of the overseas Chinese societies]" in *Guojia zhengce luntan -National Policy Forum* 1/7 (2001), pp. 129-134.

Hall, Stuart (1993) "Cultural Identity and Diaspora" in Stuart Hall (ed.) (1993) *Colonial Discourse & Postcolonial Theory: A Reader*, Hemel Hempstead: Harvester Wheatsheaf, pp. 392-403.

Harding, Harry (1995) "The Concept of 'Greater China': Themes, Variations and Reservations" in Harry Harding (ed.) (1995) *Greater China: the Next Superpower?*, Oxford, New York: Oxford University Press, pp. 8-34.

Hu-DeHart, Evelyn (2005) "Afterword: Brief Meditation on Diaspora Studies" in *Modern Drama* 48/2 (2005), pp. 428-439.

Huang Kunzhang 黃昆章 (1999) "Cong luoye dao shenggen – shijie huaren" 從落葉歸根到落地生根 - 世界華人研究文集 [From luoye guigen to luodi shenggen – shijie huaren yanjiu wenji research collection ethnic Chinese worldwide], Guangzhou: Zhongguo Guangzhou Jinan daxue chubanshe.

Huang, Philip C. C. (2000) "Biculturality in Modern China and in Chinese Studies" in *Modern China* 26/1 (2000), pp. 3-31.

Huang, Weiwu 黃慰吾 (1955) "Haiwai qiaobao de huigu yu qianzhan" 海外僑報的回顧與前瞻[Retroperspective and future trends of the overseas Chinese newspapers] in *Huaqiao wenti lunwenji* 2 (1955), pp. 37-53.

Hung, Chin-fu (2004) "The Internet and the Changing Beijing-Taipei Relations: Toward Unification or Fragmentation?" in Hung, Chin-fu (ed.) (2004) *Cyber China: Reshaping National Identities in the Age of Information*, New York: Palgrave Macmillan, 125-151.

Kalathil, Shanthi (2002) "Community and Communalism in the Information Age" in *The Brown Journal of World Affairs* 9/1 (2002), pp. 347-354.

Lee, Erika and Naoko Shibusawa (2005) "Guest Editor's Introduction: What is Transnational Asian American History?: Recent Trends and Challenges" in *Journal of Asian American Studies* 8/3 (2005), pp. vii-xvii.

Liao, Ching-ting 廖經庭 (2007) "BBS zhan de Kejia qunzhong rentong jiangou: yi PTT 'Hakka Dream' ban weili BBS 站得客家群眾認同建構：以 PTT「Hakka Dream」版爲例 in Zixun shehui yanjiu – Journal of Cyber Culture and Information Society 13 (2007), pp. 257-293.

Liao, Ping-hui 廖炳惠 (2003) "Zai quanqiuhua guocheng zhong de haiwai huaren lisan shequn: shijue yishu zhong zhengzhi yu wenhua gongminquan de fenhe" 在全球化過程中的海外華人離散社群：視覺藝術中政治與文化公民權的分合 [Overseas Chinese

Communities in Global Diasporas: Visualizing Political and Cultural Citizenships] in *Zhongwai wenxue - Chung-Wai Literary Monthly* 32/4 (2003), pp. 17-28.

McKeown, Adam (2004) "Global Migration, 1846-1940" in *Journal of World History* 15/2 (2004), pp. 155-189.

Meyer-Clement, Elena and Gunter Schubert (2004) "Greater China – Idee. Konzept. Forschungsprogramm. Zur Einführung in einen neuen Arbeitsschwerpunkt am Seminar für Sinologie und Koreanistik der Universität Tübingen" *Greater China Occasional Papers*/1. <http://www.gcs.uni-tuebingen.de/index.php?id=34>, accessed 10 May 2007 (2004).

n.a. (2006) "Jizai huaren fendou yu chengjiu nongsuo lishi de haiwai huaren bowuguan" 記載華人奮鬥與成就 濃縮歷史的海外華人博物館 [The struggle and the success of the ethnic Chinese: synopsis on museums on overseas Chinese] in *Xinhuanet*. http://news.xinhuanet.com/overseas/2006-08/25/content_5006947.htm accessed 31 July 2008.

Ng, Wing Chung (1999) *The Chinese in Vancouver, 1945-80: The Pursuit of Identity and Power*, Vancouver: University of British Columbia Press, 1999.

Ong, Aihwa (2003) "Cyberpublics and Diaspora Politics among Transnational Chinese" in *Interventions* 5/1 (2003).

Ong, Aihwa (2005) "Chinese Diaspora Politics and Its Fallout in a Cyber Age" in Aihwa Ong Aihwa (ed.) (2005) *Encyclopedia of Diasporas: Immigrant and Refugee Cultures around the World*, New York: Springer, pp. 65-76.

Ong, Aihwa and Donald Nonini (1997) "Chinese Transnationalism as an Alternative Modernity" in Aihwa Ong and Donald Nonini (eds) (1997) *Ungrounded Empires: The Cultural Politics of Modern Chinese Transnationalism*, New York and London: Routledge, pp. 3-33.

Pan, Lynn (1999) *The Encyclopedia of the Chinese Overseas*, Cambridge, MA: Harvard University Press.

Parker, David and Miri Song (2006) "Ethnicity, Social Capital and the Internet: British Chinese Websites" in *Ethnicities* 6/2 (2006), pp. 179-202.

Pollard, Vincent D. (2007) "From Southern Seas to Cyberspace: Chinese Diaspora Websites in Southeast Asia and in the South Pacific" in *Chinese Southern Diaspora Studies* 1 (2007), pp. 138-146.

Pollard, Vincent D. (2008) "Chinese Cultures Abroad" <http://www2.hawaii.edu/~pollard/chculture.html>, accessed 3 May 2008.

Sassen, Saskia (2000) "Understanding the Impact of Global Networks in Local Social, Political and Cultural Values" in Saskia Sassen (ed.) (2000) *The Impact of the Internet on Sovereignty: Unfounded and Real Worries*, Baden Baden: Nomos, pp. 195-209.

Saunders, Robert A. and Sheng Ding (2006) "Digital Dragons and Cybernetic Bears: Comparing the Overseas Chinese and Near Abroad Russian Web Communities" in *Nationalism & Ethnic Politics* 12/2 (2006), pp. 255-290.

Shi, Cheng-feng 施正鋒 (1999) "Taiwan yishi de tansuo"台灣意識的探索（上）[About the Taiwanese identity] in *Gongheguo zazhi - The Republic* 10. <http://www.wufi.org.tw/republic/rep1-10/no10_15.htm>, accessed 18 May 2008.

Siapera, Eugenia (2006) "Multiculturalism Online: The Internet and the Dilemmas of Multicultural Politics" in *European Journal of Cultural Studies 9/1,* pp. 5-24.

Su, Ping 酥餅 (2007) "Gongmin meiti yu wanglu shehui yundong, buluoge de mengxiang yu xianshi" 公民媒體與網路社會運動，部落格的夢想與現實 [Civil media and social movements on the net, dream and reailty of blogs] in *Gongheguo zazhi –The Republic* 54. <http://www.wufi.org.tw/dbsql/showrwork.php?sid=262>, accessed 18 May 2008 (2007).

Suryadinata, Leo (1971) *The Pre-World War II Peranakan Chinese Press of Java: a Preliminary Survey*, Athens: Ohio University.

Suryadinata, Leo (2007) "Resurgence of Ethnic Chinese Identity in Post-Suharto Indonesia: Some Reflections" in *Asian Culture* 31 (2007), pp. 11-17.

Tu, Weiming (1994) "Cultural China: The Periphery as the Center" in Tu, Weiming (ed.) (1994) *The Living Tree: the Changing Meaning of Being Chinese Today*, Stanford: Stanford University Press, pp. 1-34.

Tu, Weiming (1996) "Cultural Identity and the Politics of Recognition in Contemporary Taiwan" in *The China Quarterly* 148 (1996), pp. 1115-1140.

Wang, Gungwu (1993) "Greater China and the Chinese Overseas" in *The China Quarterly* 136 (1993), pp. 926-948.

Wang, Gungwu (2002) "New Migrants: How New, Why New?" in Wang, Gungwu (ed.) (2002) *Essays on Ethnic Chinese Abroad, Vol. 1, Migration, Entrepreneurs and Commerce* Taipei: Huaqiao xiehui zonghui, pp. I-XI.

Wang, Gungwu (2003) "Preface" in Wang, Gungwu (ed.) (2003) *The Chinese Diaspora, Vol. 1*, London: Eastern Universities Press/Marshall Cavendish, pp. vii-ix.

Wang, Ling-Chi (2003) "On Luodi-shenggen" in Wang, Ling-Chi (ed.) (2003) *The Chinese Diaspora, Vol 1*, London: Eastern Universities Press/Marshall Cavendish, pp. x-xi.

Watson, James L. (2004) "Presidential Address: Virtual Kinship, Real Estate and Diaspora Formation - The Man Lineage Revisited" in *The Journal of Asian Studies* 63/4 (2004), pp. 893-910.

Wu, Xu (2007) *Chinese Cyber Nationalism: Evolution, Characteristics, and Implications*, Lanham: Lexington Books.

Yang, Guobin (2003) "The Internet and the Rise of a Transnational Cultural Sphere" in *Media, Culture & Society* 25 (2003), pp. 469-490.

Yu, Jung-hui 尤榮輝 (2007) *TOCL.net zai wang lu shi jie wei tai wan jian guo fa sheng TOCL.net* 在網路世界爲台灣建國發聲 [TOCL.net: a voice on the net for the establishment of a Taiwan Republic] in *Gongheguo zazhi - The Republic* 53. <http://www.wufi.org.tw/dbsql/showrwork.php?sid=243>, accessed 18 May 2008 (2007).

Yuen, Peter Yui Chi (2003) *Civilisation Online: How the Internet Challenges Elite Discourses of the Chinese* Nation(s) Hawai'i.

Zheng, Yanfen 鄭彥棻 (1953) "Haiwai qiaobao de rongyu yu dangqian shiming" 海外僑報的榮譽與當前使命 [The honor and the current tasks of the overseas Chinese newspapers] in 僑務月報 16 (1953), pp. 1-2.

Umweltpolitik der Volksrepublik China, Konfuzius-Institut an der Freien Universität Berlin, 8. Dezember 2007

Zur aktuellen Thematik von Klimawandel, Ressourcennutzung und den Konsequenzen für die *Umweltpolitik der Volksrepublik China* veranstaltete am 8. Dezember 2007 das Konfuzius-Institut an der Freien Universität Berlin einen wissenschaftlichen Workshop mit Experten aus Deutschland und China.

Liu Hongyan, Professor für Umweltstudien an der Peking Universität (Department of Ecology, College of Environmental Sciences) und Stipendiat der Alexander-von-Humboldt-Stiftung am Potsdam-Institut für Klimafolgenforschung (PIK), legte in seinem Eröffnungsreferat zu „Climate Change and Environmental Policy" den Schwerpunkt auf geophysikalische Gegebenheiten und geothermische Fakten. Bereits über die gesamte chinesische Geschichte wurden Naturkatastrophen im Zusammenhang mit lokalen Gegebenheiten verzeichnet. Dazu zählen beispielsweise Überschwemmungen und Flutkatastrophen am Verlauf des Gelben Flusses oder Dürreperioden in Zentralchina. Die heute im Rahmen des Klimawandels diskutierte globale Erderwärmung ist Resultat des Anstiegs von Kohlendioxid-(CO_2)-Emissionen seit der industriellen Revolution im 19. Jahrhundert. Allein für China hat sich in Langzeitmessungen (1951-2001) eine Erwärmung von 1,5 Grad Celsius ergeben. Dies bedeutet wärmere Winter und für immer größere Regionen trockeneres Klima. In der Inneren Mongolei, die ein Sechstel des chinesischen Territoriums ausmacht, wächst der Anteil an verlorenem Land durch Verwüstungen (Desertifikation). Gleichzeitig erreichen die Ausläufer von Sandstürmen weiter entfernte Gegenden, z.B. nicht allein Peking, sondern auch Japan – und in Extremfällen sogar die USA. Desweiteren begünstigt wird das Abschmelzen von Eis, dem so genannten *Perma-Frost*. Betroffen ist das Qinghai-Tibet-Plateau, hier befindet sich über 80 Prozent der Eisfläche des Landes. *Liu* benannte als konkrete politische Maßnahmen gegen die skizzierten Umweltprobleme exemplarische Programme z.B. zu Waldaufforstung, Erhöhung von Vegetationsanteilen oder Bodenqualität (*Green Great Wall Program*, *Three North Shelter Program*, *Grain for Green Program*). Als Reaktion darauf, dass China ebenfalls durch die eigene, stark gewachsene Industrie zu den CO_2-Emissionen beiträgt und beitragen wird, ist die im 11. Fünf-Jahres-Plan formulierte Nachhaltigkeitsstrategie der Regierung zu bewerten: Durch die Schaffung eines *Green GDP* soll der Energieverbrauch pro Einheit BSP um 20 Prozent gesenkt werden – bei einer angestrebten Verdopplung des Bruttosozialprodukts (BSP) von 2000-2010.

Gu Xuewu, Lehrstuhl Politik Ostasiens an der Ruhr-Universität Bochum, konkretisierte den Zusammenhang zwischen Chinas Wirtschaftswachstum und dem damit gestiegenen Energieverbrauch. In seinem Beitrag zu „Chinas Energiemix und seine Umweltprobleme" formulierte er, dass die Energiepreise in China derzeit viel zu niedrig angesetzt sind und ökologische sowie soziale Belastungen eingerechnet werden müssen. Zudem sei beim Energiemix die Dominanz durch den Verbrauch von Kohle mit 70 Prozent als Hauptverursacher der Luftverschmutzung ungebrochen. Der Anteil von Erdöl sei zwar auf 22 Prozent gestiegen, jedoch stamme nur die Hälfte aus inländischer Produktion und die Importabhängigkeit werde entsprechend der Ausweitung der Industrieproduktion weiter steigen. Alternative Energiequellen aus Wasserkraft spielen mit 7 Prozent derzeit eine untergeordnete Rolle, stattdessen wird die Nutzung von Atomenergie auch in den nächsten Jahren ausgeweitet. *Gu* wies auf den Zusammenhang von China als Standort innerhalb der globalisierten Industrieproduktion hin. Dies erkläre den berechtigten Anspruch Chinas, auf umfangreichen Technologietransfer auch unter Umweltgesichtspunkten zu bestehen. Daneben sollten die

Staatsbetriebe den Einsatz von Umwelttechnik vorantreiben. Insgesamt werde die internationale Diskussion z.B. um Pro-Kopf-Berechnungen/Abgaben als eine Debatte um globale Gerechtigkeit geführt. Die Bereitschaft zum Handeln sei allerdings in China wesentlich größer als in den USA oder anderen westlichen Ländern. Laut *Gu* differiert allerdings die Perspektive: „Für China bedeutet es einen Verzicht auf Wachstum, während es für den Westen ein Verzicht auf Luxus ist."

Dem Komplex Wachstum, Entwicklung und Ökologie widmete sich *Edgar Endrukaitis*, Deutsche Gesellschaft für Technische Zusammenarbeit GmbH (GTZ). Sein Beitrag analysierte „Chinas rasantes Wachstum – Eine ökologische Herausforderung." Die rasante Industrieentwicklung und die damit einhergehende Urbanisierung haben zu über 170 Millionenstädten geführt. Im weltweiten Vergleich befinden sich von den 30 am meisten durch Umwelteinflüsse belasteten Städten 20 in China. Nur 52 Prozent des Siedlungsabfalls und 29 Prozent des städtischen Abwassers werden umweltgerecht behandelt. Auch wenn die Regierung mit ihrem Nachhaltigkeitsprogramm *Green GDP* auf qualitatives statt quantitatives Wachstum umschwenkt, steht die Durch- und Umsetzung der Umweltgesetzgebung noch am Anfang. *Endrukaitis*, selbst langjähriger Berater der GTZ bei der SEPA (*State Environmental Protection Administration*), plädierte für eine stärkere Demokratisierung der Umweltpolitik unter Berücksichtigung einer „ökologischen Performanz" der Verwaltung, mehr öffentlicher Beteiligung und der Einbeziehung der Medien. In der Volksrepublik selbst bedarf die Umweltverwaltung weiteren Auf- und Ausbaus. Der Schritt, die Umweltverwaltung SEPA (seit 1998 mit ministeriellem Rang) 2008 endgültig zu einem Ministerium umzugestalten, sei richtungsweisend.

Joachim Nibbe, Hochschule Bremen, stellte seinen Beitrag unter den Titel „Chinas Wirtschaftswachstum unter besonderer Berücksichtigung der Umweltproblematik." Die Gesamtkosten für Umweltverschmutzung in China werden – auch von der chinesischen Umweltbehörde (2006) – auf etwa 8 bis 13 Prozent des Bruttoinlandsprodukts beziffert, d.h. etwa so hoch wie das jährliche Wirtschaftswachstum. Die nachhaltige Umgestaltung eines auf quantitativem wirtschaftlichem Wachstum orientierten Entwicklungsmodells sei unabdingbar. *Nibbe* plädierte für die Organisation des umweltpolitischen Dialogs und der umweltpolitischen Beratung in Zusammenarbeit mit den relevanten staatlichen und privaten Institutionen in China auf zentraler und lokaler Ebene. Kernbereich wäre der Klimaschutz. Auf der internationalen Bühne habe China schon vielfach seine Problemlösungskapazitäten bewiesen. So hat China als erstes Land 1992 zwei Jahre nach dem UN-Umwelt-Gipfel von Rio de Janeiro seine *Agenda 21* vorgelegt und internationale Konventionen umgesetzt (Montreal Protokoll zum Ausstieg FCKW, UN Rahmen-Konvention zum Klimawandel, Kyoto-Protokoll, UN Konvention zur Bekämpfung von Verwüstungen).

In der abschließenden Diskussion unter der Leitung von *Bettina Gransow*, Ostasiatisches Seminar der Freien Universität Berlin, zeigte sich die – nicht nur für China – große Herausforderung, die das Thema Umweltpolitik begleitet. Die Beurteilung von geothermischen Ursachen und Wirkungen sind durch eine teilweise unvollständige Datenlage, teilweise widersprüchliche Prognosen unterschiedlicher Modelle sowie durch Langfristigkeit und Interdependenzen additiver Effekte schwierig. Diskutiert wurden neben konkreten Politikmaßnahmen weitere Anwendungsmöglichkeiten für China wie Konzepte einer Öko-Steuer, mögliche negative Effekte bei der Nutzung sauberer Energie (z.B. bei Bau von Staudämmen/Wasserkraftwerken) und die sozialen Auswirkungen von Umweltmaßnahmen (ökologieinduzierte Migration). Als wichtiges Handlungsfeld wurde trotz des gestiegenen

Umweltbewusstseins von Regierung und Wirtschaft eine bislang nicht genügend entwickelte adäquate Umweltverwaltung auf zentraler und lokaler Ebene identifiziert.
Der Workshop machte für alle Teilnehmerinnen und Teilnehmer deutlich, dass bei einer globalen Diskussion zur Umweltpolitik angesichts von weltweiten Akteuren/Verursachern von Umweltproblemen es unverständlich und sachlich falsch ist, dass China derzeit oft als dominierender Problemverursacher benannt wird. Die Lösung von Umweltfragen ist global entscheidend und für und mit China auch zukünftig nur im Zusammenhang mit weltweiter wirtschaftlicher und gesellschaftlicher Entwicklung im Spannungsfeld von Wachstums-, Industrie- und Energiepolitik aller Beteiligter zu betrachten. (Simona Thomas)

Taiwan's 2008 Presidential Election

The 2008 presidential elections in Taiwan were not only the subject of wide-spread reports in the global media (with the notable exception of the PRC), but were also a focus of attention for scholars, journalists, NGO-activists and international party organizations. Various post-election workshops were organized which analyzed the landslide-victory of the KMT candidate, Ma Ying-jeou, who was inaugurated on 20 May 2008. Ma Ying-jeou and his running mate for the vice-presidency, Vincent Siew, gained 58% of the votes, while Frank Hsieh and Su Teng-chang gained 42 % of the votes. This mirrored almost exactly the outcome of the Legislative Yuan elections in January 2008 and, as a result of the newly introduced electoral system, led to a disproportionate allocation of seats, with the blue camp gaining 76 % of the seats, and the green camp 24 % of the seats, giving the KMT the power to make significant changes to the constitution.
Various groups of election observers were invited by Taiwanese Foundations to observe the election processes with the dual aim of ensuring that the election proceeded smoothly and that the outcome of the election would be discussed and analyzed from various perspectives: first of all, with regard to foreign and international issues, that is, how the outcome will influence relations between Taiwan and China, and between Taiwan and the United States and Japan; secondly, with regard to the internal political situation, that is, assessing the level of maturity and stability attained by Taiwan as a democracy, in which direction the DPP will develop after losing the election, how the KMT will deal with their newly gained power and whether Taiwan will continue on the road towards becoming a fully fledged democracy.
Immediately after the election, an international roundtable on "Assessing the Meaning and Implications of the March 22 Presidential Elections." was hosted by the New Taiwanese Cultural Foundation and the Center for China-US Corporation, University of Denver, at the Taipei International Convention Center. This workshop focused on the topics of cross straits relations, the future of Taiwan-US relations, and Taiwan's domestic issues. The first panel, "Implications for Taiwan's Democracy and Political Development," was chaired by *Yun-Han Chu* (Institute of Political Science, Academia Sinica). *Emile Sheng* (Department of Political Science, Soochow University) stressed that the main reasons for the election result was the poor performance by Chen Shuibian; the DPP had not been able to attract the middle-of-the-road/undecided voters. *Emile Sheng* was optimistic that the newly elected President Ma Ying-jeou would be able to improve cross strait relations significantly; he was, however, aware of the continuing distrust among large sections of Taiwanese society which is rooted in the fear that Ma as a mainlander born in Hong Kong might "sell out" Taiwan to the mainland. Regarding the development of Taiwan's democracy, *Emile Sheng* was convinced of the transition to a matured democracy – with the emergence of more individual and topic-

oriented citizens with less enthusiasm for party politics. *Shirley Rigger* (East Asian Politics, Davidson College) agreed that many of the DDP's failures were self-inflicted and that the election outcome was influenced by a deep distrust of Chen Shuibian; she also emphasized the successful campaigning for median voters by the KMT. She stressed that Ma Ying-jeou must take decisive action against factionalism within the KMT. In addition, while in opposition, the KMT had learned to depend less on the power of local factions (most of the *lizhang*, the village chairmen, were personally connected to the KMT), and more on governance performance. With regard to the DPP, *Shirley Rigger* stressed the need to go back to the center, and not to tell – especially young voters – that "to love Taiwan, means to vote for the DPP" a slogan which alienated at least the better-educated. *Fu-hsiung Shen*, a former DPP lawmaker and now a critical and "blue-ized" TV moderator, mentioned the poor governance performance as one of the main reasons for the defeat of the DPP. *Larry Diamond* (Hoover Institution) expressed the opinion that with "an eloquent and smart winner," the gridlock in Taiwan's policy could be broken. He described the huge majority obtained by the KMT in the Legislative Yuan, however, as "unhealthy" and spoke of a "suboptimal" election system. He further warned the Grand Jury, Control Yuan, and Executive Yuan against being taken over by the old KMT cadres. *Nat Bellochi* (former AIT Chairman) focused on the economic aspects, that is, on the expected greater integration of Taiwan in a common market, which could improve Taiwan's economic performance. *Jonathan Pollack* (Asian Pacific Studies, Strategic research Department, US Naval War College) also offered advise to Ma Ying-jeou on how to heal the wounds of a divided nation. He regarded Taiwan's relations with China as an interesting test case for China from two points of view: Chen Shuibian had so obviously been an enemy of China that China had not had to react; with Ma, however, China could have talks, but only if she did not set strict preconditions. And the comeback of the KMT could set an example for China: an authoritarian party which allows democratic development is not necessarily excluded from power forever.

The second panel focused on "Implications for US-Taiwan and Cross-straits Relations" and was hosted by *Suisheng Zhao* (Center for China-US Cooperation, Graduate School of International Studies, Denver), who regarded the election outcome as a new opportunity for the Chinese government to adopt a new approach towards Taiwan. *Alan Romberg* (Stimson Center) discussed the possibility that China might now allow Taiwan to obtain observer status with the WHO. He warned against any assumption that everything will go smoothly as hardliners in Beijing could press for many preconditions for talks with Ma. This would be unacceptable for Taiwan which has become much more "Taiwanese" than it was eight years ago. *Doug Paal* (Former AIT Director) stressed the better atmosphere between the US and the newly elected president. *Szu-Yin Ho* (Political Science, National Chengchi University) was convinced that Ma's power within the KMT was strengthened by the election result and that the era of corruption will come to an end. Michael Swaine (Carnegie Endowment for International Peace) was optimistic that a new pragmatic approach would be employed on both sides of the Taiwan Strait. *Lynn White* (Politics and International Affairs, Woodrow Wilson School, Princeton) emphasized that the US is willing to protect Taiwan's liberalism, but not Taiwan's formal and de jure independence. He expected the "three links" (santong) to be established very soon. *Richard Baum* (Political Science, UCLA), further suggested that both sides could reach an agreement whereby Taiwan would promise not to strive for independence if China would promise not to strive for unification within a certain time.

A second forum organized by the Taiwan Thinktank, "2008 Presidential Election: Impacts and Implications" took place on Monday. The workshop was chaired by *Chih-Cheng Lo* (Political Science, Soochow University). *Jih-Wen Lin* (Political Science, Academia Sinica) referred to the large group of median voters whom he did not regard as extremely sophisticated swing voters, but as a large, rather apolitical group, easily influenced by the mass media and merely followers of the general trend. In particular, the local factions in central Taiwan, which had swung to the DPP/Chen Shuibian in 2005, when Chen was considered to be a strong leader who could support the local factions financially, had now once more become more supportive of the KMT. *Michael H.H. Hsiao* (Center for Asia Pacific Area Studies, Academia Sinica) mentioned several unresolved issues: the validity of Ma's green card, the one party dominance of the KMT and Ma's ambiguous position regarding national identity, that is, Taiwan or ROC nationalism. *Cheng-Yi Lin* (Institute of European and American Studies, Academia Sinica) examined Beijing's sophisticated "carrot and stick" policy: Beijing uses the Taiwanese business associations in China to exert pressure on Taiwanese voters to vote for the KMT; Hu Jintao will push for a "one-China joint communiqué" with Japan; Hu Jintao will again offer two panda bears (named Tuantuan and Yuanyuan, which together mean "unity" or "reunion") as a gift to the Taipei Zoo; Beijing will propose direct links and economic benefits, but at the same time, will continue to increase the number of missiles pointing in the direction of Taiwan. *Chih-Cheng Lo* also expressed the fear that more and more Taiwanese business people will be taken as "hostages" by the PRC – and that this number would increase within a common market. He also drew parallels with Hong Kong, by pointing to the increasing self-censorship of the Taiwanese media with regard to PRC- related reports. *Raymond R.K. Wu* (Fu Jen Catholic University) dealt more with inner party factions within the DPP and stressed again the unsatisfactory performance by Chen Shuibian, and Frank Hsieh's inability to distance himself from Chen.

Another roundtable on "Taiwan's 2008 Presidential Election: A New Beginning for Cross-Strait Relations?" was organized by the Institute for National Policy Research (INPR), the Taiwan and Asia Research Centre, and the London School of Economics (LSE), UK on March 23, 2008. The Welcome Remarks were addressed by *Lin Cheng-Yi* (Academia Sinica) and *Chris Hughes*, Professor of International Relations at LSE. *Hughes* briefly summarized the experiences of the group of foreign researchers who had been observing the final week of election campaigning. *Hughes* then made a general post-election assessment that issues of governance and economics, corruption, poor performance, loyalty and leadership qualities had determined the election outcome in favor of Ma. The first session focused on the "Significance of the Result of the 2008 Presidential Election." Speakers were *Shih Cheng-Feng* (National Dong Hwa University) who emphasized that, in the 2008 election, identity politics were no longer decisive, and that a mainlander had been preferred over a native Taiwanese. Shih, however, questioned the extent to which the Taiwanese voters had matured. *Tom Hart* (Stockholm School of Economics) reflected on the elections as the coming of age of Taiwanese democracy. He also phrased the outcome of this election in optimistic terms of new opportunities being created for a dialog between the KMT and the PRC that could generate a long-term modus vivendi in the cross-strait development. *Ho Szu-yin* (Overseas Affairs of the KMT) evaluated the type of reform that the DPP could undertake in the realm of political economy: What are the party's strategies for developing a meaningful dialog between "protectionism" and free trade across the strait. *Phil Deans* (Temple University) focused on the perception of Ma in Japan. Deans remarked that even if the Japanese revisionist right-wing favored a president who was pro-Taiwan independence, the Japanese government does not have a coherent China-policy, and will most likely follow US policy. The second session dealt with "Interpreting the Two Referenda." *Gunter Schubert* (University of Tübingen) briefly assessed the electoral turn-out at the referenda, expressing the view that the result revealed a sad degradation of the value of referenda in society and politics. He concluded that the leadership of both parties was to blame. *Lin Cheng-Yi* gave a detailed overview of the six referenda. With regard to the 2008 referendum, he argued that the DPP had been fighting on three fronts: the million Taiwanese investors in the PRC, the negative attitude of the USA towards the referendum, and the opposition from KMT diplomats. With the change in power, it still remains to be seen whether Taiwan will be able to participate in international institutions in the future. In the third session, "The Implications for Cross-Strait Relations," *Lai I-Chung* (International Affairs of the DPP) put forward the view that the election result was not tantamount to the downgrading of identity issues in Taiwan. He referred to Ma's vacillating stances that "the future of Taiwan should be determined by Taiwanese (and Chinese) people." *Jean-Pierre Cabestan* (Hong Kong Baptist University) warned against exaggerated optimism, pointing out some of the obstacles that will surface when the newly elected KMT government attempts to normalize relations with China. *Cabestan* also drew attention to strategic issues, such as how to convince the Taiwanese economic and political elite of the need for closer integration with the PRC. *Huang Chieh-Cheng* (Tamkang University) observed that the general impression was one of stable cross-strait relations. However, a closer look reveals that entering into negotiations for participation in international organizations would require a positive attitude on the part of the PRC if there were to be any chance of success. These were major concerns. On the other hand, there was the hope that Ma would most likely continue with a policy of transparency, and avoid a back-door style in dealing with the PRC. Finally, *Gudrun Wacker* (Stiftung Wissenschaft und Politik, SWP, Berlin) drew attention to the EU dimension. On the election results, she noted that the return to power of the KMT with Ma as president will have the support of the EU as a guarantee of stability and that cooperation is anticipated. She also warned against exaggerated expectations. She commented that the EU parliament has indicated strong support for improving Taiwan's position internationally. Although the EU has become more critical of China, this does not take away the reality that significant differences still exist between individual EU member-states. *Chris Hughes* concluded that with this election, dynamics have certainly changed, but it is not clear how this will affect China's pressure on a KMT Taiwan. In that sense, Ma's visit to Japan may build the framework for the development of cross-strait relations and the relationship with Japan. During the open discussion, *Bruce Jacobs* (Monash University) drew attention to the lack of international interest in the importance of the election outcome for domestic affairs and pointed out that Ma appears to hold contradictory views with regard to cross-strait relations. *Fiorella Allio* (CNRS, France) asked how the new government would present Taiwanese culture in view of the opening up to PRC tourists and emphasized the differences in political culture between the north (Taipei) and the south (Tainan). *Jerome Keating* (National Taipei University) made the useful comment that identity in Taiwan was not just a card played for the purposes of *domestic* ethnic politics, but that identity and the struggle for democracy was as always a real issue in Taiwanese society and that this was made quite clear in the election result. Ending on an encouraging note, Tom Hart mentioned the recent trend towards pro-Taiwan editorials in

Sweden which could set an example for the international community to follow with regard to advocating the democratic cause in Taiwan and elsewhere. (Jens Damm/Ann Heylen)

China in Africa: Who benefits? Interdisciplinary Perspectives on China's Involvement in Africa, International Conference, Johann Wolfgang Goethe-Universität, Frankfurt am Main, 14.-15. Dezember 2007

Die gemeinsam vom Interdisziplinären Zentrum für Ostasienstudien (IZO) und dem Zentrum für interdisziplinäre Afrikaforschung (ziaf) an der Johann Wolfgang Goethe-Universität in Frankfurt am Main und dem Institut für Ethnologie und Afrikastudien an der Johannes Gutenberg Universität in Mainz organisierte und hauptsächlich von der Deutschen Gesellschaft für Technische Zusammenarbeit (GTZ) finanzierte Konferenz „China in Africa: Who benefits?" wurde mit Ansprachen des Vize-Präsidenten der Universität Frankfurt, *Inger Ebsen*, und des Leiters des Afrikareferates der GTZ, *Andreas Proksch*, eröffnet.

Darauf folgten Grundsatzreden von *Helmut Asche* (Universität Leipzig), *Sanusha Naidu* (Stellenbosch, Südafrika) und *Gu Xuewu* (Ruhr-Universität Bochum) unter dem Vorzeichen „China in Afrika: Chance oder Bedrohung?". Alle drei machten jedoch schnell deutlich, dass sie über pauschale Fragestellungen dieser Art hinausgehen wollten und diese als polarisierend und insgesamt wenig erhellend ablehnten.

Helmut Asche unterschied vier Ebenen des aktuellen chinesischen Engagements in Afrika: Handel, Investitionen, Entwicklungshilfe und Migration, alle im Jahr 2007 an einem Höhepunkt angelangt. Ungeachtet der – weder prognostizier- noch belegbaren – langfristigen Effekte sei es an der Zeit, dieses Engagement als ein Beispiel gewachsener Multipolarität hinzunehmen und dem (endlich) mit einer flexiblen europäischen Geopolitik und effektiven trilateralen Verhandlungsmechanismen zu begegnen.

Sanusha Naidu stellte die These auf, nicht China, sondern afrikanische Regierungen selbst behinderten Entwicklung. Aktuelle chinesisch-afrikanische Beziehungen seien hierfür nur ein weiteres Beispiel. Wolle man negative Folgen des chinesischen Engagements in Afrika verhindern, so müssten afrikanische Regierungen stärker in die Verantwortung genommen, Regierungsführung verbessert und Bevölkerungen an der Gestaltung der Beziehungen zu China stärker beteiligt werden. Aufgabe westlicher Wissenschaftler und Analysten sei es, möglichst konkret Verhandlungsspielräume im Umgang mit China vor Augen zu führen und eine aktive afrikanische Chinapolitik voranzubringen.

Auch *Gu Xuewu* wechselte die Perspektive: China in Afrika sei vielleicht gar kein Nullsummenspiel. Chinas Vorteile seien offensichtlich: Energiesicherung, Multipolarität und Bündnispolitik. Afrika habe aber auch hinzugewonnen: neben materiellen und strukturellen Vorteilen auch Prestige und Selbstbewusstsein. Und selbst Europa könne diese neue Konstellation als Chance zur Neudefinition der eigenen Afrikapolitik wahrnehmen.

Im nächsten Abschnitt wurden beispielhaft „Auswirkungen des chinesischen Engagements in Afrika" diskutiert. Beobachter kritisieren Beijings indirekte Unterstützung von Diktaturen durch Hilfsleistungen ohne politische Konditionalität („Beijing Consensus"). *He Wenping* (Chinesische Akademie der Sozialwissenschaften, Beijing) argumentierte dagegen, es brauche ohnehin erst einen gewissen wirtschaftlichen Entwicklungsgrad, bevor Demokratie und gute Regierungsführung greifen könnten. Chinesische Erfahrungen der letzten 25 Jahre und Gemeinsamkeiten beider Regionen (Kolonialismus, Agrargesellschaft, autoritäre kulturelle Tradition) führten sie zu dem Schluss, ökonomische Aktivitäten seien momentan der einzig sinnvolle Entwicklungsbeitrag in Afrika. *Wolfgang Saam* (Universität Potsdam) schilderte am Beispiel Nigerias typische Nachteile der Zusammenarbeit mit China in Infrastrukturprojekten: asymmetrische Geschäftsbeziehungen, nicht eingelöste Zusagen, Arbeitskräfte aus China, Gewinnströme nach China u.ä. Andererseits habe Nigeria spezifische Standort- und Wettbewerbsvorteile in Verhandlungen mit China überhaupt noch nicht in die Waagschale geworfen. Wichtig für eine Win-Win-Situation seien aber gerade jeweils eigene Chinastrategien einzelner afrikanischer Länder auf der Basis ihrer relativen Vorteile. *Sabrina N'Dayes* (Freie Universität Berlin) Untersuchungen vor Ort zeigen, wie sich die wachsende Zahl chinesischer Kleinhändler auf Märkten in Dakar, Senegal, durchaus auch positiv auf vorhandene lokale Strukturen auswirkt: Marginalisierte Marktakteure erhielten neue Beteiligungschancen und die jüngsten Händler Möglichkeiten, aus familiären Abhängigkeiten auszubrechen und bei chinesischen Händlern eigene Karrieren zu begründen. *Antoine Kernen* (Institut d'Etudes Politiques de Paris) meint aufgrund seiner Beobachtungen chinesischer Kleinhändler und -Unternehmer in Senegal und Mali, die Rolle des chinesischen Staates und die Staatsnähe chinesischer Unternehmen in Afrika würden stark überbewertet. Tatsächlich müsse man beginnen, verschiedene chinesische Akteure, Handlungsmotive und Strategien der Begegnung zu unterscheiden – sogleich würde Chinas Afrikastrategie heruntergebrochen auf viele verschiedene Einzelstrategien auf der Graswurzelebene.

Den Abschnitt „Begegnung der Kulturen" begann *Liu Haifang* (z.Zt. Institute of Social Studies, Den Haag) mit einer kleinen Geschichte der chinesischen Kulturdiplomatie in Afrika, welche trotz der heutigen Ökonomisierung der Beziehungen starke Traditionslinien und Kontinuitäten seit Mao Zedong betonte, die vom westlichen Publikum zu Unrecht kaum wahrgenommen würden. *Conal Ho* (University of Carolina, Santa Cruz) hat sich mit Prozessen chinesischer Vergemeinschaftung in Ghana beschäftigt. Wieder seien nicht staatliche chinesische Konzepte oder Organisationen ausschlaggebend, sondern individuell erlebte Vor-Ort-Dynamiken, Ver- bzw. Misstrauen, Klatsch, Rassismus und Vorurteile. Trotz deren bindender Kraft würde der Aufenthalt aber selbst nach 40 Jahren noch als „vorübergehend" und die eigene Identität entlang ethnischer Kriterien definiert. *Gregor Dobler* (Universität Basel) hat Interdependenzen zwischen namibischer Politik und chinesischem Händlerverhalten in der Grenzstadt Oshikango untersucht und festgestellt, dass Händler strategisch auf strengere Einwanderungskontrollen, beschränkte Erteilung von Arbeitserlaubnissen und Übersättigung von Teilmärkten reagierten. Im Umkehrschluss sieht Dobler hier Möglichkeiten der Regulierung und gezielten Steuerung chinesischen Händlerverhaltens durch die namibische Regierung. *Basile Ndjio* (University of Buea, Kamerun) hat chinesische Prostitution in Douala und den Wandel von Konzepten chinesischer Frauenkörper bei der afrikanischen Klientel untersucht. Innerhalb weniger Jahre wechselten Vorstellungen von begehrenswerten exotischen Frauenkörpern zu Bildern billiger, unechter „Einwegartikel".

Den letzten Abschnitt „Strategien und Perspektiven" eröffnete *Nehru Pillay* (MINTEK, Randburg, Südafrika). Er zeigte die Chancen für Afrika angesichts Chinas anhaltenden „Energiehungers" auf: Globale Diskussionen über Klimawandel und chinesisches Umweltverhalten setzten China unter Druck. Afrika erhalte dadurch Gelegenheit, den chinesischen Zugriff auf seine Bodenschätze neu zu verhandeln, deren Verarbeitung vor Ort und Wertschöpfung für afrikanische Ökonomien zur Bedingung zu machen. *Anna Katharina Stahl* (College of Europe, Brügge) verzeichnete Annäherungen europäischer und chinesischer Afrikapolitik. Chinas Interesse an politischer Stabilität in Afrika sei gewachsen, sein Prinzip der Nicht-Einmischung in innere Angelegenheiten aufgeweicht. Die Europäische Union hingegen habe das Prinzip und die Rhetorik der gleichberechtigten Partnerschaft mit Afrika in den Vordergrund gestellt als auch trilaterale Gesprächsforen geschaffen. Über die übliche Analysetiefe hinaus untersuchte *Sara Van Hoeymissen* (Katholieke Universiteit Leuven) den Wortlaut chinesisch-afrikanischer Erklärungen im Hinblick auf Konvergenzen und die konkrete Unterstützung Chinas für afrikanische Integration und Multilateralität. Erwartungsgemäß ist die chinesische Unterstützung/Beteiligung im wirtschaftlichen und sozialen Bereich (bi- und multilateraler Infrastrukturbau, Technologietransfer, Wiederaufbau, Förderung von Ownership u.ä.) ungleich größer als im politischen (Förderung der kritischen Selbstbewertung innerhalb der Afrikansischen Union (APRM), Wahlbeobachtung, Korruptionsbekämpfung u.ä.) jedoch auch vorhanden (Annäherung Chinas an afrikanische Haltung zur Notwendigkeit von Inverventionen). *Stefan Stähle* (GTZ Beijing) setzte den häufig geäußerten Befürchtungen, Chinas Vergabepraxis bei der Entwicklungshilfe und Projektfinanzierung in Afrika hebele bisherige Standards aus, konkrete Handlungsempfehlungen entgegen: Er betonte, Deutschland sei vor dem Hintergrund seiner Erfahrungen hinsichtlich technischer Zusammenarbeit, Armutsbekämpfung, nachhaltiger Entwicklung und sozialer Verantwortung von Unternehmen (CSR) prädestiniert, China stärker in offiziellen Vergabemechanismen zu engagieren.

In der Schlussdiskussion wurde festgestellt, dass die Auswirkungen des chinesischen Engagements in Afrika bislang kaum beurteilt werden können. In den einzelnen Beiträgen habe jedoch gezeigt werden können, dass diese Auswirkungen auf einzelne Bereiche heruntergebrochen wahrscheinlich meistens sehr viel positiver bewertet werden müssten als dies gemeinhin passiere. Der Wert aktueller Feldforschungen zum chinesischen Engagement in Afrika könne daher nicht genug betont werden; sie sei hier das probate Mittel, die Forschung und auch Paradigmenwechsel voranzutreiben.

Die Konferenz hat die Diskussion insofern vorangebracht, als hier Annäherungen zwischen den beteiligten Akteuren herausdestilliert wurden und nicht die Unvereinbarkeit der Interessen betont wurde. Man hat Chancen für Afrika herausgearbeitet, anstatt das Gefahrenpotenzial überzubetonen, und man hat sich nicht zuletzt bereit gezeigt, statt der weiterhin verbreiteten Abstrafung Chinas und Bevormundung Afrikas möglicherweise auch voneinander zu lernen. (Nathalie van Looy)

Erinnerungen, Mythen, Reflektionen: Vergangenheitsbewältigung in der Volksrepublik China, Vertretung des Freistaats Thüringen beim Bund in Berlin, 10.03.2008

Die Bundesstiftung zur Aufarbeitung der SED-Diktatur veranstaltete diesen Workshop anlässlich des Erscheinens des Jahrbuchs für Historische Kommunismusforschung 2008. Thema waren historische Traumata der jüngeren chinesischen Geschichte, ihre Aufarbeitung sowie die Frage nach einer chinaspezifischen Vergangenheitsbewältigung.

Susanne Weigelin-Schwiedrzik (Universität Wien) stellt Jung Changs (Zhang Rong) „Mao Zedong: Das Leben eines Mannes, das Schicksal eines Volkes" in den Mittelpunkt ihres Vortrages. Weigelin-Schwiedrziks Kritik ist vernichtend: Das Werk erscheine kaum wissenschaftlich fundiert, seine Erkenntnisse seien wenig neu und es reduziere die Komplexität einer vielschichtigen historischen Phase auf die behauptete Herrsch- und Rachsucht einer Einzelperson. Interessant sei allerdings, dass Zhang den Stil ihrer Auslassungen an ‚typisch chinesische' Formen der Geschichtsschreibung anlehnt („Lob und Tadel"). Historische Ambivalenzen fielen unter den Tisch, gehe es doch erklärtermaßen einzig darum, Mao in seiner historischen Rolle zu desavouieren. So trage das Werk zur

Festigung einer fragwürdigen historischen Narrative bei, die eindimensional die Rolle Maos in den Blick nimmt. Rongs Buch stoße wohl nicht zuletzt deshalb im „Westen" auf positive Resonanz, weil es inhaltlich an bereits existierende Muster der Stalin- und Hitlerperzeption anknüpfe und gleichzeitig das Stereotyp von Mao als „asiatischem Despoten" bediene.
Auch *Nora Sausmikat* (Universität Köln) kommt in der Präsentation der Ergebnisse ihrer 10jährigen Langzeitbeobachtungen und Tiefeninterviews mit Zeitzeugen der Kulturrevolution (1966-1976) zu dem Schluss, dass offzielle historiographische Narrativen den Erinnerungsdiskurs dominierten und die Erinnerung und Trauerkultur entsprechend ritualisiert und homogenisiert sei. Differenzierungen seien nur entlang enger, nuancenfreier Kategorien möglich: So werteten zum Beispiel Menschen, die auf ihr Leben entlang machtpolitischer Sinnkategorien zurückblickten, die Kulturrevolution tendenziell eher als Desaster; wohingegen sie von Solchen, die in familiären Sinnkategorien dächten, häufiger „als intensives Erlebnis mit geistiger Bereicherung" erinnert würde. Gerade diese Nostalgie aber habe bislang eine Aufarbeitung verhindert und eine Amnesie und Verharmlosung von Gewalt und Verbrechen befördert. Sausmikat stellt fest, dass die Historisierung der Kulturrevolution in China zu früh erfolge, prognostiziert aber auch vorsichtig mit Martin Walser, dass sich das Gedächtnis der Öffentlichkeit nicht „auf Dauer manipulieren" lasse.
Im Rahmen des dritten Vortrags beschäftigte sich *Felix Wemheuer* (Universität Wien) mit der Erinnerung an das gewaltsame Ende der studentischen Massenunruhen im Juni 1989. Bis heute ließe sich kein einheitlicher gesellschaftlicher Diskurs erkennen: Während die offizielle parteistaatliche Geschichtsschreibung in China den „Tian'anmen-Zwischenfall" bis heute tabuisiere, konkurrierten multiple (nichtoffizielle) Narrativen des Geschehenen um gesellschaftliche Anerkennung. „19 Jahre nach dem Massaker: Wem gehört die Bewegung vom Platz des Himmlischen Friedens?" ist somit die provokante Frage, die Wemheuer seinen Ausführungen voranstellt. Seine Antwort: Die Erinnerung an 1989 findet in Fraktionen statt und wird in den Dienst aktueller Bedürfnisse und Interessen gestellt – eine Tendenz zur Annäherung der Diskurse sei nicht zu erkennen. Weltweit als epochales Ereignis konstruiert, funktionierten Bilder des „Tian'anmen-Zwischenfalls" vielmehr inzwischen als popkulturelle Referenz. Besondere Relevanz entwickelte das Gedächtnis auch auf der Ebene politischer Diskurse: Wemheuer skizziert in diesem Zusammenhang die „globalisierungskritische" Erinnerung, deren Vertreter_innen den massiven Militäreinsatz zur Beendigung der studentischen Proteste 1989 als wegweisenden Sündenfall eines zunehmend neoliberal orientierten chinesischen Staates verhandeln.
Der Workshop verdeutlichte, dass Erinnerungsdiskurse in China gegenwärtig einerseits durch parteistaatliche Normierungen geprägt sind und auf ausgewählte Phasen der chinesischen Geschichte begrenzt werden, während man andere konsequent tabuisiert. Unterhalb der offiziösen Narrativen existieren zwar durchaus alternative, differenziertere Erinnerungskulturen; scheinbar fehlen momentan jedoch adäquate Kanäle sowie ein ausreichendes kollektives Interesse, diese auch mit Anspruch auf breite gesellschaftliche Anerkennung zu artikulieren.
Die Beiträge des Workshops sollen im Jahrbuch für Historische Kommunismusforschung 2009 veröffentlicht werden. (Hauke Neddermann und Nathalie van Looy)

Xiaoming Chen: From the May Fourth Movement to Communist Revolution. Guo Moruo and the Chinese Path to Communism. Albany, NY: State University of New York Press 2007, 156 S. (ISBN 978-0791471371)

„Zwei Seelen wohnen, ach! in meiner Brust ..." So hatte es Goethe seinen Faust einst verzweifelt ausrufen lassen. Verse, die selbst im fernen China ihre Wirkung entfalteten: Fausts legendäre Klage sprach auch den jungen Guo Moruo ganz intuitiv und unmittelbar an. Im Jahr 1920 nutzte er sie gar als Einleitung seines Briefbandes *Sanyeji* [Kleeblatt]. Kaum verwunderlich, fühlte sich doch auch der junge chinesische Dichter innerlich zerrissen – und er sollte es in seiner politisch-weltanschaulichen Identität wie auch in seinen moralischen Überzeugungen noch jahrzehntelang bleiben. Denn: Leitsätze des Konfuzianismus und des Kommunismus überlagerten und verbanden sich in der Persönlichkeit Guos auf einzigartige Weise – er habe sich, so Chen Xiaoming, langfristig zu einem „konfuzianischen Kommunisten" entwickelt. Dass er dabei immer wieder Kämpfe mit sich selbst und seinem sich wandelnden (und phasenweise dogmatisch radikalisierten) Umfeld auszufechten hatte, liegt auf der Hand.

Die Formierung der politischen Identität Guos mag in ihren Details und Ausprägungen einzigartig gewesen sein. Dass sie gleichzeitig jedoch durchaus Anhaltspunkte für die Erfahrung chinesischer Intellektueller im Allgemeinen bietet, zeigt Chen in seiner hervorragenden Studie „Von der 4.-Mai-Bewegung zur kommunistischen Revolution: Guo Moruo und der chinesische Weg in den Kommunismus". Die Biografie Guos bildet einen überaus passenden Hintergrund, förmlich den roten Faden für das faktenreiche historische Panorama, welches Chen – als Historiker und ausgewiesener Experte für die Geschichte der chinesischen Intellektuellen an der Ohio State University bestens für das ehrgeizige Ziel seiner Studie gerüstet – in dem schmalen Band entwickelt und vor dem Leser ausbreitet. Die forschungsleitende Fragestellung: Warum war die kommunistische Idee so außerordentlich attraktiv für die chinesische Studierenden- und Gebildetenschicht?

Chen wartet mit einer überraschenden Antwort auf: Nicht – wie man annehmen könnte – weil sie einen totalen Bruch mit den konfuzianischen Traditionen des chinesischen Staates in Aussicht gestellt habe, sondern weil sie einen solch radikalen Schnitt im Verständnis der chinesischen Intellektuellen eben gerade nicht verlangt habe. Zwar begehrten sie im Kontext der 4.-Mai-Bewegung gegen einzelne Grundpfeiler der konfuzianischen Ordnung erfolgreich auf, so u.a. gegen den traditionell üblichen Brauch der Zwangsverheiratung und die Leitlinie, seine Familie (durchaus in autoritärem Sinne) in „Ordnung" zu halten *[qijia]*. Allerdings waren andere Maximen des traditionellen konfuzianischen Gesellschaftsmodells aus Sicht der jungen chinesischen Intelligenz keineswegs überkommen oder veraltet: Die Staatsverwaltung ordentlich zu organisieren *[zhiguo]* und Harmonie auf der ganzen Erde zu schaffen *[pingtianxia]* galten ihr als zeitgemäße Ideale – und mit den Versprechen marxistischer Programmatiken durchaus vereinbar. Schien der Kommunismus nicht als einziger Weg zu ihrer Realisierung? Auch die konfuzianische Weisung zur moralischen Selbstkultivierung *[xiushen]* verwarf sie nicht, sondern suchte sie sozialistisch zu interpretieren und in die angestrebte neue, moderne Gesellschaft zu integrieren. Nicht zuletzt war es das marxistische Ziel einer endgültigen und völligen Befreiung des Individuums in der kommunistischen Gesellschaft, das (nicht nur jugendliche) Intellektuelle vor allem im städtischen China begeisterte.

Aspekte, welche die Analyse Chens bewusst aufgreift. Sie besteht im Kern aus vier übergeordneten Kapiteln: Nacheinander untersucht der Autor darin die Hoffnung (I) auf Emanzipation des Individuums, (II) auf nationale Erlösung, (III) auf Befreiung der gesamten Menschheit und (IV) die endgültige Lösung der dramatischen Krise der chinesischen Intelligenz.

Den intellektuellen Entwicklungsweg Guo Moruos zeichnet der Autor – stets mit Blick auf die Zeitläufe und die Situation der Intellektuellen – gewissenhaft nach: Seine (Ver-)Wandlung vom konfuzianischen Sohn zuerst zum kompromisslosen Individualisten, dann zum „konfuzianischen Kommunisten" im Laufe der 1920er Jahre verdeutlicht der Autor anhand einer ganzen Vielzahl von Äußerungen und Werkszitaten des Dichters. Obwohl die Analyse dabei immer wieder den Aspekt der Literarizität insbesondere der Lyrik Guos außer Acht lässt und die Analysen somit teilweise methodisch unsauber erscheinen, gelingt es Chen (schon allein durch die Fülle an Indizien und Beweisen) letztlich, seine These überzeugend zu belegen.

So legt Chen Xiaoming mit „Von der 4.-Mai-Bewegung zur kommunistischen Revolution" einen insgesamt überzeugenden und durchaus lesenswerten Band vor, der weit über das Feld der Guo-Moruo-Studien hinausweisen dürfte. Zwar wird die Analyse dem wissenschaftlichen Anspruch auf methodische Nachvollziehbarkeit nicht durchgängig gerecht – insbesondere fehlen klärende Hinweise auf den (Bedingungs-) Zusammenhang zwischen literarischen Texten und dem zeitgenössischen soziokulturellen und -politischen Kontext. Doch dürften die Denkanstöße, die sich aus der Lektüre des Bandes ergeben, für jede ernsthafte Beschäftigung mit der Geschichte der chinesischen Intelligenz sowie der kommunistischen Bewegung von überaus großem Wert sein. (Hauke Neddermann)

J. M. Galenovič, *Rossija – Kitaj – Amerika. Ot soperničestva k garmonii interesov?* (Russland – China – Amerika. Von der Rivalität zur Harmonie der Interessen?), Moskau: Russkaja Panorama 2006, 575 S. (ISBN 5-93165-113-6)

Der Sinologe J. M. Galenovič (1932) hat als Hochschullehrer und stellvertretender Direktor der sowjetischen Akademieinstitute für Afrika (1978-1982) und des Fernen Ostens (1982 – 1988) gearbeitet. Als Experte und als Mitarbeiter der Abteilung Internationale Verbindungen des ZK der KPdSU und im Moskauer Außenministerium wirkte er über viele Jahre an der Konzipierung und Gestaltung der sowjetisch-chinesischen Beziehungen mit. Er nahm an den sowjetisch-chinesischen Grenzverhandlungen 1964-1970 und 1979 teil und warnte im Januar 1969 vor chinesischen militärischen Aktionen, die dann im März begannen. Über die Verhandlungen berichtete er, gestützt auf amtliche Niederschriften, in seinem 2001 erschienenen Buch "Russland und China im XX. Jahrhundert: Die Grenze" (russ.). In mehreren Monografien beschäftigte er sich immer wieder mit Fragen der sowjetisch-chinesischen Beziehungen. J. M. Galenovič zählt zu denjenigen russischen Wissenschaftlern und Politikern, die den russisch-chinesischen Beziehungen sehr skeptisch und der Moskauer China-Politik kritisch gegenüberstehen.

Die vorliegende Publikation ist ein aufschlussreiches Beispiel für die Schwerpunkte und die aktuelle Kultur der Diskussion zwischen russischen und chinesischen Autoren über die Beziehungen zwischen Russland und China. Es ist ein in mehrfacher Hinsicht ungewöhnliches Buch. Auf 450 Seiten befasst sich Galenovič mit den russisch-chinesischen Beziehungen in Vergangenheit und Gegenwart, was in weiten Teilen den Charakter eines kommentierten Lesebuchs über chinesische Ansichten zum Thema angenommen hat. Diese werden mit umfangreichen Auszügen aus jüngsten chinesischen Veröffentlichungen belegt. So entstand ein Überblick von repräsentativen Meinungen und Einschätzungen aus China zu den wichtigsten Aspekten der russisch-chinesischen Beziehungen des vergangenen Jahrhunderts und zu Beginn des 21. Jahrhunderts, verbunden mit den Positionen des Autors dazu.

Fast ein Drittel des Buches ist eine Auseinandersetzung mit der 2001 in Peking erschienenen Veröffentlichung von Dong Baocun: *Feng qi Diaoyutai* (Sturm über den Senkaku-Inseln). Galenovič sieht sie als repräsentativ für die offizielle Geschichtsauffassung der chinesischen Führung zu den verschiedenen Abschnitten und Stationen der chinesisch-sowjetischen Beziehungen an. Seine über Jahrzehnte gewonnenen Erfahrungen und Eindrücke aus Verhandlungen, Gesprächen und Analysen haben ihn nachhaltig geprägt und widerspiegeln sich in seinen Ansichten wie auch in den Methoden der Auseinandersetzung. Nicht selten erinnert das an die Polemik der Konfrontation in den 1960er und 1970er Jahren. So war Deng Xiaoping für Galenovič bis ans Ende seines Lebens ein „getreuer Fortsetzer der feindseligen Linie Mao Zedongs gegenüber unserem Lande" (S. 150). Das Resümee der Auseinandersetzung mit Deng besteht u.a. in der These: „Die Feindseligkeit in der Propaganda des ZK der KPCh gegenüber unserem Lande wird beibehalten, vertieft und auf die Erziehung auch der heranwachsenden Generationen der Chinesen an allen Schulen der VR China und auf die Soldaten der chinesischen Armee ausgedehnt" (S. 172). Es bestätige sich „das Bestehen von Plänen bei den Nachfolgern Mao Zedongs, jene Forderungen durchzusetzen, die sowohl er als auch Deng Xiaoping unserem Land gestellt hatten" (S. 177).

Im August 2003 sprach der Mitarbeiter der Abteilung Militärgeschichte der Akademie für Militärwissenschaften Chinas, Liu Zhiqing, auf einer Konferenz in Harbin über die Ausbildung chinesischer Militärs durch die Sowjetarmee und wie sie in den 1950er Jahren abgebrochen wurde. Galenovič hebt hervor, dass die wesentlichen Leistungen der sowjetischen Hilfe und die Art des Abbruchs durch die chinesische Seite zutreffend dargelegt wurden. Davon kann sich der Leser durch 30 Seiten Text der Rede Lius überzeugen, die von Galenovič durch einige Angaben ergänzt werden.

Dem stand der Beitrag eines Mitarbeiters vom Institut für Wirtschaft und Leitung der Pädagogischen Universität Shenyang auf derselben Konferenz entgegen. Er verteidigte die Theorie Mao Zedongs vom „UdSSR-Zentrismus". Für Galenovič, der dagegen polemisiert, gab es hingegen auf Seiten der KPdSU und der UdSSR keine Fehler, nicht einmal Schwächen oder Unvollkommenheiten.

Des Weiteren setzt sich Galenovič mit einem chinesischen Zeitungsartikel aus dem Jahre 2004 auseinander, der sich mit der relativ hohen Entlohnung sowjetischer Spezialisten in China in den 1950er Jahren beschäftigt. Galenovič sieht ihn als Versuch an, die Gleichberechtigung zwischen beiden Ländern in jener Zeit zu bestreiten.

Im Oktober 2003 führten Galenovič und andere russische Kollegen einen Meinungsaustausch mit chinesischen Kollegen zu den internationalen Beziehungen, zum Platz Russlands in der Weltpolitik und zu regionalen Problemen. Galenovič gibt den Inhalt und einige Positionen wieder. Alle Teilnehmer schätzten das gegenseitige Vertrauen als wichtigste und aktuellste Frage ein. Strittig waren die Methoden zur Vertrauensbildung. Für Galenovič war der Abschluss des Abkommens über Maßnahmen des Vertrauens und der Reduzierung der Streitkräfte an der gemeinsamen Grenze ein Fehler Gorbatschows (S. 290). Der wichtigste und unverzichtbare Schritt auf diesem wie auf allen Gebieten wäre seiner Ansicht nach der Abschluss eines Vertrages über die Grenze. Nur so wäre ein für allemal die Frage "ungleiche Verträge" aus den Beziehungen verbannt. Erfolge das nicht, müsse die russische Seite immer

wieder mit dem Aufwerfen dieser Frage rechnen, und so käme kein dauerhaftes Vertrauen auf. Das ist eine zentrale Position Galenovičs, auf die er wiederholt zurückkommt.
In der Diskussion vom Oktober 2003 war man sich darüber einig, dass Unverständnis und sogar Feindschaft unter der Bevölkerung beider Seiten groß sind und dass dagegen Entscheidendes getan werden muss. Die chinesischen Wissenschaftler kennzeichneten die Situation der letzten zehn Jahre in den bilateralen Beziehungen mit der Formel „oben warm, aber unten kalt". So verloren die Beziehungen ihre Lebenskraft, und der Abstand, der beide Nationen trennt, vergrößert sich. Galenovič formuliert daher als Aufgabe: „Es wäre gut, wenn abgesehen von den Führern unserer beiden Länder auch die gesamte Staatsmaschinerie Russlands und Chinas, alle gesellschaftlichen Kräfte beider Länder sich der beunruhigenden Lage bewusst würden, die sich in unseren bilateralen Beziehungen herausbildet und vertieft und Anstrengungen unternehmen würden, diese Situation zu verändern" (S. 301).
Vier Wochen vor dem Besuch Hu Jintaos in Moskau im Mai 2003 veröffentlichte Galenovič einen kurzen Leserbrief in einer Moskauer Zeitung (S. 307 f.), in dem er seine Beunruhigung über den Zustand der Beziehungen mit China ausdrückte. Drei Fragen müssten gelöst werden, um eine wirklich dauerhafte ideelle Grundlage der Beziehungen zu schaffen. Das seien: ein neuer Vertrag über die Grenze anstelle der bestehenden Verträge, die von einer Seite als „ungleich" bezeichnet werden; die Aufhebung des Abkommens über die 100-km-Zone, da von Russland keine militärische Bedrohung ausgehe; schließlich sollten lediglich Ausländer die russische Staatsbürgerschaft erhalten, die die russische Kultur übernehmen, nicht aber solche, die zwar russische Staatsbürger mit entsprechenden Rechten werden wollen, in Wirklichkeit aber Eigentum ihres Staates blieben. Galenovič schlug dafür regelmäßige Gipfelgespräche von mindestens einer Woche Dauer vor, über deren Inhalt öffentlich zu informieren wäre. So könne allmählich das Misstrauen auf beiden Seiten beseitigt werden. Außerdem schlug er vor, dass beide Staatsoberhäupter Schritte zur Schaffung eines dreiseitigen Mechanismus für einen Meinungsaustausch zwischen Russland, China und den USA zur Vorbereitung von Beschlüssen des UN-Sicherheitsrates unternehmen.
Diese ungewöhnliche öffentliche russische Meinungsäußerung löste eine massive chinesische Antwort aus. Sie beinhaltete eine umfassende und allseitige Analyse des Standes der chinesisch-russischen Beziehungen, wie es sie seit Jahren nicht gegeben hatte. Auf der erwähnten Konferenz in Harbin 2003 legten der Leiter des Forschungszentrums zum Studium der internationalen Strategie der Zentralen Parteischule des ZK der KPCh, Jiang Changbin, und Li Chuanxun von der Universität Heilongjiang einen umfangreichen Bericht vor. Sein Titel: "Befreit euch vom engen Nationalismus, vertieft das Verständnis und Erkennen. Ein Aufruf an die Freunde aus Russland, dem Nachbarstaat". In den darauf folgenden Monaten wurde er in China mehrfach veröffentlicht. Galenovič widmet ihm in seinem Buch 100 Seiten. Die gegensätzlichen Positionen zu allen wichtigen bilateralen Problemen werden behandelt und die dazu verwendeten Argumentationslinien treten dabei deutlich hervor.
Jiang und Li kritisieren in ihrem Harbiner Überblick neben Galenovič eine ganze Reihe russischer Publikationen zu den russisch-chinesischen Beziehungen. Sie wenden sich gegen russische Auffassungen von einer „gelben Gefahr" und die „Theorie von der Bedrohung durch China". Sie verweisen auf Erscheinungen von „Großmachtchauvinismus und typischen Dogmatismus". Von russischer Seite kommt der Vorwurf, Russland solle sich der Politik Chinas unerordnen, und die chinesische Auffassung von der Existenz „ungleicher Verträge" bestehe fort. Für Galenovič widerspiegelt die russisch-chinesische Deklaration vom 27. Mai

2003, dass am Beginn des 21. Jahrhunderts hinsichtlich der Grenzverträge „erneut scharf und direkt die Frage von Meinungsverschiedenheiten prinzipieller Natur zwischen beiden Seiten" hervortrat (S. 335). Russland habe sich im Übrigen während des gesamten vergangenen Jahrhunderts gegenüber China in der Defensive, nicht aber in der Offensive befunden und nur seine nationalen Interessen verteidigt (S. 350). Die Aussagen Mao Zedongs und Deng Xiaopings hinsichtlich des „territorialen Schuldners Russland" seien nicht zurückgenommen worden. Galenovič kritisiert das 2002 erschienene chinesische Geschichtsbuch für Mittelschüler, in dem die Geschichte der Grenzverträge nachgezeichnet wird. M. S. Gorbatschow habe nach seiner Auffassung im Gespräch mit Deng Xiaoping im Mai 1989 nicht die Interessen Russlands vertreten (S. 362 f.). Ein Ausweg aus der bestehenden Situation wäre, die Charakterisierung der bestehenden Verträge von der Unterzeichnunge eines neuen zu trennen (S. 365). Aber bei der Erörterung des chinesischen Wunsches nach Pacht des Hafens Zarubino an der Mündung des Tjumen erhebt Galenovič es zur Vorbedingung, dass ein neuer Grenzvertrag abgeschlossen wird, beide Staaten sich vor der UNO feierlich verpflichten, die bestehende Grenze für unverletzlich und ewig zu erklären sowie die Aussagen Mao Zedongs 1964 und Deng Xiaopings 1969 über die Grenze aufgehoben werden (S. 390). Kontrovers sind die Positionen auch in Bezug auf den 2003 vereinbarten Verlauf der Pipeline Angarsk-Daqing und der Verbindung der Transsibirischen Eisenbahn mit der Koreanischen Halbinsel. Die massenhaften illegalen Einreisen von Chinesen nach Russland in der ersten Hälfte der 1990er Jahre waren für Galenovič der „größte Schaden für den Zustand unserer Beziehungen und die Vorstellungen, die beide Nationen voneinander haben, nach dem Tod Mao Zedongs" (S. 397).

Galenovič sieht in dem von Jiang und Li vorgelegten Überblick den Versuch, feindselige Gefühle gegen Russland wiederzubeleben. Er zieht daraus den Schluss, dass es Aufgabe der gegenwärtigen Parteipropaganda in der VR China sei, innenpolitisch das russische Scheitern gegenüber dem chinesischen Erfolg nachzuweisen sowie in der Weltarena nach gemeinsamen Interessen mit den USA zu suchen (S. 404).

Schließlich wendet sich der Autor den Möglichkeiten für eine normale Entwicklung der bilateralen Beziehungen zu. Das geschieht in Auseinandersetzung mit einem Artikel, den die in Moskau erscheinende chinesische Zeitung „Luxun cankao" am 25.12.2003 veröffentlichte. Darin war von einer „neuen Situation und neuen Problemen" in den bilateralen Beziehungen die Rede, bezogen auf Ausführungen Hu Jintaos gegenüber W. W. Putin in Bangkok vom 19. Oktober 2003. Galenovič spricht sich dagegen aus, die Geschichte der Beziehungen überwiegend im schlechten Licht zu betrachten und die Russen als alleinige Feinde Chinas anzusehen. In Wahrheit verfolge die chinesische Führung langfristige Pläne „zur Umsiedlung von Teilen der Bevölkerung Chinas auf unser Territorium und zur wirtschaftlichen Nutzung unserer Ressourcen und unseres Marktes im Interesse ausschließlich der chinesischen Seite" (S. 422). Als aktuelles Beispiel wird u. a. erneut die Pipeline Angarsk-Daqing genannt.

Angesichts all dessen plädiert der Autor dafür, gestützt auf die wirtschaftliche und militärische Macht Russlands standhaft abzuwarten, bis in China alternative Ansichten zu den heute vorherrschenden entstehen (S. 434).

Am 14. Oktober 2004 wurde zwischen Russland und China ein Zusatzabkommen zum Grenzverlauf im Ostabschnitt unterzeichnet. Damit besteht erstmals in der vierhundertjährigen Geschichte der bilateralen Beziehungen eine durchgehende, genau festgelegte, beiderseits anerkannte Grenzlinie. Galenovič zeichnet die Vorgeschichte dieses Abkommens präzise nach und erinnert wiederum daran, dass damit die Frage nach einem neuen

Grenzvertrag nicht gelöst wurde. Er verweist außerdem darauf, dass nun zahlreiche neue Fragen entstanden sind. Sie reichen von gemeinsamen Wirtschaftsräumen und Sonderwirtschaftszonen über die Zusammenarbeit in der Shanghaier Organisation für Zusammenarbeit bis hin zum Wettbewerb und zur Harmonisierung der Interessen in den dreiseitigen Beziehungen Russland-China-USA (S. 446f.). Der Autor verweist auch auf mögliche Richtungen globaler Partnerschaft, um dann abschließend acht Vorschläge zur Entwicklung der bilateralen Beziehungen zu unterbreiten. Sie gehen wiederum von einem neuen Grenzvertrag bis zur Harmonisierung der nationalen Interessen Russlands, Chinas und der USA durch einen Mechanismus regelmäßiger Konsultationen und Treffen der Staatsoberhäupter dieser drei Staaten (S. 460ff.).

Im zweiten Teil seines Buches befasst sich Galenovič mit den Beziehungen zwischen China und den USA sowie dem weltpolitischen Dreieck Russland-China-USA nach dem Jahre 2001, wobei er von einer Charakterisierung der Partner und ihrer Interessenlage ausgeht. China und die USA seien in einer beispiellosen Position, keinen Krieg fürchten zu müssen und keiner Kriegsgefahr ausgesetzt zu sein. Galenovič schließt nicht aus, dass beide Staaten mit der Zeit „zu einer zentralen Achse der Beziehungen zwischen den Nationen der Welt werden können" (S. 501). Sie könnten ihre Beziehungen allerdings nicht gestalten, ohne die Interessen der anderen Staaten zu berücksichtigen. Der Autor verweist auf grundlegende Unterschiede zwischen beiden Staaten und Nationen. Dazu gehören die unterschiedlichen Vorstellungen von der Welt. Während in der VR China ein totalitär-autoritäres System existiert, besteht in den USA ein demokratisches (S. 500). Die sozialökonomischen Systeme sind unterschiedlich. Es fehlt bisher ein Mechanismus zur Regulierung von Gegensätzen und Meinungsverschiedenheiten hinsichtlich Sicherheit, Handel und Menschenrechte.

Galenovič geht dann auf Wege zur Abstimmung der Interessen zwischen den drei Mächten ein, bei der Frieden, Gleichberechtigung und Unabhängigkeit zu beachten seien (S. 558). Keine der drei Seiten könne ihre Interessen allein durchsetzen. Galenovič spricht sich nochmals für eine Harmonisierung der Interessen aus, wobei er gegenwärtig eine größere Annäherung zwischen Russland und den USA als zwischen China und den USA sieht.

Der Autor schließt mit dem Satz, dass zukünftig bei „äußerst wahrscheinlichen und sogar sicheren Komplikationen zwischen Moskau und Washington Peking sich als die Kraft erweisen könnte, an die Moskau sich anlehnt" (S. 570). (Joachim Krüger)

Li Hua-yu, *Mao and the Economic Stalinization of China, 1948-1953*, Lanham et.al: Rowman & Littlefield Publishers, Inc., 2006, XII+215 S. (ISBN 0-7425-4053-7)

Das Buch von Li Hua-yu ist eine überarbeitete Version ihrer Dissertation in Vergleichenden Politikwissenschaften an der Columbia University. Diese gut recherchierte und sehr detaillierte Arbeit untersucht die Hintergründe der Aufnahme der „Generallinie der Partei für die Übergangsperiode" im Jahr 1953 und zeigt auf, dass der scheinbar spontane Wechsel von einer moderaten hin zu einer radikalen Wirtschaftspolitik keineswegs der aktuellen Notwendigkeit entstammte, sondern von Mao Zedong initiiert und bereits im Vorfeld vorbereitet wurde.

Lis Hauptthese besteht darin, dass Maos Entscheidung für eine radikale Umgestaltung des Wirtschaftssystems der stalinistischen wirtschaftlichen Entwicklungslinie aus den 1920er und 1930er Jahren entsprach, wie sie in der „Geschichte der Kommunistischen Partei der Sowjetunion (Bolschewiki), kurzer Lehrgang" (fortan „Kurzer Lehrgang") formuliert worden waren. Nach Li war Mao ein treuer Stalinist, der paradoxerweise nicht dem moderaten Stalin treu war, von dem er Ende der 1940er – Anfang der 1950er Jahre in vielerlei Hinsicht abhängig war, sondern dem radikalen Stalin der 1920er und 1930er Jahre. Damit liefert sie einen weiteren Anhaltspunkt gegen die weit verbreitete Vorstellung von Mao als innovativen Theoretiker des Marxismus, der nur ungern Stalins Politik verfolgt habe.

Die Autorin stützt sich dabei auf publizierte Archivmaterialien aus China, die seit Mitte der 1980er Jahre zur Verfügung stehen, eine Auswahl an Materialien aus zwei russischen Archiven in chinesischer Übersetzung aus der Sammlung des chinesischen Historikers Shen Zhihua, Memoirenliteratur und parteigeschichtliche Veröffentlichungen. Außerdem hat sie seit Anfang der 1990er Jahre Interviews mit Akademikern und Parteiforschern durchgeführt.

Das Buch besteht aus fünf chronologischen und thematischen Kapiteln, ausgenommen Einleitung und Schlussteil. Im ersten Kapitel „The Historical Background and Contemporary Setting" werden die innerchinesischen und internationalen, historischen und zeitgenössischen Bedingungen vorgestellt, unter denen Mao sein neues Programm der „Generallinie der Partei für die Übergangsperiode" formulierte. Es wird kurz auf die Auswirkungen des Korea-Krieges auf die innerchinesische Situation eingegangen. Den Kern des Kapitels stellen die sino-sowjetischen Beziehungen in den 1940er und Anfang der 1950er Jahre dar. Hervorzuheben ist hier besonders, dass die Studie auf die Beziehungen vor 1949 Bezug nimmt – im Gegensatz zu vielen anderen Arbeiten, welche die sino-sowjetischen Beziehungen Anfang der 1950er Jahre zum Thema haben.

Das zweite Kapitel „Mao, Stalin, and Transforming China's economy: 1948-1952" liefert die Beweise für Lis Hauptthese, indem es darstellt, wie Mao auf Stalins Ratschläge in drei wichtigen wirtschaftlichen Fragen in den Jahren 1948-1952 reagierte. Die Reaktionen Maos waren zwar unterschiedlich und er musste auf Stalin Rücksicht nehmen, doch zusammenfassend lässt sich sagen, dass Stalins pragmatische und moderate Ratschläge von Mao weitgehend ignoriert wurden. Stalins Ratschläge konnten Maos radikale Tendenzen, die er dem „Kurzen Lehrgang" entnahm, höchstens hemmen, nicht aber verhindern.

Der „Kurze Lehrgang" und sein Einfluss auf Mao und die KPCh ist das Hauptthema des dritten und m.E. aufschlussreichsten Kapitels „Stalin's Short Course and Mao's Socialist Economic Transformation of China in the Early 1950s". Nach einem Überblick über den Einfluss des Buches seit seinem Erscheinen in China im Jahre 1938 bis in die 1960er Jahre, in dem klar wird, wie außerordentlich zentral dieser Text für Maos Verständnis des Kommunismus war, werden zwei Perioden vorgestellt, in denen Mao die Ideen aus dem „Kurzen Lehrgang" am intensivsten angewandt habe: die Periode der „Ausrichtungskampagne" in Yan'an (1941-1944) und die wirtschaftliche Umgestaltung seit 1953.

Im vierten Kapitel „Mao's Formulation of the General Line for Socialist Transition: October 1952-September 1953" wird Mao noch klarer als der alleinige Gestalter der neuen Generallinie dargestellt. Es wird ausführlich beschrieben, welche Maßnahmen er ergriff, um jeglichen Ausdruck von Meinungsverschiedenheiten innerhalb der Parteiführung und der gesellschaftlichen Eliten zu unterbinden. Außerdem werden die Rahmenbedingungen für die neue Politik untersucht und die einzelnen politischen Maßnahmen für sozialistische Umgestaltung der Industrie und des Handels dargestellt.

Das fünfte Kapitel „Mao's General Line for Socialist Transition: October-December 1953" stellt die Durchführung der neuen Wirtschaftspolitik im Bereich der Landwirtschaft dar. Nach Stalins Tod stand es Mao frei, ohne Rücksicht auf den „großen Bruder" seine radikalen Ideen zu verfolgen. Im Herbst 1953 nutzte er die Getreidekrise, um die sozialistische Umgestaltung der Landwirtschaft voranzutreiben.

Die Einleitung und der Schlussteil des Buches sind sehr stark aufeinander abgestimmt und greifen die Hauptthesen des Buches auf. Was die Einleitung vermissen lässt, ist eine Einordnung dieser Arbeit in den Forschungsstand sowie ein theoretischer oder methodischer Rahmen, in dem sie zu verorten wäre. Stärker ausgearbeitete Bezüge zwischen den Ergebnissen der Studie und größeren Kontexten wie z.B. dem Verständnis des Sozialismus in China oder den sino-sowjetischen Beziehungen wären im Schlussteil wünschenswert.

Li leistet mit dieser Arbeit einen wichtigen Beitrag zum Verständnis der chinesischen Wirtschaftspolitik der 1950er Jahre. Das Buch ist sowohl für Historiker und Politikwissenschaftler von großem Interesse, als auch für all diejenigen, die an einer detaillierten Analyse des Jahres 1953 als Wendepunktes interessiert sind. (Izabella Goikhman)

Antje Richter und Helmolt Vittinghoff (Hg.) ***China und die Wahrnehmung der Welt.*** **(Jahrbuch der Deutschen Vereinigung für Chinastudien 3), Wiesbaden: Harrassowitz Verlag 2007, 355 S. (ISBN 978-3-447-05539-0)**

Dieser lesenswerte Sammelband präsentiert die Ergebnisse der XV. Jahrestagung der Deutschen Vereinigung für Chinastudien (DVCS), die im Jahre 2004 in Leipzig stattfand. In 19 Beiträgen, die drei großen Themenbereichen zugeordnet werden können, nähern sich die Autorinnen und Autoren der Problematik von Selbst- und Fremdwahrnehmung Chinas. Im ersten Themenbereich geht es um die chinesische Wahrnehmung der chinesischen Welt. Dabei wird die Wahrnehmung von Armut (Antje Richter, Freiburg) ebenso thematisiert wie das prekäre Verhältnis von Dichtung und Wirklichkeit (Volker Klöpsch, Köln) oder Identitätsfindung in chinesischen Romanen (Carsten Storm, Dresden). Der chinesische Blick auf die nicht-chinesische Welt bestimmt den zweiten Themenbereich. Raoul David Findeisen (Bochum) behandelt chinesische Reiseberichte aus der ersten Hälfte des 20. Jahrhunderts, Erhard Rosner (Göttingen) befasst sich mit der Darstellung der Außenwelt in der spätkaiserzeitlichen Biji-Literatur und Hans Kühner (Berlin) analysiert die Wahrnehmung des Westens in der chinesischen Literatur des 20. Jahrhunderts – um nur einige Beiträge zu nennen.

Eine dritte Gruppe von Beiträgen hat das Wechselverhältnis zwischen Wahrnehmung der Welt und der Wahrnehmung Chinas aufzuzeigen versucht. So untersucht u.a. Martina Eglauer (München) Zhang Junmais Positionen als Beispiel für die Wahrnehmung der westlichen Moderne, während Fang Weigui (Trier) die Frage aufwirft, ab wann man von einer chinesischen Nation sprechen könne.

Die empirisch sehr gut fundierten Beiträge bilden insgesamt ein relativ breites Spektrum chinawissenschaftlicher Themen und methodischer Herangehensweisen ab und geben damit über die Thematik im engeren Sinne hinaus auch einen allgemeinen Einblick in die sinologische Forschungssituation in Deutschland. Gerade für die jüngeren Nach- wuchswissenschaftlerInnen bleiben die Jahrestagung der DVCS und die hiermit gegebene Publikationsmöglichkeit außerordentlich wichtig, um ihre Forschungsergebnisse einem breiteren Kreis präsentieren zu können. (Mechthild Leutner)

Notes on Contributors

Yiu Fai Chow (周耀輝) is a PhD candidate at the Amsterdam School of Communications Research, University of Amsterdam. His project concerns young Chinese living in the Netherlands and their use of popular culture, in particular martial arts films, beauty pageant and pop music. Next to his PhD project, Chow is active as lyric writer for Chinese language pop songs. He has collaborated with a variety of pop artists in Hong Kong, Taiwan and mainland China since 1989.

Jens Damm is Wissenschaftlicher Assistent (Assistant Professor) at the Institute of East Asian Studies, Freie Universität Berlin. His research interests include the Chinese diaspora in Southeast Asia, gender studies, and new media.

Cord Eberspächer is a Research Fellow at the Secret Prussian State Archive in Berlin. He is currently working on the Prusso-German-Chinese Relations 1842-1911. His research interests further include military history, history of shipping, Germany in the early 20th century and Qing history.

Andrew Field is Academic Director for the China in a Global Context program for CIEE in Shanghai. He is currently finishing a book manuscript on jazz-age nightlife in Shanghai in the 1920s-40s and a documentary film on the contemporary independent rock music scene in China.

Martin Gieselmann is a researcher and graduate programme manager at the Cluster of Excellence "Asia and Europe in a Global Context" at Heidelberg University. Research foci are with contemporary Chinese literature, performing arts, visual culture and transnational Chinese cinema.

Izabella Goikhman is a Research Associate and PhD candidate at the Institute for East Asian Studies, Free University Berlin. Her main research interests are: Jews in China, history of Science, cross-cultural science- and knowledge transfer and gender studies.

Jeroen Groenewegen is a junior researcher funded by the Hulsewé-Wazniewski Foundation (HWS) at the School of Asian, African and Amerindian Studies (CNWS), Leiden University. His current project is titled "The Performance of Identity in Chinese Popular Music."

Heather Inwood is Assistant Professor of Modern Chinese Cultural Studies in the Department of East Asian Languages and Literatures at the Ohio State University. Her current research focuses on the impact of new media upon contemporary literature and culture in the PRC.

Jeroen de Kloet is Assistant Professor of Mediastudies at the University of Amsterdam and works on the cultural implications of globalization in China. His current research project focuses on the Beijing Olympiad and is titled "Celebrations and Contestations of

Chineseness – The Beijing 2008 Olympics and 21st Century Imaginations of Place, Culture and Identity."

Joachim Krüger (Dr. rer. Pol.) was a Professor at the Insitute for International Relations at Potsdam-Babelsberg. He is currently envolved as a co-editor in the research project "The Comintern and China" at Freie Universität Berlin. Other research interests include the history of GDR-Chinese relations.

Mechthild Leutner is a professor and currently holding the chair of Chinese Studies at the Institute for East Asian Studies, Free University Berlin. Her main research interests are on Chinese social and political history, German-Chinese relations and Chinese women's history.

Hauke Neddermann is a Research Associate and PhD candidate at the Institute of East Asian Studies, Freie Universität Berlin. His research interests include history and society of modern China; especially regional history of Xinjiang and the social history of the 1950s and 1960.

Andreas Steen is Assistant Professor of Modern Chinese History and Culture at the Department of East Asian Studies, Aahrhus University, Denmark. His research focuses on various topics of Chinese popular culture and the German-Chinese Relations.

Carsten Storm is Lecturer at the Centre for East Asian Studies, Technische Universität Dresden, and at the Department of Chinese Studies, University of Cologne. His research focuses on genre theory and narrative structures, historicity, mentality, and identity.

Simona Thomas is a Scientific Author and PhD candidate at the Center for Chinese and East Asian Politics, Department of Political and Social Sciences, Freie Universität Berlin. Her main research interests include China's economic development, especially e-commerce/e-business and its effects on Chinese and foreign companies in the PRC.

Nathalie van Looy is a Research Associate and PhD candidate at the Institute for East Asian Studies, Free University Berlin. Her main research interests are: labor relations and conflict, recent social developments and transformation processes in the People's Republic of China, as well as China's foreign policy strategy towards Africa.

Anne Wedell-Wedellsborg is Professor of Modern Chinese Literature and Culture at the Department of East Asian Studies, Aarhus University. She specializes in modern and contemporary Chinese literature. Other research interests include the contemporary Chinese cultural scene and Sino-European cultural relations.

China *aktuell*

Journal of Current Chinese Affairs

Call for Papers

China aktuell – Journal of Current Chinese Affairs is an internationally refereed academic journal published by the Institute of Asian Studies (part of GIGA German Institute of Global and Area Studies), Hamburg. The bimonthly journal focuses on current developments in Greater China. It has a circulation of 1,200 copies, making it one of the world's most widely distributed periodicals on Asian affairs. *China aktuell* reaches a broad readership in the academia, administration and business circles. Articles to be published should be written in German or English and submitted exclusively to this publication.

China aktuell is devoted to the transfer of scholarly insights to a wide audience. The topics covered should therefore not only be orientated towards specialists in Chinese affairs, but should also be of relevance to readers with a practical interest in the region.

The editors welcome contributions on contemporary China including Hong Kong, Macau and Taiwan that are concerned with the fields of international relations, politics, economics, society, education, environment or law. Articles should be theoretically grounded, empirically sound and reflect the state of the art in contemporary Chinese studies.

All manuscripts will be peer-reviewed for acceptance. The editors respond within three months. Research articles should not exceed 10,000 words (incl. footnotes and references). Manuscripts should be submitted to the editors in electronic form: china-aktuell@giga-hamburg.de. For detailed submission guidelines see: www.giga-hamburg.de/ias/stylesheet.

Recent topics:

- *Approaches towards Sustainable Development in China*
- *Between Denial and Acceptance – Human Rights and History in Modern China*
- *China's Economic Policy towards Taiwan*
- *Authority, Trust, and Legitimacy in the PRC*

Editors: Karsten Giese • Heike Holbig

Institute of Asian Studies
GIGA German Institute of Global and Area Studies
Rothenbaumchaussee 32 • 20148 Hamburg • Germany
Phone: +49 40 4288740 • Fax: +49 40 4107945
Website: www.giga-hamburg.de

GIGA
German Institute of Global and Area Studies
Institute of Asian Studies